Governing From Center Stage

White House Communication Strategies During the Television Age of Politics

The Hampton Press Communication Series
Political Communication
David L. Paletz, Editor

Eastern European Journalism
Jerome Aumente, Peter Gross, Ray Hiebert, Owen Johnson, and Dean Mills

The In/Outsiders: The Mass Media in Israel
Dan Caspi and Yehiel Limor

Islam and the West in the Mass Media:
Fragmented Images in a Globalizing World
Kai Hafez (ed.)

Mass Media, Politics, and Society in the Middle East
Kai Hafez (ed.)

Governing from Center Stage: White House Communication Strategies
During the Television Age of Politics
Lori Cox Han

Eden Online: Re-inventing Humanity in a Technological Universe
Kerric Harvey

Civic Dialogue in the 1996 Presidential Campaign:
Candidate, Media, and Public Voices
Lynda Lee Kaid, Mitchell S. McKinney, and John C. Tedesco

Mediated Women: Representations in Popular Culture
Marian Meyers (ed.)

Public Opinion & Democracy: Vox Populi—Vox Dei?
Slavko Splichal (ed.)

Gender, Politics and Communication
Annabelle Sreberny and Liesbet van Zoonen (eds.)

War in the Media Age
A. Trevor Thrall

forthcoming

The Holocaust and the Press
Nazi War Crimes Trials in Germany and Israel
Akiba A. Cohen, Tamar Zemach-Marom, Jürgen Wilke, and Birgit Schenk

American Dreams, Hebrew Subtitles
Notes From the Receiving End of Globalization
Tamar Liebes

Business as Usual: Continuity and Change in Central and
Eastern European Media
David L. Paletz and Karol Jakubowicz (eds.)

Women, Politics, Media
Uneasy Relationships at the New Milennium
Karen Ross

Governing From Center Stage

White House Communication Strategies During the Television Age of Politics

Lori Cox Han
Austin College

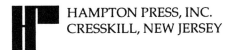
HAMPTON PRESS, INC.
CRESSKILL, NEW JERSEY

Printed in the United States of America

Library of Congress Cataloging-in-Publication Data

Han, Lori Cox.
    Governing from center stage : White House communication
    strategies during the television age of politics / Lori Cox Han.
        p. cm. -- (The Hampton Press communication series. Political
    communication)
    Includes bibliographic references and index.
    ISBN 1-57273-356-X (cl) -- ISBN 1-57273-357-8 (pb)
        1. Presidents--United States--Press conferences. 2. Press and
    politics--United States. 3. Communication in politics--United
    States. I. Title. II. Series.

    JK554.H35 2001
    320.973'01'4--dc 21

                                                                    2001039297

Hampton Press, Inc.
23 Broadway
Cresskill, NJ 07626

To the memory of my dad,
J.D. Cox

Contents

Acknowledgments   xi

1. White House Communication Strategies:
   The Impact on Governing   1
      The Limits of Presidential Leadership   3
      Presidential Rhetoric and Speechwriting in Context   5
      Presidential Public Activities: Beyond the Rhetoric   7
      The Presidential Public Agenda: Prioritizing Policies   11
      Understanding the Presidential/Press Relationship   12
      Assessing White House Communication Strategies   15
      Case Studies   18
      Endnotes   21

2. Kennedy: The Television Age Arrives   27
      Kennedy and the Press   28
      Kennedy's Public Activities   33
      The Kennedy Policy Agenda   34
      The First Tier: The Tax Cut Proposal of 1963   36
      The Second Tier: Aid to Education in 1961   39
      Conclusion   42
      Endnotes   43

3. **Johnson and Nixon: Playing Ball in the Kennedy's Court**   **47**
    Johnson and the Press   48
    Johnson's Public Activities   63
    The Johnson Policy Agenda   66
    The First Tier: Medicare-1965   69
    The Second Tier:
       The Safe Streets and Crime Control Act of 1968   74
    Nixon and the Press   78
    Nixon's Public Activities   87
    The Nixon Policy Agenda   89
    The First Tier: Welfare Reform in 1971-1972   92
    The Second Tier: Environmental Protection in 1970   96
    Conclusion   99
    Endnotes   102

4. **Ford and Carter: The Aftermath of Watergate**   **111**
    Ford and the Press   112
    Ford's Public Activities   128
    The Ford Policy Agenda   130
    The First Tier: The Tax Cut of 1975   132
    The Second Tier: Energy Corporation   137
    Carter and the Press   141
    Carter's Public Activities   155
    The Carter Policy Agenda   158
    The First Tier: Energy   159
    The Second Tier: Civil Service Reform   165
    Conclusion   170
    Endnotes   171

5. **Reagan and Bush: Stagecraft and its Legacy**   **179**
    Reagan and the Press   180
    Reagan's Public Activities   192
    The Reagan Policy Agenda   196
    The First Tier: Social Security Reform of 1982-1983   199
    The Second Tier: Student Aid Cuts in 1982   201
    Bush and the Press   203
    Bush's Public Activities   209
    The Bush Policy Agenda   210
    The First Tier: The Education Excellence Act   212
    The Second Tier: The Clean Air Act of 1990   216
    Conclusion   219
    Endnotes   221

6. Clinton: Years of Scandal and Spin   **227**
    Clinton and the Press   228
    Clinton's Public Activities   235
    The Clinton Policy Agenda   237
    The First Tier: The Anti-Crime Bill of 1994   238
    The Second Tier: The National Service Plan of 1993   240
    Conclusion   242
    Endnotes   245

7. Is Governing from Center Stage Possible?   **247**
    A Comparison of Presidents   248
    White House Communication Strategies:
      Useful or Futile?   261
    Endnotes   265

Bibliography   267
Author Index   279
Subject Index   285

Acknowledgments

As with many first books, this project began as my doctoral dissertation at the University of Southern California under the direction of Bill Lammers. I could not have asked for a better advisor and mentor; his patience, guidance, and vast knowledge of the presidency gave this project a strong focus from the start. The completed manuscript represents what began as a conversation in Bill's office on a rainy afternoon in November 1995 about my "thoughts and ideas" on a dissertation topic. Along the way, his enthusiasm never waned, and his comments on the early drafts proved invaluable. At my dissertation defense in July 1997, Bill, along with my other committee members, Herbert Alexander and Terry Seip, encouraged me to pursue publication with the requisite changes from dissertation to book manuscript. Bill passed away less than three months later. And, while I feel a tremendous sense of accomplishment having completed this more-than-four-year project, it will always seem like it is not quite finished without Bill's comments, suggestions, and seal of approval. His dedication to his students will never be forgotten, and I will always consider myself incredibly lucky to be counted among them.

I am grateful for the financial support that I received while conducting the research for this project. The Joan Shorenstein Center on the Press, Politics and Public Policy at the Kennedy School of Government,

Harvard University, provided a Goldsmith Research Grant that funded travel to the John F. Kennedy Library in Boston and the Nixon Project at the National Archives in College Park, Maryland. I also received travel grants from the Lyndon Baines Johnson Foundation in Austin, Texas, and the Gerald Ford Library in Ann Arbor, Michigan. And finally, I received a Richardson Grant from Austin College which funded travel to the Jimmy Carter Library in Atlanta, Georgia. I also conducted research at the Ronald Reagan Library in Simi Valley, California, but was fortunate to live ten minutes away before moving to Texas in August 1998. My experience at all six of the libraries/archives was tremendously positive, and all of the staffs were most helpful.

Many colleagues have also offered support and assistance throughout the completion of this manuscript. Michael Genovese has been a wonderful mentor in all areas of my professional development as a presidency scholar. The Presidency Research Group, and in particular Martha Joynt Kumar, has provided a wonderful support network to welcome and encourage the work of junior scholars in this field. The enthusiasm for this project from Barbara Bernstein at Hampton Press, as well as David Paletz, the editor of this series, was always appreciated. The reviewer's comments were also tremendously encouraging and helpful, especially at those times when I had reached a temporary impasse. I would also like to acknowledge those who provided support at Austin College. Thanks to my political science colleagues Shelly Williams and Kenneth Street for reading drafts of this manuscript and providing important feedback, as well as to one of my hardest working students, Micah Pardun, for volunteering to do some last-minute copy-editing. I would also like to thank the former and current Deans of Social Science, Janet Huber Lowery and Howard Starr, for their support and understanding. I am also grateful to my presidency students, both at Austin College and at UCLA, who provided inspiration on a regular basis, and all of whom probably now know more than they ever bargained for about White House communication strategies.

I would also like to thank Ann Gordon, both friend and colleague, for always reminding me how far we have come since graduate school, while still remembering how far we have to go. And finally, I owe the largest debt of gratitude to my family. This project would have never been completed without the never-ending love, support, and understanding of my husband, Tom. Words cannot describe how much that has meant to me, both professionally and otherwise. My daughter, Taylor, and my son, Davis, motivate me as no one else can, and always remind me of what is most important. My only hope is to make them proud.

1

White House Communication
Strategies:
The Impact on Governing

Bill Clinton's presidency, from start to finish, may be remembered best as a tale of survival. While candidates and politicians in today's media-dominated society have come to expect attacks on both their professional and personal lives by the press, the Clinton years witnessed many new developments in the complex and intertwined relationship between media and politics. As early as the 1992 presidential primaries, and as late as early 1999 as the spectacle of the impeachment trial and the Monica Lewinsky scandal finally began to fade from public view, Clinton's team of advisors worked overtime to protect both his image and message to the American public. Perhaps no other recent adminis-tration better illustrates the importance of an effective communication strategy, the complexities of the presidential/press relationship, and their impact on presidential leadership better than the Clinton years do. However, communication strategies have been a crucial aspect of presi-dential leadership since the early 1960s, as presidents during the televi-sion age of politics have learned to rely on a myriad of strategies to effectively get their message out to the public. The use of a communica-tion strategy represents an important step in allowing a president to set his policy agenda with the public, Congress, and other political participants, especially the news media. Therefore, successful presidential leadership in the media age relies heavily on developing effective communication strategies in order to implement policy goals and to ultimately create a lasting historical legacy.

As it has evolved with recent administrations during the last four decades, a White House communication strategy consists of various components, including the leadership style of the president, presidential rhetoric and speechwriting, presidential public activities, the presidential policy agenda, and the presidential/press relationship. The use of a strategy in the area of communications has not only become more important with the rise of the rhetorical presidency during the twentieth century, but has become more complex as well. The presidency itself has become more institutionalized and, as a result, politicized.[1] The news media have also contributed to the expansion of the executive branch as an institution. The extent to which the White House handles both press and public relations is evidenced by the number of people now employed in both the press and communication offices.[2] However, presidents still implement and rely on strategies in an attempt to control as much of the political environment as possible. As a result, communication strategies emerge for every president, and can shape, to varying degrees, the relationship that the president has with both the press and the public, which in turn can help determine the overall success of the administration and its policies.

As this book will demonstrate, various factors play a role in whether or not a president develops a successful communication strategy, which has become an integral part of the day-to-day operation of the White House. An effective presidential communication strategy can be a critical factor, at least for presidents since the emergence of the television age, in developing and implementing the administration's policy goals. To understand how a president communicates is to understand an important base of power for the modern presidency. Developing an effective strategy for press relations is also a top priority for new administrations since the news media is the primary link between the president and the public, especially in terms of setting the national political agenda. Each administration has also developed its own unique style of communicating with both the press and public, providing an instructive comparison between recent administrations which can lead to a better understanding of the development of presidential leadership in the public realm. Communication strategies have become an important and permanent part of the everyday operation of the White House. Since the presidency is now more institutionalized and politicized, presidents and their staffs have found it necessary to learn over time how best to deal with the news media, which have become more institutionalized and politicized in their own right.[3] Presidents must use the press to govern, but they do not have much control over the final message, which creates many challenges for successful presidential leadership.

Taking into consideration the many works that currently exist on similar and/or related topics, this book will bring together many of the strategic components of presidential communications to provide a unique perspective. A better understanding of the behind-the-scenes strategies of White House advisors, as well as a comparative analysis of specific strategies that have been used by presidents over the years, presents a clearer picture of the impact that communication strategies can have on presidential leadership. Presidents during the television age have worked hard at trying to control both their image and message as it is portrayed to the public and to other political actors through the news media. However, not many presidents have had much success in this area. Yet, why presidents continue these communication efforts explains not only how the institution of the presidency has evolved during the television age, but also shows the current disconnection between communicating and governing from the Oval Office. Many limitations already exist for successful presidential leadership within our constitutional framework, and the ever-increasing need for presidential communication may seem to aid a president in leading the nation, but it actually gives a false sense of presidential power. Communicating is not necessarily governing, and this study will demonstrate—through a detailed comparative analysis of the specific aspects of communication strategies—how many presidents have been frustrated by their inability to lead effectively and live up to public expectations during the media age.

THE LIMITS OF PRESIDENTIAL LEADERSHIP

First, it is important to demonstrate the previous research, conducted in a variety of areas, which not only influences this work, but also helps to place it within its proper academic context. Many scholars have documented a shift during the twentieth century to a style of presidential leadership that is increasingly based on rhetorical skills. In turn, the expanding role of the rhetorical presidency in American politics, along with the growing technology and influence of the mass media, have forever changed the definition of presidential leadership. For presidents in the modern era, communicating with both the public and other political participants, especially Congress, has become a key component of both effective leadership and successful policy making. Most often, the mass media provide the primary means of presidential communication. In

Richard Neustadt's classic study of the presidency, real presidential power is defined as the power to persuade, with successful presidents relying on a leadership style based on bargaining.[4] Many scholars have since further examined—and some have redefined—how presidential communication and public opinion can affect policy making by the president and his attempts to control the political agenda. By the mid-1960s, the president had become a central focus of news from Washington, and hence began to have more power over shaping the national agenda by rapidly reaching, through both television and print, his national audience. The ability to help shape public opinion, through televised and/or highly covered speeches and press conferences, began to provide the president an important advantage during the legislative process. As the influence of television increased, presidents worked even harder to keep the initiative and/or control over the policy agenda coming out of the White House.[5]

Presidential personality, character, and leadership style can either help or hurt the president's policy objectives since the office of the presidency can be greatly defined by its occupant. However, the office is considered both fluid and institutionalized. So, while the character and personality of each president, as well as the staffing of the oval office, can have an impact on presidential leadership, the structure of the office and the executive branch can place limits on presidential leadership. According to Mary Stuckey, these aspects of leadership are tied closely to the creation of presidential strategies, which she defines as being "situationally grounded, purposeful adaptations of individual style and preferences (character) to accommodate institutional expectations (role) and promote a specific, policy-oriented goal." A president's success with his legislative agenda, therefore, can be limited by the political and institutional environment, his own leadership style, and in the area of communication, how well he meets public expectations.[6] The limitations placed on leadership potential by unrealistic public expectations represent paradoxes for the presidency; for example, Americans want and often demand strong leadership from the president, yet they place strong limits on the powers of the office due to suspicions about the abuse of power.[7]

Much has also been written on the variety of ways presidents are limited in their attempts to influence the national policy agenda, ultimately determining whether or not their administrations will be viewed as successful. The organization, behavior, and structure define the institutional parameters of the presidency, and while presidents can make marginal changes to that organization, the office is not reinvented with each new occupant in the White House. Also, presidents tend to behave in similar ways since they are faced with similar political and institutional environments. As a result, "the institution of the presidency shapes presidents as much as presidents, during their short tenures, shape the institution."[8] The individuality of the president himself is still an important consideration, including the effect on events and institutions, but only if historical situations and other environmental factors are considered as well. Individuals do make a difference, since a president deals with practices that are institutionalized, as well as those that are not. For example, much of a president's day-to-day job may be out of his control due to the institutionalized nature of the office, such as regular dealings with the White House press corps, which all presidents must face. Nonetheless, individual presidents can still "lend their touch" to media strategies, thereby playing a part in effecting the outcome of press coverage. Other individual activities of presidents that are not institutionalized can also contribute to strategies involving press coverage, such as how a president presents himself in public or his initial selection of a policy agenda.[9] Presidential policy making is also considered a relevant determinant of presidential success or failure, especially in terms of leadership. All presidents pursue policies, and how they do so reveals much about their "ideology and world view," as well as the "overall operation, productivity, and quality of a given administration all of which reveal something in turn about a president's design, manufacturing, and marketing sense."[10] Clearly, many factors can play an important role in whether or not a president is viewed as an effective leader.

PRESIDENTIAL RHETORIC AND SPEECHWRITING IN CONTEXT

Recent attempts have been made to define and articulate the scholarly and disciplinary differences between the "rhetorical presidency" and "presidential rhetoric." The literature that has emerged in the past two decades on the rhetorical presidency, mostly from political scientists, has examined the effectiveness of presidential governance—specifically, the ways presidents have been able to accomplish their policy and broader ideological objectives through rhetorical skills. In his seminal work on the subject, Jeffrey Tulis argues that the presidency, as an institution, experienced a fundamental transformation by becoming a "rhetorical presidency" during the early part of the twentieth century, causing an institutional dilemma for the modern presidency. The current political culture now demands presidents to be popular leaders, with "a duty constantly to defend themselves publicly, to promote policy initiatives nationwide, and to inspirit the population." Presidential rhetoric is now a means for mobilizing the masses, and is a primary tool used by presidents in their attempts to implement policy objectives. However, by fulfilling popular functions and serving the nation through mass appeal, the presidency has now greatly deviated from the original constitutional intentions of the Founders, removing the buffer between citizens and their representatives that the framers established.[11] Roderick Hart also believes that the rhetorical presidency is a twentieth century creation and a constitutional aberration. The president is not merely a popular leader vested with unconstitutional powers, but also one who uses rhetoric as a "tool of barter rather than a means of informing or challenging a citizenry." Presidents, through rhetoric, now play an elaborate game with the public in the hopes of maintaining high public opinion ratings.[12]

Stuckey has also aptly labeled the president an "interpreter-in-chief" and the "nation's chief storyteller." Beyond the institutional aspects, when viewed as a fluid institution, the presidency allows each occupant of the White House to utilize his own personal preferences and leadership style by which to govern. Presidential rhetoric has changed over time as media technologies have continued to expand, providing citizens with more in-depth coverage of the president. Due especially to television coverage, presidential advisers now develop communication strategies that seek more support for the president and less support for specific policy proposals. This has led to an emphasis on ceremonial, rather than deliberative, speech.[13] Some would suggest that the presidency is in a rhetorical crisis, resulting from the increasing amount of time that presidents spend on public speaking, and the time they must also spend on defending misstatements they inevitably make that the press routinely covers as "real news." Trust, competence, and consistency are all necessary images that a president must maintain publicly in order to achieve rhetorical success. But if one of these should erode, then the president will often focus his rhetorical strategy on protecting his image, which weakens his ability to exercise presidential leadership.[14]

In contrast, other scholars view presidential rhetoric as a positive institutional and constitutional feature, as well as one imagined by the Framers as a necessary element of a properly-functioning republic that allows presidents to speak directly to the public. Rhetoric also plays an important role in the institutional setting of the presidency by enabling different presidents to shape the presidency in a stable and constant manner.[15] One such way is the depiction of the office through public addresses. Presidents often rely on the persuasiveness of describing the powers and responsibilities of the office to maintain public and congressional support for policy initiatives. Lyndon Johnson, Richard Nixon, Ronald Reagan, and George Bush were all considered monarchical in the way they spoke about their responsibilities as president—the forceful leadership of commander-in-chief and chief of state. On the other hand, Jimmy Carter and Bill Clinton attempted to develop an intimacy with the American people, placing the emphasis on the "people's presidency"; each had "promised change, requested public sacrifice, and committed himself to reviving the national economy." However, most presidential depictions of the office promise more than can be delivered.[16]

Those scholars, mostly within the fields of speech and communication, studying presidential rhetoric—as opposed to the rhetorical presidency—are less concerned with the institutional implications on the office of the presidency and more concerned with the persuasiveness of a particular speaker within a particular setting. According to Martin Medhurst, the art of rhetoric is more than just an attempt at persuasion, but includes "the intellectual powers displayed by the rhetorician in the selection of what to say, how to say it, to whom, under what conditions, and with what apparent outcome." Studying the formal dimensions and content of language can also reveal methods of argument, style, and delivery, as well as how the message serves to construct the political thoughts and ideology of the speaker.[17] Certainly, an understanding of presidential speechwriting, as well as the oratory styles of each president, would fit under this category. While it is important and instructive to acknowledge the vast contribution that scholars of both the rhetorical presidency and presidential rhetoric have contributed to a better understanding of various aspects of the American presidency, with works relevant to each discipline dating back to both Aristotle's *Politics* and *Rhetoric* respectively, this book is not an attempt to provide a descriptive or comparative analysis of presidential rhetoric. Nor does it attempt to refute any of the above-mentioned theories and/or findings. Instead, it is an attempt to place the use of rhetoric within the proper context as part of the overall communication strategy of modern American presidents. Tulis argues that speechwriting has become "an institutional locus of policymaking in the White House."[18] So, too, has the use of communication strategies in the broader context.

PRESIDENTIAL PUBLIC ACTIVITIES: BEYOND THE RHETORIC

More than just presidential rhetoric and speechwriting, the venues and audience also help to define the presidential message. The presidential image as constructed through these events, as well as public opinion of both the man and the office, is also an important strategic consideration for the White House. According to Sam Kernell, presidents of the modern era have utilized public support by "going public," a style of presidential leadership that includes "a class of activities that presidents engage in as they promote themselves and their policies before the American public." Addresses to the nation, press conferences, and other public appearances are examples of how a president attempts to sell his agenda or other presidential actions, not only to the public, but to other political actors as well. Certainly, the technological developments of the mass media in recent years have allowed presidents to go public more often, and with much greater ease. Going public for some presidents can also occur simply through frequent or impromptu discussions with members of the press. Recent trends also show that "the more recent the president, the more often he goes public."[19] Going public, however, is contradictory to some views of democratic theory, but it is now practiced by presidents as a result of a weakened party system, split-ticket voting, divided government, the increased power of interest groups, and the growth of mass communication systems.[20]

Public opinion can also play an important role in a president's effectiveness as a leader or success as a policymaker. The White House is now obsessed with popularity and how the president rates in public opinion polls since high approval ratings can translate into more successful dealings with Congress. This is influenced by the press and its expectations of presidential performance.[21] Public opinion about the president, as well as approval ratings, is derived by the public from daily reports in the media about policy outcomes. Events such as the presidential honeymoon, White House rallying events to sell an agenda item, or economic performance alone do not affect presidential approval ratings. News reports about policies in the news media help to shape how citizens evaluate their president. Opinions about the president are usually formed following reports in the media of policy outcomes, which contribute to a one-sided response by the president: a chance to take credit for the outcome of a successful policy.[22] Popular presidents also have much greater success at influencing public opinion than do unpopular presidents. The relationship between presidents and public opinion can be reciprocal, with presidents taking a stand on an issue in response to or in anticipation of public opinion. Also, popular presidents can influence public opinion on a particular policy issue by their actions as reported by the media.[23]

Several studies on presidential rhetoric have attempted to answer a variety of questions about how, when, and why presidents participate in public activities. The "perpetual campaign" of the modern presidency now exists, which results from, among other things, the decline of party influence during elections that "personalize[s] the presidency and make[s] imagery one of its cornerstones." While speaking styles may differ between presidents, all presidents of the modern era have utilized public appearances, which include national activities (press conferences, addresses to the nation, foreign travel), group activities (minor policy addresses and other symbolic appearances), and partisan activities (the role as party leader). The extent to which public appearances occur represents "institutional behavior that shows different individuals facing similar circumstances and engaging in similar behavior."[24]

Key predictors have been found to exist which determine when a president is likely to deliver a national address, as well as when he is not. Changes in public attitudes toward the president, as well as changes in national conditions, increase the likelihood of a presidential address, whereas worsening economic conditions or an increase in military activities decreases the chance of a president addressing the nation.[25] In general, the use of public opinion polling by the White House has emerged in recent years as an important tool in both the designing of presidential rhetorical strategies and the building of policy agendas.[26] Conversely, a president can also significantly increase his own standing in public opinion polls by addressing the nation on an important topic; an increase in both popularity and job approval ratings often occur immediately following a major address.[27]

Presidents also now rely so heavily on attention-focusing activities that they do not necessarily need to change their public strategies during the reelection campaign at the end of the first term. In general, presidents now partake in extensive public exposure efforts, such as public addresses and other appearances throughout their first term in office, not just during the reelection campaign, due in part to the increased news media attention toward the presidency over the past 40 years. Presidents are now "motivated by a realization that public exposure can be more helpful to them for reelection when it is undertaken in their role as president rather than in the role of a candidate for reelection."[28]

Other important moments have been discovered for public activities during distinct time periods of a president's tenure in office. Presidential transitions prior to first taking office—a time traditionally spent staffing administrations, developing congressional relationships, and building coalitions to gain support of a new policy agenda—often find presidents relying heavily on public rhetoric to develop support for their policy agendas and shape the political context of their administration. This is especially true if the incoming president is a member of the opposite party of the incumbent he is replacing.[29] Presidential inaugurals also provide the president with a critical rhetorical moment at the

start of his administration. Inaugural addresses have become part of a
"rhetorical genre" with five key elements: unifying the audience, high-
lighting traditional values, setting the political principles of the new
administration, showing the president's respect for his new duties as
president, and focusing on the present, as well as the past and future, to
maintain the democratic values of government—of which the presidency is an integral part.[30] Since the first inaugural address by George
Washington in 1789, most presidents still follow his original script: outlining goals and discussing the constitutional duties of the office.[31]

Presidents have also used press conferences as a tool to promote
their agendas, although some have more frequently than others.
However, since these are not controlled events and include other participants, the ability to control the agenda is not always predictable. The
president's opening statement may include several minor policy
announcements, or may be a reaction to a single event, such as an international crisis. During the latter, the president more easily maintains
control of the agenda during the press conference. Despite what he says
in his opening remarks, the president may also have a hidden agenda,
which may be an attempt to respond to an event or a critic within the
political realm. Allowing a reporter to bring up the issue can let the
president respond without placing high importance on a political antag-
onist through a response in a public speech.[32] Since the days of Franklin
Roosevelt and Harry Truman, presidents have relied less on frequent
and regular press conferences due to such factors as an increase in international involvement, presidential personalities, and the advent of televised news conferences during the 1960s. Presidents are also more likely
to avoid the press during times of national uncertainty, when major policy options are being considered within the White House, or when a situation arises that could embarrass the administration.[33] Ronald Reagan,
however, provides an excellent example of how to hold a press conference while still avoiding the press. Reagan rarely provided a direct
answer to questions by reporters during press conferences (only roughly
20 percent of questions about policies were answered), while the
remaining responses showed his mastery of avoiding a question with a
variety of rhetorical tactics, such as delaying, discrediting the opposition, blaming the media, making personal or historical references,
deflecting through humor or anecdote, or providing other symbolic,
nonspecific answers.[34]

THE PRESIDENTIAL PUBLIC AGENDA:
PRIORITIZING POLICIES

Several scholars have addressed presidential agenda setting and how presidents attempt to utilize the power of their office to have an impact on the policymaking process. E.E. Schattschneider wrote in 1960 that ". . . the definition of alternatives is the supreme instrument of power. . . . He who determines what politics is about runs the country, because the definition of the alternatives is the choice of conflicts, and the choice of conflicts allocates power."[35] Political issues arise from group conflict, and they are placed on the agenda when they increase in scope, intensity, and visibility. Two types of agendas exist—a systemic agenda includes all issues that are both legitimate and salient to the entire political community, and the formal agenda, which includes those issues that are recognized and considered by government officials.[36] Three factors can influence why an issue gets placed on the formal government agenda. First, issues viewed as problems, rather than just existing conditions, usually take precedence as being more urgent. Second, political events—such as elections, shifts in public opinion, and interest group activities—can often change the prominence of issues on the agenda. Third, visible participants in the political process, such as the president, key members of Congress, political party leaders, and the news media, greatly influence which items are placed on the agenda, while hidden participants such as career bureaucrats, congressional staffers, and academics help shape the list of alternatives to proposed public policies.[37] The president also plays a decisive role in placing issues high on the agenda. The president can provide a clear focus on an issue, as well as influence other political actors, more than any other participant in the policymaking process.[38]

The president's ability to control the agenda can be viewed as functioning to both gain and utilize power. For the president, his agenda is a "signal" of which issues he considers important and what alternatives exist for dealing with the issue. Five factors have influenced the changes in the formation of presidential domestic agendas since the 1950s: stronger competition from Congress to control the agenda; the increased complexity of Congress following its decentralization of the committee structure during the late 1960s and early 1970s; the weakened state of political parties in Congress; increased congressional and media surveillance of the president's actions; and the emergence of "constituentless" issues, such as welfare reform, social security funding, and health care reform, that play better to a national audience than to the constituencies represented in Congress. Timing is also crucial for a president to gain passage of his agenda by capitalizing on his resources, including internal ones such as time, information, expertise and energy, and external ones such as public approval, congressional support, and the electoral margin by which he was elected.[39]

Timing is especially crucial for newly elected presidents who must have an effective strategy with which to "hit the ground running" so as to achieve policy agenda success. The power to control the political agenda must be seized early in an administration; only constitutional authority is automatic since the "power of the presidency—in terms of effective control of the policy agenda—must be consciously developed."[40] What a presidential candidate talks about during the general election campaign—especially if he discusses specific domestic policy proposals—is a good indication of what his agenda will look like once in office. However, presidents alone do not control their destinies since outside political actors, such as Congress or interest groups among others, are important players in the agenda-building process. Presidents only have control over the policies they choose to initiate and the strategy behind that initiation.[41] An important tool for that strategy is, of course, the use of public activities, since a president can affect to some degree the public's policy agenda through public speeches. A specific policy will often rise on the public's agenda if a president gives a high-profile speech on that specific issue. The public also responds to the emphasis a president gives to a particular policy during multi-policy speeches, especially the State of the Union address, and the president's popularity in public opinion polls does not seem to affect his ability to place an issue on the public's agenda.[42]

UNDERSTANDING THE PRESIDENTIAL/ PRESS RELATIONSHIP

This is one of the most crucial factors for a president and his advisors to consider when developing a communication strategy. The news media can certainly help in getting out the president's message, but they have also been known to distort the message. Historically, the press has always been among the most influential political actors with which presidents must contend. During the twentieth century, the White House and the Washington press corps have often struggled to define the political agenda. Each wants to control the content of the news, but like it or not, one cannot do its job without the other. Reporters have maintained a presence at the White House for more than 100 years, but an "ideal" relationship in which each side was satisfied with the other has never existed between the president and the press.[43] This love-hate relationship has also been fueled over the years by a credibility gap between an investigative press and a government bent on managing news.[44] The press, however, can be useful to a president by providing information about current events, keeping the executive branch apprised of major concerns of the public, enabling executives to convey their messages to the public and political elites, and allowing the president to remain in full public view on the political stage.[45]

A cyclical view of the relationship between the press and the president has been shown to exist, which is based on both cooperation and continuity between the two institutions. While the extent of cooperation varies throughout each administration, the relationship is not always adversarial since each side must cooperate with the other to get its job done. The growth of the president's communication staff in recent years can be attributed to the systematic approach of handling the news media, not out of a desire to control the content of the news. The larger news outlets have also kept up with this level of growth, putting some members of the White House press corps on equal footing with the president's communication advisors. And, since both the president and major news organizations gain from coverage that is favorable and prominent, both sides try to work together to avoid conflict.[46] However, reporters on the White House beat are rarely experts on the policy issues that presidents promote since many reporters receive their assignment after covering the president as a candidate during the previous election. Stories, then, can often lack substance since reporters, unlike presidential advisers, do not become more specialized in handling policy issues.[47]

White House reporters are most often comfortable reporting on what they know best, which is the politics of Washington: suspected scandal, dissension within an administration, verbal and visual gaffes, and tactical political blunders. Few are policy experts, but most have expertise in covering the horse race aspect of politics. This contributes to the focus on politically oriented, rather than policy oriented, stories. The press is open to public criticism and does not want to be wrong, so they avoid hard-core analyses of complicated issues, often following the lead of the White House press team on specific policy issues. Presidents have attempted control over the news with the knowledge of the news media's preference to report on politics, but only the subject matter can be controlled, not the tone of the news. Ultimately, the bias toward writing about politics rather than government is a nonhistorical approach to covering the presidency, does a great disservice to the public, and can project a misperception about a president's competence.[48]

The president, however, makes news by virtue of being the "ideological symbol of American democracy and nationhood" for both journalists and the public. The president's relationship with the press is a combination of both strengths and weaknesses. Presidential power can be undermined by a failure of the administration to effectively manage the news, by newsgathering norms within the journalism industry, and by the skepticism of the press. While presidents can usually enjoy deference from the press in terms of coverage during times of crisis or certain ceremonial occasions, usually reporters place presidential actions within a political context that reduces the symbolic nature of the presidency to just another politician seeking to retain political power. The president is under constant scrutiny by the press, but he must be careful in his criticisms of reporters, who not only give voice to his opponents, but can also present the news in a manner unflattering to the president's public image.[49]

Several factors can increase the tensions between the president and the press. Presidents have historically viewed the press as a hindrance to achieving the public's support for policies, mostly due to the content of the majority of news originating from the White House. First, an administration, as well as other top government officials, often attempts to use the press to its advantage through leaks. Top aides—or even the president himself—will leak information as a "trial balloon" to test public reaction to a proposed policy. In this instance, the press agrees to serve as a communication tool of the government in order to remain competitive with other news outlets. Second, many stories on the president tend to have a superficial or trivial quality. Stories focusing on the personal aspects of the president's life often gain more prominent coverage than stories analyzing policies. Again, competition among reporters, as well as a lack of expertise on many national political issues, fuels this type of coverage. Finally, while most studies on media coverage of news show no systematic bias along partisan or ideological lines, distortion still occurs in coverage of the president. The presentation of news contains a structural bias in how stories are selected since all issues do not receive coverage. Due to deadlines and limited time and/or space for stories, important issues are often oversimplified.[50]

The role of the White House Office of Communications in maintaining a president's public image has also increased in recent years. The news media are obsessed with covering conflicts, which often results in serious discussions of policy issues within the White House being depicted as dissent among top presidential advisers. As a result, the goal of the White House is to stop any news reports of internal conflict and push for positive coverage of the president's policy agenda. The White House Office of Communication handles this through a long-term public relations strategy. Advisers usually spread the "line of the day" throughout the administration, which then takes it to the press; the office also takes the White House message directly to the people when necessary. The ultimate goal is to set the public agenda through the use of focus groups, polls, sound bites, and public appearances by the president.[51]

Press coverage of the president, and the generation of stories out of Washington, have continued to evolve during the 1990s as a result of the increasing technological capabilities of the news media as well as the changing political environment. Intense competition between the various mediums for both audience and advertising revenue has altered both the content and tone of many political stories. Newspapers now must compete with television as a result of CNN's emergence during the 1980s, which created the 24-hour news cycle. Now, other all-news networks, such as MSNBC, compete to have the most up-to-the-minute news headlines available. The Internet has also influenced the availability and quality of political news. Competition and the dramatically shortened news cycle have resulted in the frequent use of questionable news sources and many factual errors in reporting, all done with the zeal to become the "first" to provide an "exclusive" to the American audience. As the first baby-boomer president raised during the television age, Bill Clinton has routinely used alternative media formats such as talk shows and live townhall meetings to speak directly to the American people, often bypassing the traditional Washington press corps. These factors, among others, have led news coverage of both politics in general and the presidency in particular to become more personal, intrusive, and obsessed with scandal.[52]

ASSESSING WHITE HOUSE COMMUNICATION STRATEGIES

Taking into consideration the many works that have been written in recent years on presidential communications, this book will add to an already robust and interdisciplinary discussion by examining the evolution of White House communication strategies during the television age, and by discussing the resulting impact on presidential leadership. Specifically, the research provides a case study analysis of communication strategies during the administrations of the eight most recent presidents: John F. Kennedy, Lyndon B. Johnson, Richard Nixon, Gerald Ford, Jimmy Carter, Ronald Reagan, George Bush, and Bill Clinton. While the television age of politics initially began during the Eisenhower administration of the 1950s, this study begins with the Kennedy administration in 1961 since Kennedy innovated the skillful use of the news media through such tactics as live televised press conferences. Each president offers a distinct case study in not only presidential communication, but in leadership style as well, and each provides the opportunity to observe and analyze changes in communication strategies and also in the relationship between the presidency and the press over the past four decades. Communication strategies were examined in terms of the types of forums used for public activities to determine how and where each president discussed various issues, as well as the issue content of public addresses to determine policy prioritization. Also of concern were the specific goals each administration set forth in order to achieve in the area of communications, as well as the resulting news coverage on certain domestic issues in the *New York Times*.

Each presidential case study will analyze the following five areas of communication strategies: presidential public activities, policy prioritization and the public agenda, administrative goals for communication, domestic policy issues, and newspaper coverage.

Presidential Public Activities

To determine the total number of public activities of each president, as well as the different forums used, each public event chronicled in the *Public Papers of the Presidents* was placed into one of the following categories: national addresses, policy addresses, radio addresses, press conferences (president only), brief statements/nonpolicy remarks, partisan remarks or campaign speeches, press conferences with foreign dignitaries, signing ceremonies, teleconference remarks, roundtable discussions, town meeting/question-and-answer sessions, and exchanges with or remarks to reporters.[53]

Policy Prioritization and the Public Agenda

To determine the frequency with which each president discussed policy issues, each major presidential address from the *Public Papers of the Presidents* was content analyzed. Major presidential addresses were considered those falling into the first four categories as mentioned above: national addresses (inaugurals, state of the union or other addresses to a joint session of Congress, addresses to the nation that are broadcast live on television and radio); policy addresses (other major addresses that presidents use to outline policy goals, including addresses to business, labor, or other interest groups, or university commencement addresses);[54] news conferences (the prepared opening statement given by the president); and radio addresses. A total of 12 policy categories were developed for coding.[55] Each reference to a particular policy within a speech was then counted to measure the frequency with which presidents discussed issues on their agendas.[56] Policy topics for the speeches were then ordered by rank based on how often each was mentioned.

Administration Goals for Communication

Extensive research for the case studies was conducted for each presidency (with the exception of Bush and Clinton) at presidential libraries and archives. White House files of key advisors and other staff members were examined to locate information on presidential communication strategies in general, and for information on strategies involving relationships with the press, presidential image, speech writing, and specific communication strategies involving selected domestic policies for each president.

Domestic Policy Issues

Two domestic policy issues from each president's domestic agenda were selected for the case study analysis. While presidents may only have marginal control over which domestic issues to emphasize, foreign and economic issues were excluded since, traditionally, presidents have even less control over how and when these items may appear on their agendas, due to events such as war or other instabilities within foreign governments, trade imbalances, and the rise and fall of the American economy.[57] The domestic issues were then separated into the categories of first-tier and second-tier policies, with one of each selected for each president. A first-tier issue was considered a top priority for the president to pursue through public activities and/or a policy that would, once enacted, create sweeping legislative change or reform. On the other hand, a second-tier issue was considered as not as high of a priority during public activities for the president, or was perhaps a pet policy initiative with a smaller impact that the president was pursuing.

Newspaper Coverage

Finally, each case study concludes with a content analysis of newspaper coverage appearing in the *New York Times* on each domestic policy issue. All news items on each issue were first categorized by both the type and the source of the item. The type of item included a news story, a news analysis, a column, or an editorial. (Texts of presidential speeches or news conferences, and letters to the editor, were excluded.) The source of the news item (that is, the political activity that generated the coverage) included three categories: presidential activity, congressional activity, and interest group or other political participant activity. Next, the news items generated by presidential activity were coded for tone of content. Four categories were used for coding tone: positive, negative, neutral, or balanced/mixed.[58] An obvious limitation to this study is the inclusion of only one news source. However, throughout the twentieth century, the *New York Times* has been widely recognized as the nation's "newspaper of record," and is often the trendsetter in coverage for which other news outlets, both print and broadcast, follow. The *Times* also remains one of the most widely-read newspapers in the country, as it began printing a national edition available throughout the country in 1980, and it has the largest Sunday circulation of any newspaper within the United States with more than 1.5 million readers. Not only is the *Times* a recognized leader of news coverage within the journalism industry, but it is also considered an influential political player within Washington.[59]

CASE STUDIES

The case studies for each president are presented in Chapters 2 through 6. Remembered best for holding the first televised news conferences, Kennedy's communication strategies are analyzed in chapter 2. During a time when television was still new to presidential politics, key advisors did not shy away from meeting the challenge of the increasing size of the White House press corps nor the expanding communication technologies. The administration held a generally positive attitude toward the press in terms of what it could provide to Kennedy—an outlet for the President to inform the American public about issues of importance. A majority of the Kennedy agenda of the early 1960s was dominated by foreign policy issues, such as the Cold War, or domestic issues with an international outlook, such as the Peace Corps or the space program. While the Kennedy administration did not represent an overly broad domestic agenda, the proposed income tax cut in 1963 provided analysis of a first-tier issue, while the federal aid to education package proposed in 1961, which was not a high-profile piece of legislation, offers analysis of how the Kennedy team dealt with a second-tier policy issue.

Chapter 3 examines the Johnson and Nixon presidencies. Unlike the Kennedy years, both the Johnson and Nixon White Houses had a much different, and in Nixon's case, harsher view of the press and its role in politics. Following the communicative successes of Kennedy, especially with the use of image building through the increasingly powerful medium of television, advisors to both Johnson and Nixon faced a daunting task. The stage had been set for the White House to continue to present both the president and his policy agenda to meet the demands and expectations of the news media as well as the public. While Johnson was known as an effective and persuasive communicator both on a personal level and as a legislator, he had difficulty transmitting that image through television to the American public as president. Despite a vast domestic policy agenda, the escalation of America's involvement in Vietnam would hinder the fulfillment of Johnson's overall legislative record. His Great Society programs provided many domestic issues for study; those selected included the first-tier issue of Medicare in 1965 and the passage of the Safe Streets Act in 1967-1968 for a second-tier issue. By 1969, convinced that the "liberals" in the national news media were out to destroy a Republican in the White House, the Nixon administration utilized a daily news summary to keep tabs on how various media outlets were portraying its actions, and it continually strategized on how to counter-balance the bias of the "Eastern-establishment" press, most notably the *New York Times* and the *Washington Post*. Nixon was also one of the least publicly accessible presidents, holding few press conferences. Like Kennedy, Nixon's agenda was dominated by foreign policy. However, he also had an extensive domestic agenda, which included efforts to combat crime and to reform various federal programs. Two interesting policies emerged for case studies from Nixon's first term. First, the Family Assistance Plan, Nixon's proposed changes to welfare programs first introduced by the administration in 1969, was still a first-tier issue during 1971 and 1972 as Congress continued consideration on the issue of welfare reform; and second, while environmental issues were a top priority with the public, Nixon's creation of the Environmental Protection Agency in 1970 remained a second-tier issue at the White House.

Chapter 4 analyzes the post-Watergate years of Ford and Carter. As an unelected president, Ford found himself in the role of introducing himself to the American people following Nixon's resignation. He worked hard to portray himself as an everyday, common, and honest man who could recapture the trust of the American people and restore public confidence in the office of the presidency. However, his image was forever tarnished following his pardon of Nixon in September 1974. And, while he relied heavily on public activities to take his message to the American people during his short tenure in office, he never presented an effective communication style through the news media. He also had little time to develop a domestic policy agenda, relying quite heavily on the veto power to counteract a reform-minded Democratic congress. However, Ford's proposed tax cut in 1975 is considered a first-tier issue, while the so-called Energy Corporation proposal is assessed as a second-tier issue. Carter did not fare any better in presenting an image as an effective communicator to the public. He was virtually an unknown when he entered the 1976 presidential primaries, and as president, proved that the skills needed to win the presidency are much different than those needed to govern effectively. Carter was helped tremendously during the election by his image as an outsider, and was also perceived as honest and down-to-earth. His style of governing and communicating reflected his desire to maintain the image of an outsider. This hurt his relationship with Congress tremendously, and it also hurt the clarity of his message to the American people. Carter had many policy ideas and initiatives, especially in the domestic area, but he could not communicate the bigger picture to the public. The first-tier issue of an energy policy and the second-tier issue of civil service reform are considered.

Chapter 5 looks at Ronald Reagan, whom many called the "Great Communicator," and his successor, George Bush. The Reagan administration was considered one of the most successful at orchestrating press coverage to focus on the president's agenda, and is remembered as a highly symbolic presidency. Advisers perfected the art of feeding the press a "line of the day" to highlight a particular White House policy. Public activities were also geared toward helping a particular policy issue make the evening network newscasts, complete with photo opportunities and sound bites. Following the flurry of economic proposals from the Reagan administration during 1981, in 1982 Reagan began to focus his domestic agenda on other issues, such as entitlement programs, various federal government deregulations, a balanced-budget constitutional amendment, and the controversial issues of school prayer and abortion. The two policy issues selected for analysis include the first-tier issue of Social Security reform in late 1982 and early 1983, and the second-tier issue of proposed cuts in federal student aid in 1982. Upon his election in 1988, Bush worked hard to distance himself from the stagecraft of the Reagan years. A Washington insider who was less conservative than the man for whom he had served eight years as vice president, Bush talked of a "kinder, gentler America". While much more accessible to the press than Reagan had been, Bush was not as gifted in the area of communication skills. His former boss had left a tough legacy to follow in the area of public relations. Bush also had difficulty in articulating a domestic policy agenda and a broader national vision to the American public. Issues selected for study included the first-tier issue of the Education Excellence Act, and the second-tier issue of environmental policies, specifically the amendments to the Clean Air Act of 1990.

The Clinton administration provides the last case study, and it is presented in chapter 6. Like many of his predecessors in the White House, Clinton has not always had an easy time in dealing with the press. However, he does rely quite heavily on public activities to sell items on his policy agenda to both the press and the public. The Clinton White House has also relied on campaign-like public strategies in an attempt to win passage of key pieces of legislation. From the start, the

Clinton policy agenda has been dominated by domestic issues, including deficit reduction, job creation, health care reform, and welfare reform, among the more notable first-tier issues. Also a first-tier issue, the anticrime bill debated during 1994, is analyzed, followed by an assessment of the 1993 national service program, a second-tier policy issue.

Finally, chapter 7 provides a concluding analysis about the evolution of White House communication strategies during the television age, the impact on presidential leadership, and the role the press plays in how presidents govern. Ultimately, any study suffers from the limitation of the inability to provide definitive answers to some of the larger questions, especially when studying the presidency. (For example, how much political power does the president really have?) However, the uniqueness of the office, when compared with others in our political system, provides an excellent starting point. The president has emerged during the twentieth century as a dominant rhetorical figure in American politics, representing a national constituency with many opportunities to influence the national agenda. A president's public activities, as well as media strategies to get his message out, are important in understanding the parameters of presidential leadership and policy outcomes during the media age of politics in which we now live. Therefore, this comparative analysis of eight presidents during the modern era of the presidency, where the news media play such an influential role in politics, provides a basis for discussing the following questions: Are presidents capable of developing successful communication strategies to get their message out to the public, most often through the press, or does the institution of the presidency, and the role that the press plays within it, so limit a president's options that attempts to develop strategies are futile? And, perhaps more importantly, what impact does this political environment, so focused on the public aspects of the presidency, have on a president's ability to effectively govern?

ENDNOTES

1.   See Terry M. Moe, "The Politicized Presidency," in *The New Direction in American Politics*, Eds. John E. Chubb and Paul E. Peterson (Washington, DC: The Brookings Institution, 1985), and "Presidents, Institutions, and Theory," in *Researching the Presidency: Vital Questions, New Approaches*, Eds. George C. Edwards, III, John H. Kessel, and Bert A. Rockman (Pittsburgh: University of Pittsburgh Press, 1993); John Burke, *The Institutional Presidency* (Baltimore: Johns Hopkins University Press, 1992); and Thomas J. Weko, *The Politicizing Presidency: The*

White House Personnel Office, 1948-1994 (Lawrence: University of Kansas Press, 1995).

2. See John Anthony Maltese, *Spin Control: The White House Office of Communications and the Management of Presidential News*, 2nd rev. ed. (Chapel Hill: University of North Carolina Press, 1994).

3. Matthew Robert Kerbel, *Remote and Controlled: Media Politics in a Cynical Age*, 2nd ed. (Boulder, CO: Westview Press, 1999), 106.

4. Richard Neustadt, *Presidential Power and the Modern Presidents: The Politics of Leadership From Roosevelt to Reagan* (New York: Macmillan, 1990).

5. See Elmer E. Cornwell, Jr., *Presidential Leadership of Public Opinion* (Westport, CT: Greenwood Press, 1965), 3-7; and Theodore J. Lowi, *The Personal President: Power Invested, Promise Unfulfilled* (Ithaca, NY: Cornell University Press, 1985), 138-9.

6. Mary Stuckey, *Strategic Failures in the Modern Presidency* (Cresskill, NJ: Hampton Press, 1997), 1-11.

7. For a thorough discussion on presidential leadership and the paradoxes of the office, see Thomas E. Cronin and Michael A. Genovese, *The Paradoxes of the American Presidency* (New York: Oxford University Press, 1998), 1-28.

8. Lyn Ragsdale, *Vital Statistics on the Presidency: Washington to Clinton* (Washington, DC: Congressional Quarterly Inc., 1996), 7-13.

9. Erwin C. Hargrove, "Presidential Personality and Leadership Style," in *Researching the Presidency*, 69-72.

10. Paul C. Light, "Presidential Policy Making," in *Researching the Presidency*, 161-3.

11. Jeffrey K. Tulis, *The Rhetorical Presidency* (Princeton, NJ: Princeton University Press, 1987), 4-23.

12. Roderick P. Hart, *The Sound of Leadership: Presidential Communication in the Modern Age* (Chicago: University of Chicago Press, 1987), 110, 212.

13. Mary E. Stuckey, *The President as Interpreter-in-Chief* (Chatham, NJ: Chatham House, 1991), 1-3.

14. Craig Allen Smith and Kathy B. Smith, *The White House Speaks: Presidential Leadership as Persuasion* (Westport, CT: Praeger, 1994), 191-3.

15. Karlyn Kohrs Campbell and Kathleen Hall Jamieson, *Deeds Done in Words: Presidential Rhetoric and the Genres of Governance* (Chicago: University of Chicago Press, 1990), 1, 213-9.

16. Paul Haskell Zernicke, *Pitching the Presidency: How Presidents Depict the Office* (Westport, CT: Praeger, 1994), 2-3, 145.

17. Martin J. Medhurst, "A Tale of Two Constructs: The Rhetorical Presidency Versus Presidential Rhetoric" in *Beyond the Rhetorical Presidency*, Ed. Martin J. Medhurst (College Station, TX: Texas A&M University Press, 1996).

18. Tulis, 185.

19. Samuel Kernell, *Going Public: New Strategies of Presidential Leadership*, 3rd ed. (Washington, DC: CQ Press, 1997).

20. See both Kernell and Richard Rose, *The Postmodern President* (Chatham, NJ: Chatham House Publishers, 1991), 132.

21. Paul Brace and Barbara Hinckley, *Follow the Leader: Opinion Polls and the Modern Presidents* (New York: HarperCollins, 1992), 6-9, 22-4.

22. Richard A. Brody, *Assessing the President: The Media, Elite Opinion, and Public Support* (Stanford, CA: Stanford University Press, 1991), 168-76.

23. Benjamin I. Page and Robert Y. Shapiro, *The Rational Public: Fifty Years of Trends in Americans' Policy Preferences* (Chicago: University of Chicago Press, 1992), 348-50.

24. Ragsdale, *Vital Statistics*, 145-54.

25. Lyn Ragsdale, "The Politics of Presidential Speechmaking, 1949-1980," *American Political Science Review* 78 (December, 1984): 971-84.

26. For example, see Diane J. Heith, "Presidential Polling and the Leadership of Public Thought." Paper prepared for delivery at the "Presidential Power: Forging the Presidency for the 21st Century" conference sponsored by the Presidency Research Group of the American Political Science Association, Columbia University, New York, November 15-16, 1996.

27. See Ragsdale, "The Politics of Presidential Speechmaking;" and Brace and Hinckley, *Follow the Leader*, 55-6.

28. William W. Lammers, "Presidential Attention-Focusing Activities," in *The President and the Public*, Ed. Doris Graber (Philadelphia: Institute for the Study of Human Issues, 1982), 145-71.

29. A.L. Crothers, "Asserting Dominance: Presidential Transitions From Out-Party to In-Party," *Polity* 26 (Summer 1994): 793-814.

30. Campbell and Jamieson, 15.

31. Lee Sigelman, "Presidential Inaugurals: The Modernization of a Genre," *Political Communication* 13 (January-March 1996): 81-92.

32. Carolyn Smith, *Presidential Press Conferences: A Critical Approach* (New York: Praeger, 1990), 79-85.

33. William W. Lammers, "Presidential Press-Conference Schedules: Who Hides, and When?" *Political Science Quarterly* 96 (Summer 1981): 261-78.

34. Mary E. Stuckey, *Playing the Game: The Presidential Rhetoric of Ronald Reagan* (New York: Praeger, 1990), 15-22.

35. E.E. Schattschneider, *The Semisovereign People: A Realist's View of Democracy in America* (New York: Harcourt Brace, 1975), 66.

36. Roger W. Cobb and Charles D. Elder, *Participation in American Politics: The Dynamics of Agenda-Building* (Boston: Allyn and Bacon, 1972), 160-1.

37. John W. Kingdon, *Agendas, Alternatives, and Public Policies* (New York: HarperCollins, 1995), 196-200.

38. Frank R. Baumgartner and Bryan D. Jones, *Agendas and Instability in American Politics* (Chicago: University of Chicago Press, 1993), 241.

39. Paul C. Light, *The President's Agenda: Domestic Policy Choice from Kennedy to Reagan* (Baltimore: Johns Hopkins University Press, 1991), 1-12.

40. James P. Pfiffner, *The Strategic Presidency: Hitting the Ground Running*, 2nd ed. (Lawrence: University Press of Kansas, 1996), 3.

41. Jeff Fishel, *Presidents & Promises: From Campaign Pledge to Presidential Performance* (Washington, DC: CQ Press, 1985), 187-8.

42. See Roy L. Behr and Shanto Iyengar, "Television News, Real-World Cues, and Changes in the Public Agenda," *Public Opinion Quarterly* 49 (1985): 38-57, and Jeffrey E. Cohen, "Presidential Rhetoric and the Public Agenda," *American Journal of Political Science* 39 (February 1995): 87-107.

43. See Martha Joynt Kumar, "The Relationship Between the White House and the Press: One Hundred Years in the Making," Paper prepared for delivery at the 1997 Annual Meeting of the Midwest Political Science Association, Chicago, Illinois.

44. Michael Emery and Edwin Emery, *The Press and America: An Interpretive History of the Mass Media*, 8th ed. (Needham Heights, MA: Simon & Schuster, 1996), 443-52.

45. Doris Graber, *Mass Media and American Politics*, 5th ed. (Washington, DC: Congressional Quarterly, Inc., 1997), 272-3.

46. Michael Baruch Grossman and Martha Joynt Kumar, *Portraying the President: The White House and the News Media* (Baltimore: Johns Hopkins University Press, 1981), 3-16.

47. Stephen Hess, *Presidents and the Presidency* (Washington, DC: The Brookings Institution, 1996), 114-23.

48. James Fallows, "The Presidency and the Press," in *The Presidency and the Political System*, Ed. Michael Nelson (Washington, DC: CQ Press, 1990), 315-33.

49. David L. Paletz and Robert M. Entman, *Media Power Politics* (New York: Macmillan, 1981), 55-65.

50. George C. Edwards, III, *The Public Presidency: The Pursuit of Popular Support* (New York: St. Martin's Press, 1983), 140-69.

51. Maltese, 2-5.

52. For relevant discussions on how the press covers politics, particularly scandal, see Kerbel, and Larry Sabato, *Feeding Frenzy: How Attack Journalism Has Transformed American Politics* (New York: Free Press, 1991).

53. Lyn Ragsdale in *Vital Statistics on the Presidency* uses a similar, but not as detailed, breakdown of categories after which this system was modeled.

54. See Ragsdale, *Vital Statistics*, 149-52.

55. Categories included: diplomatic and international military policy; international trade and economic policy; domestic fiscal and

monetary policy; unemployment, job creation, and industrial policy; defense and defense conversion policy; political reform policy; anticrime policy; health care reform and other health policy; welfare reform and other entitlements policy; education policy; environment, land management, and energy policy; and science, technology, and transportation policy.

56. When using content analysis, measurement is defined as "counting the occurrences of meaning units such as specific words, phrases, content categories, and themes." See Robert Philip Weber, *Basic Content Analysis*, 2nd ed. (Newbury Park, CA: Sage Publications, 1990), 70.

57. See Ragsdale, *Vital Statistics*, 10-1, and Fishel, *Presidents & Promises*.

58. Several studies in political communication, especially those assessing campaign coverage, rely on a similar coding technique to determine the tone of news stories. For example, see Kim Fridkin Kahn, *The Political Consequences of Being a Woman: How Stereotypes Influence the Conduct and Consequence of Political Campaigns* (New York: Columbia University Press, 1996). For example, a news item coded as positive was one that included a predominantly optimistic outlook for the success of the president's policy and/or highlighted the benefits of the policy, especially through quotes from political supporters. A negative story was one that was predominantly pessimistic about a policy, and/or outlined how the policy would cause harm to existing programs. Neutral news items included those that did not portray the president or his policy in either light, and a balanced news item was one that presented both sides of the issue. A similar technique was used in assessing coverage of the Eisenhower through Carter administrations in Grossman and Kumar, *Portraying the President*.

59. The influence of the *New York Times*, both politically and within the journalism industry, has been well documented. For example, see Graber, *Mass Media and American Politics*, 5th ed.; Emery and Emery; and Dean E. Alger, *The Media and Politics*, 2nd ed. (Belmont, CA: Wadsworth Publishing, 1996).

2

Kennedy:
The Television Age Arrives

No discussion of the mass media and its effects on the American political process would be complete without mentioning the much studied 1960 presidential election. The story of how the young Democratic nominee, Senator John F. Kennedy from Massachusetts, outperformed the Republican nominee, Vice President Richard Nixon, in front of the television cameras during the televised debates between the two candidates has become almost legend. When looking back at the campaign, some scholars credit the first televised debates with giving Kennedy the slightest of edges over Nixon, allowing him to capture the presidency. Using television as an effective tool by which to portray a positive image would remain a top priority for Kennedy once he took office. The communication strategy that would follow during Kennedy's brief tenure in the White House would focus on imagery, rhetoric, and utilizing the emerging power of television to capture and deliver the youthful energy of the new administration to the American people. The Kennedy years would also set a new standard for presidential uses of public activities and the news media as means to expand the influence of presidential power in an attempt to govern from center stage.

KENNEDY AND THE PRESS

A key aspect of the Kennedy communication strategy focused on culti-vating favorable coverage by the press. Following the 1960 campaign, Kennedy and his advisors continued their trail-blazing attitude toward the press, especially television, and how it would best suit the goals of the administration.[1] Top advisors in the White House, including Special Counsel Theodore Sorensen and Press Secretary Pierre Salinger, consid-ered the press an important player in the political process, especially as the vehicle through which the President would educate the masses on both his policy initiatives and the role of the federal government. In a White House memorandum on presidential/press relations dated April 17, 1961 to Sorensen, Salinger writes that he believes that the administra-tion had been successful to date in educating Americans: "I believe that we are getting through [to] the people. . . . [N]o administration has given the people a better glimpse of the Presidency and the President and the inner workings of the executive branch of the government."[2] To some, Kennedy and his attempts at public education represented a paradox of sorts. Early assessments of the administration in the press pointed to Kennedy's preoccupation with selling his image more than his ideas to the American public. But Arthur Schlesinger, Jr., historian and Kennedy White House staff member, argues that Kennedy actually did more to educate the public than his predecessors through his skillful use of the mass media: "[I]n later years the age of Kennedy was seen as a time of quite extraordinary transformation of national values and purposes." In retrospect, Kennedy was not perceived as doing too little to educate the public, but "too much too quickly, . . . [putting] over too many new ideas in too short a time."[3]

   Of all the press strategies employed by the Kennedy White House, the innovative use of live televised press conferences provided perhaps the best forum to use the press as a political weapon, a "plat-form from which [Kennedy] could speak over the heads of reporters and editors, the anchormen and the commentators," to take his message directly to the American public.[4] Salinger's idea of holding the press conferences live on television, now viewed as one of the most successful communication strategies during the Kennedy years, initially met with much resistance from not only the print press, who feared an unfair advantage to television reporters, but other top advisors in the White House as well. As Salinger recalled:

> It was my initial advice to President Kennedy that he hold his press conferences live on television and the President agreed with me. Sorensen was opposed to the idea; [Special Assistant] Kenny

O'Donnell was not wildly enthusiastic about it; [Dean] Rusk was dead against it when he became Secretary of State; [National Security Advisor] McGeorge Bundy was dead against it. The primary feeling of Sorensen, Bundy, and Rusk was that the President, if he made some very serious error on television, would cause a great international problem. My counter argument was that the communications in the world had reached the point that if any President in the United States made that kind of a critical mistake, he was going to destroy whatever situation he had around the world anyway. The fact that he was seen on live TV would not have a great effect. Anyway, Kennedy felt very strongly that we should go ahead with this.[5]

Both Salinger and Kennedy believed that live press conferences would be a smart strategic move, given the success that Kennedy had enjoyed on television during the Nixon debates in 1960. This would give the administration the chance to take its message directly to the American people, beyond the many conservative leaning newspapers that Salinger believed were opposed to a Democratic president at the time. An uncut and uncensored version of the President's message to the public highlighted Kennedy's strong television appeal. And according to Salinger, it was his job as press secretary to establish "a pattern of operation as far as the press [was] concerned which reflects the manner of the man that you work for and his idea of how the job should operate."[6]

While the use of the press conference itself was a definite part of the overall press strategy, the Kennedy administration also gained an unexpected advantage in the battle for public approval as a result of the televised events. Sorensen had made the decision to move press conferences from the Executive Office Building to the State Department Auditorium. He was accused by members of the press of trying to ruin the intimacy and atmosphere of the presidential/press ritual, and he was told that the television cameras would "make actors out of everybody."[7] However, despite the fact that the White House press corps continued to do its job as usual, the American public was disturbed by what it saw—a pack of unruly Washington reporters being rude to the President. As Salinger noted to Sorensen in April 1961, the televised press conference had

opened up to full view of 60,000,000 people the workings of the American reporter. And the fact is that the people are not particularly enchanted with what they see. They consider the reporters rude, their questions inept. In fairness to the reporters, it should be noted that their questions are no better or worse than they have been in the past. For the first time, however, they are subjected to a critical eye.[8]

During this formal gathering of the press before the cameras, Kennedy knew how to use individual reporters to his advantage while putting on a good show; he was young, charming, stylish, and funny—the actor at center stage. Press conferences were usually held late in the afternoon, just in time for the nightly newscasts.[9] Kennedy was the first president to not only successfully use television to his advantage, but also to understand its worth to the presidency; he was also the first president "to recognize that a president could appear on [press conferences] as a newsmaker even when there was no real news to make."[10] Salinger summed up the ultimate goal of the presidential press conference in its importance "for the American people to know the President's views on issues of importance," as well as its function as "a window to the world for the President. It gives him an indication about what problems are on the minds of the people."[11]

Kennedy has been credited with changing the art of Washington journalism forever. He knew how to entertain both the press and the public through his press conferences, and as a result, the size and influence of the White House press corps grew tremendously in his first two years in office. News organizations began to place more correspondents in Washington, and especially at the White House. Kennedy also began to perfect the new skill of news management. By giving the press more access than ever before, Kennedy managed to direct the attention of the media to the presidential core of power within government, away from Congress and the bureaucracy.[12] Efforts were also made to coordinate the message coming out of the White House and various departments and agencies. This was often an added bonus when preparing Kennedy for his press conferences. Meetings with advisors from other departments allowed Salinger "to find out what the other guys were doing, in order to reinforce the lines of communication . . . we also did a lot of the coordination work that we wanted to do."[13]

Other press strategies beyond the press conferences did exist, and many proved both innovative and successful for the Kennedy White House. These included: greater access than previously allowed by reporters to members of the White House staff, which was a big change from the Eisenhower years; television specials focusing on in-depth interviews with the President; in-depth interviews for print media as well, including several photo essays in magazines on "a day in the life" of the President; off-the-record background briefings for key White House reporters on major policy initiatives, as well as invitations to major social events; and White House luncheons for numerous editors and publishers from across the nation.[14] Kennedy was constantly concerned with his administration's image, as well as his own, and is remembered as "one of the most image-conscious presidents of his century." Family was an important theme to promote with the press, because he and his advisors had realized that "personal style could counter political frustration, mask ineptness, and create popularity in a media-dominated society."[15]

As a result, Kennedy gave frequent individual interviews to members of the press. Having once been a newspaperman himself after returning from military service in World War II, he was comfortable being around the press, as they were with him. He was also friends with several correspondents, as well as with editors and publishers, and he was not afraid to lobby them to gain favorable coverage of his policy initiatives. Like most presidents, he was interested in how he and his administration were covered in the press, and as a result read half a dozen leading newspapers on a daily basis, while expecting his staff to do the same.[16] Despite the fact that the Kennedy team had given television broadcasters a great advantage in the dissemination of news during press conferences, print journalists still remained the top priority of the White House, especially the wire services, the leading eastern dailies such as the *New York Times* and the *Washington Post*, and top newsmagazines like *Time* and *Newsweek*. The wire services were considered a top priority at press conferences, and reporters from Associated Press and United Press International were usually granted the first two questions. Salinger also worked hard to accommodate the deadlines of weekly news magazines, often providing news in a timely manner for Monday publication dates.[17]

The editor and publisher luncheons were used to cultivate not only favorable coverage, but also a better understanding among top newspaper executives of the administration's stand on issues. However, while those in attendance could ask any question they wanted of the President, they were barred from reporting his responses. Therefore, only impressions of Kennedy and the luncheon itself were printed, which resulted in mostly favorable coverage.[18] Following one such meeting in January 1962, Salinger received a letter from Paul Martin, Bureau Chief of Gannett News Service in Washington, D.C., declaring his perceived success of the luncheon:

> The consensus was that the President is an "attractive guy," well informed, with a keen mind, and a good host. "You can't help liking him," one publisher observed. Everyone agreed that the meeting was well worth while, informative, in a good atmosphere. I think there would be a better understanding among the editor-publishers of major issues discussed, and more of a tendency to resolve questions of doubt in favor of the administration.[19]

Members of the foreign press corps were also considered a valuable commodity for shaping the Kennedy message. Salinger worked hard to

cultivate contacts and favorable coverage with many foreign correspondents in Washington by holding luncheons with press representatives
from Britain, France, and various other Western European countries. He
believed that the foreign press had previously been ignored in
Washington by prior administrations, which left the United States' position on matters "completely misunderstood, misrepresented."[20]

Despite his personal charm with the press, the credibility gap
between the press, the White House, and the public did grow during
Kennedy's tenure in office. In 1961, Kennedy suffered an early defeat
with the Bay of Pigs, a plan developed by the CIA during the
Eisenhower administration to use Cuban exiles to overthrow Cuban
leader Fidel Castro. The plan was a disaster, but Kennedy took full
responsibility. Nonetheless, the press was angry about misinformation it
was given during the attempted invasion. As a result, the White House
began an attempt to control the news even more, especially during the
Cuban Missile Crisis in 1962. By then, Kennedy had been accused in the
press of being "soft" on Communism, which angered the President. He
also resented the implication that the White House was attempting to
manage the news, telling friend and journalist Ben Bradlee in March
1963, "You bastards are getting more information out of the White
House—the kind of information you want when you want it—than ever
before. Except the Cuba thing, I challenge you to give me an example of
managing the news."[21]

On October 22, 1962, Kennedy again made history on television
with his 17-minute address warning Americans of the possibility of
nuclear war and detailing his ultimatum to Soviet Premier Nikita
Kruschev. Nonetheless, in assessing the Kennedy administration's relationship with the press, coverage was generally favorable of both the
man and his administration. The press showed a great fondness for
Kennedy and his family while in office, which spared him negative coverage of his personal indiscretions.[22] Schlesinger recalls Kennedy's
famous quip during a 1962 press conference. When asked what he
thought about the press, he replied that he was ". . . reading it more and
enjoying it less." Both Kennedy and the White House press corps that
covered his brief tenure in office seemed to understand that each had a
job to do: "The reporters understood this; and, despite the animated
exchanges of 1962 and occasional moments of mutual exasperation
thereafter, the press corps regarded Kennedy with marked fondness and
admiration."[23]

KENNEDY'S PUBLIC ACTIVITIES

In addition to changing the President's relationship with the press, Kennedy has also been credited with reshaping the role of presidential leadership, starting a new era of youthful style and vigorous governing, thanks to his "rhetoric, wit, charm, youth, and Hollywood appearance."[24] Kennedy recognized the importance of public opinion polls, and strove to achieve high rankings. As a result, public relations became a key part of the everyday running of the White House and the daily communication strategy.[25] He is remembered as one of the most popular of the modern presidents, but even during his administration, his active style and the various international events that occurred between 1961 through 1963 led to high rankings in public opinion polls. An active president is not always considered popular, but Kennedy maintained both due to his flexibility, evident throughout his administration with the "fluid advisory system and pragmatic and often ad hoc responses to events."[26]

Kennedy is also remembered as a great speaker and orator, and gave one of the most memorable and perhaps most often quoted inaugural addresses, stating that "the torch has been passed to a new generation of Americans." Kennedy's style relied on delivering a "clear statement and researched information" in his speeches, with the main goal of appealing to the audience through "comprehension and comfort that translated into short speeches, short sentences when possible, a logical sequence of numbered points, and statements constructed to be clear."[27] Kennedy was also considered a good speech writer, due to his extensive reading and his ability to retain much of what he had read, but he rarely had time to write his own speeches while in the White House. Instead, he relied on key speechwriters, such as Sorensen, Schlesinger, and Richard Goodwin, as well as other advisors, as part of the system that developed his public addresses. The theory was that the more brainpower involved in the effort, the better the speech.[28] The final drafts were the responsibility of Sorensen, or occasionally Goodwin, but Kennedy remained involved in all of his speeches, from the initial concept to the final revisions. As a speechwriting team, Sorensen and Kennedy developed a style that included both an intellectual tone and a sense of humor.[29] But perhaps most important in adding to Kennedy's speaking style was the strategies behind the speeches, especially those developed for televised events: "It was the immediacy with which Kennedy invaded American living rooms that made his messages all the more striking. . . . [He] reinaugurated and expanded the rhetorical influence and potential persuasive powers of the presidency."[30]

When assessing Kennedy's use of public activities (see Table 2.1), the overall amount of events at first glance seems somewhat sparse,

Table 2.1. Kennedy—Public Activities.[31]

	1961	1962	1963
National Addresses	4	6	5
Policy Addresses	17	18	32
Press Conferences	19	27	19
Radio Addresses	0	0	0
Brief Policy/Ceremonial Remarks	126	185	206
Partisan Remarks/Campaign Speeches	8	27	5
Press Conferences with Foreign Dignitaries	0	0	0
Signing Ceremonies	16	23	13
Teleconference Remarks	2	4	0
Roundtable Discussions	0	0	0
Town Meetings/Q&A Sessions	1	1	4
Remarks to/Exchanges with Reporters	0	0	0
Total	193	291	284
Daily Average	0.56	0.8	0.87

especially when compared to some of his successors in the White House. But much of the administration's public strategy focused on television events such as press conferences, of which Kennedy held 65 during his 34 months in office. Also, since many of Kennedy's meetings with reporters or other members of the press were off-the-record discussions and remarks, they were not included in the *Public Papers of the Presidents* and therefore are not included in this data set. Kennedy did increase the number of both policy addresses and brief statements/nonpolicy remarks with each year in the White House. In total, Kennedy participated in 768 public events between the date of his inauguration, January 20, 1961, and the date of his death, November 22, 1963.

THE KENNEDY POLICY AGENDA

While Kennedy did not use public activities as extensively as some presidents during the later half of the twentieth century did, he nonetheless knew how to use speeches as an effective strategy in discussing key aspects of his policy agenda. The Kennedy White House understood that speeches "were instruments of persuasion to be used judiciously."[32] The most prominent issues on the Kennedy agenda centered on foreign policy, which goes back to the President's perceived difficulty in "educating" the public through his addresses. Unlike fellow Democrats Franklin Roosevelt and Harry Truman, both of whom faced urgent domestic, economic, and foreign issues, Kennedy came to the White House following the Eisenhower era of the 1950s, when Americans had experienced a mostly strong economy due in part to the demands of the Cold War. Kennedy, then, was "a transitional president in a transitional time who was trying desperately to cope with crises that were both self-inflicted and externally imposed."[33]

When looking at the Kennedy agenda as presented in his major public addresses (see Table 2.2), it is clear why he earned the nickname of the "Cold Warrior." His favorite topic of discussion centered on the U.S. relationship with the Soviet Union, the Cold War, and the spread of communism around the globe. Other foreign policy issues were also a high priority, including the Alliance for Progress in dealing with the diplomatic and economic developments in Latin American countries. Economic issues were also a frequent topic of Kennedy's speeches, including the administration's battle against recession and proposed tax cuts and tax reforms. For all three years, issues falling into the Diplomatic/Military category topped Kennedy's policy priorities in

Table 2.2. Kennedy's Public Agenda (Major Public Addresses).[34]

	1961	1962	1963
Domestic			
Education	41 - 3%	70 - 4%	130 - 5%
Health Care	35 - 2%	33 - 2%	20 - <1%
Welfare/Entitlements	12 - <1%	127 - 7%	27 - 1%
Anticrime	1 - <1%	3 - <1%	1 - <1%
Political Reform	1 - <1%	55 - 3%	187 - 7%
Science/Technology/ Transportation	20 - 1%	84 - 4%	18 - <1%
Environment/Energy/ Land Management	8 - <1%	3 - <1%	196 - 7%
Defense	68 - 4%	92 - 5%	40 - 2%
International			
Diplomatic/Military	968 - 61%	637 - 33%	929 - 35%
Trade/Economic	225 - 14%	313 - 16%	256 - 10%
Economic			
Domestic Fiscal/Monetary	69 - 4%	262 - 13%	512 - 19%
Unemployment/Jobs	145 - 9%	268 - 14%	331 - 13%
Total	N = 1593	N = 1947	N = 2647

major public addresses, although the totals for 1962 and 1963 dropped off by roughly 50 percent after 1961. The top category was followed by International Trade/Economic issues in 1961 and 1962, while Domestic Fiscal/Monetary issues ranked second in 1963 (due mostly to his public appeals for Congress to enact a tax cut/tax reforms). This is not to say that Kennedy did not have an extensive domestic agenda; he campaigned in 1960 on various issues and carried important domestic initiatives into the White House involving education, entitlements, and wilderness preservation, to name a few. But these issues rarely, if ever, appeared in his major addresses, with the exception of civil rights in 1963 (under the Political Reform category in Table 2.2).[35] Clearly, "going public" was not a strategy used in the fight to win passage of many of these issues. Despite Kennedy's mastery of television appearances, White House events were not covered as extensively as they would be within the next few decades, and were therefore not yet viewed as crucial to the overall communication strategy.

And while no direct correlation can be made to the lack of a public activities strategy, Kennedy did fail to gain passage of several key domestic initiatives in Congress, including Aid to Education, the Youth Conservation Corps, Medicare, creating a Department of Urban Affairs, and a tax reduction.[36]

THE FIRST TIER: THE TAX CUT PROPOSAL OF 1963

The Issue and White House Strategy

The Kennedy administration began pushing for tax revision legislation as early as 1961. In October 1962, the President signed into law the Revenue Act of 1962, which included various tax reforms, as well as a tax break for businesses intended to promote industrial investment. By the summer of 1962, the administration had begun to consider a personal income tax cut as well. But despite several recommendations for a "quickie" tax cut, by August, Kennedy had decided on a proposal that would encompass "permanent and basic reform and reduction."[37] Kennedy had closely followed economic issues since taking office, and he refused to increase the deficit by either a tax cut or increased spending in 1962 to fight a recessionary economy. For political reasons, Kennedy felt it imperative to prove to the American public, and especially the business community, that the Democratic Party could indeed be fiscally responsible. Even when the administration began pursuing the tax cut in 1963, the potential political fallout from an increased deficit was still a main concern.[38]

During the summer of 1962, White House advisors were busy devising a strategy for how and when Kennedy would pursue the tax cut policy. In a major address at the Yale University commencement in June 1962, Kennedy spoke extensively on fiscal policy in the United States, but declined to offer much specific detail about any forthcoming plans. According to Sorensen, the speech was not a trial balloon about an upcoming policy proposal, but "an academic exercise before an academic audience." However, the reaction to the speech by the business community and conservatives showed the administration that "debt and deficit spending were as unpopular as ever."[39] In July, Sorensen warned Kennedy about the crucial political timing involved with the issue: "A tax cut is a massive economic weapon. It can only be used once. It has not been used in any previous recession in my memory. . . . You did not want us to over-react in Berlin with a national emergency—I do not want us to over-react now." Sorensen urged Kennedy to seek a tax cut only if both the economic and political timing were right; that is, if employment and production continued to decline, if the cut would not result in too high of a deficit, and if both Congress and the business community seemed receptive to the move: "Once you are able to go to the Congress and country with positive answers to these items, such a move will be both right and successful. Until then, it is likely to be neither."[40] The administration continued to monitor public attitude on a tax cut, which most Americans did not favor if the result included an increased deficit, according to a Gallup Poll taken in late July 1962.[41] In August of that year, in an address to the nation, Kennedy told the American public that he would recommend to Congress a top-to-bottom cut in personal and corporate income taxes, effective January 1963, but not the "quickie" tax cut that many in the administration had suggested that summer. Sorensen believed that the August 1962 speech was "the worst speech he ever gave. . . . It isn't, however, so much because his heart wasn't in it, but that a speech announcing that you're not going to do something cannot be a very exciting speech. And economics are not very exciting under any circumstances."[42] Walter Heller, chairman of the Council of Economic Advisers, served as the Kennedy pointman in selling the new tax reduction/reform plan to the business community; the strategy included an article by Heller in the November 1962 issue of *Nation's Business* urging support of the Kennedy plan.[43] On December 14, Kennedy gave a major policy address to the Economic Club of New York outlining his economic position on a tax cut, which according to Heller was a strategic success:

Congress may be lukewarm, but powerful groups throughout the country are *ready for action*. When the Chicago Board of Commerce,

the AFL-CIO, the CED, and the U.S. Chamber are on the same side—
when repeated editorials in *Business Week* are indistinguishable from
those appearing in the *Washington Post*—the prospect for action cannot be wholly dim. Can 3000 members of the N.Y. Economic Club be
wrong?[44]

From a strategic standpoint, the administration knew that selling a $10
billion tax cut during a time of relative prosperity with an unbalanced
budget would be a difficult task. Prior to the December speech to the
conservative business group, Kennedy had not been optimistic about
passing the bill. But after the speech, Kennedy was more enthusiastic,
saying "if I can sell it to those guys, I can sell it to anyone."[45]

Kennedy continued to push for tax cut legislation throughout
1963, but congressional support and action were slow in coming. Ten days
after Kennedy's State of the Union Message on January 14, 1963, the
President submitted his tax program to Congress, stating that it was his top
priority request for the year. The administration argued that the existing
tax structure was reducing consumer purchasing power by drawing too
heavily on the nation's resources, and reducing incentives for savings and
investment.[46] Kennedy continued to discuss the tax cut in major public
addresses, including speeches to the American Bankers Association
Symposium on Economic Growth in February, the Washington Conference
of the Advertising Council in March, the American Society of Newspaper
Editors in April, the Committee for Economic Development in May, the
National Conference of the Business Committee for Tax Reduction in
September, and the Florida Chamber of Commerce in November.[47] He also
lobbied heavily for public support of the bill in an address to the nation on
September 18. This was considered by many observers to be a "masterful
speech" by Kennedy, in part, according to Sorensen, due to the simplicity
of the message. Afterward, Kennedy believed that the speech was successful and appealing to the American public.[48] However, due to partisan bickering, the tax bill made slow progress in Congress. The bill did pass in the
House of Representatives on September 25, 1963, but the congressional session ended before the Senate could reach agreement. Kennedy would not
live to see the bill enacted. The Senate finally approved the bill the following February; President Lyndon Johnson signed the Revenue Act of 1964
into law on February 26, 1964, an $11.5 billion omnibus tax reduction and
reform bill intended to promote economic growth.[49]

Press Coverage

The *New York Times* provided extensive coverage of the Kennedy tax cut
proposal between January and November 1963, with a news item

appearing, on average, slightly more often than once every two days. However, most stories were generated by either congressional or interest group activity on the proposal; only 21 percent of the coverage was generated by presidential activity (see Table 2.3).

Table 2.3. Amount and Type of *New York Times* Coverage of the Tax Cut Proposal (January 1963-November 1963).

	White House	Congress	Interest Group/Other
News Story	24	71	72
News Analysis	6	3	3
Column	4	9	2
Editorial	13	10	4
Total	47 - (21%)	93 - (42%)	81 - (37%)

Of the stories generated by Kennedy, the tone of the coverage was mixed. Most news stories were either neutral (a straight news story only describing events from the previous day), or balanced (providing quotes from both sides of the issue). Several news stories were also positive, giving extensive coverage to Kennedy's remarks during press conferences or speeches without a rebuttal from opponents and portraying the President's policy as the right course of action. All items under the news analysis and column categories were balanced in their assessments of both sides of the tax cut issue. However, of 13 editorials on Kennedy and his tax cut proposal, he received no outright endorsements from the *Times*. Seven editorials were negative, and six were balanced; the *Times* was either highly critical of both Kennedy and his policy, or in the balanced editorials, found only little merit in the proposed tax cut. Most often, the *Times* criticized what they perceived as Kennedy's ineffective political leadership with Congress over the tax cut (see Table 2.4).

THE SECOND TIER: AID TO EDUCATION IN 1961

The Issue and White House Strategy

According to those who knew him best, Kennedy believed education to be one of the most pressing policy concerns from the start of his political

Table 2.4. Tone of *New York Times* Coverage of Presidential Activities on the Tax Cut Proposal (January 1963-November 1963).

	Positive	Negative	Balanced/Mixed	Neutral
News Story	6	0	10	8
News Analysis	0	0	6	0
Column	0	0	4	0
Editorial	0	7	6	0
Total	6	7	26	8

career. During the 1960 presidential campaign, education continued to be a prominent issue, just as it was during Dwight Eisenhower's second term, with Kennedy setting the stage for education policies to become an important part of the "New Frontier."[50] Ten days after taking the oath of office, Kennedy addressed a joint session of Congress to discuss the plans of his new administration, which included federal aid to education for both public schools and colleges.[51] Then, in February, Kennedy submitted a special message to Congress on education, where he asked for $2.3 billion in grants for teachers' salaries and classroom construction, $2.8 billion in loans to colleges for construction, and $892 million for federal scholarships. The message also stipulated that no money would be used for parochial schools, relying on previous Supreme Court rulings that suggested such funding would be unconstitutional. Thus ensued the controversy over the Kennedy Aid to Education bill.[52]

Many believe that the bill had no chance of passage from the start, that it was merely a symbolic piece of legislation intended to educate the American public on the issue of federal aid to education.[53] Not only had the exclusion of church schools angered leaders of the Catholic Church, but some members in Congress refused to support federal education aid given to schools that still maintained racial segregation. Three core groups of opponents in Congress then emerged—conservative Republicans, Southern Democrats, and several Catholic members of the House. The administration, however, appeared remiss in recognizing the controversies surrounding the bill until it was too late. Strategically speaking, Kennedy and his advisers did little to ensure passage of the bill. The President failed to build coalitions both inside and outside Congress, he did not rally his supporters or neutralize his opponents, and he failed to use his political capital as president in any interventions with the Catholic Church or armtwisting in Congress; in essence, "the president hung back."[54]

Clearly, the issue of education did not rank high on the President's public agenda during 1961, despite the fact that Kennedy considered the bill his number one legislative priority. Aside from a brief mention of aid for education in his State of the Union address or a response to an occasional question during a press conference, Kennedy failed to include any discussion of the issue in his major addresses during 1961. Kennedy made no effort to get the American public to "focus on the subject, perhaps by stimulating fresh debate on education. . . . [T]here was no dramatic gesture, no attention-capturing device that would have drawn the public eye to what he said mattered most."[55] In the end, instead of Kennedy's Aid to Education proposal, Congress passed minimal extensions to the National Defense of Education Act of 1958, providing grants for school construction and augmenting teachers' salaries in areas impacted by increased federal activities.[56] The administration considered the legislative defeat on education a "major setback" and its "biggest disappointment" in 1961. However, Sorensen believed that the administration had given the bill its all, and had taken the right approach. In December 1961, he assessed the political defeat:

> Those who usually oppose such a measure over issues of segregation, states rights, academic freedom, equalization of rich and poor states and salaries versus construction, were now joined by those who wished to avoid a new religious controversy. The positions taken on each of these issues by the Administration bill were fair and constitutional. No other piece of domestic legislation received as much Administration effort, leadership, contacts, etc. A public appeal could not have changed the vote in the Rules Committee or the opposition which had hardened on the issues mentioned above, and would have only magnified the bill's defeat and embittered our Congressional relations.[57]

Press Coverage

While the White House did not place a high priority on aid to education in the use of public activities, the *New York Times* treated it like a first-tier issue in the amount of coverage between January and September 1961, with a news item appearing, on average, slightly less than once a day. And, like the coverage of the tax cut proposal in 1963, most stories were generated by either congressional or interest group activity on the proposal; only 9 percent of the coverage was generated by presidential activity (see Table 2.5). Despite the administration's low priority for discussing the issue publicly, the stories generated by Kennedy in the *Times* were fairly supportive and positive in tone. The news stories and news analysis, focusing on either comments by Kennedy at press conferences

Table 2.5. Amount and Type of *New York Times* Coverage of the Aid to Education Proposal (January 1961-September 1961).

	White House	Congress	Interest Group/Other
News Story	9	73	73
News Analysis	1	0	3
Column	4	3	5
Editorial	4	20	4
Total	18 - (9%)	96 - (48%)	85 - (43%)

or the administration's reaction to outside political events, provided a good balance in presenting both sides of the issue. In addition, the majority of columns and editorials favored Kennedy's position on education, and they often faulted Congress for politicizing an important issue. By August and September, however, the tone of editorials in the *Times* changed, being quick to point out that Kennedy's leadership on the issue had been ineffective (see Table 2.6).

Table 2.6. Tone of *New York Times* Coverage of Presidential Activities on the Aid to Education Proposal (January 1961-September 1961).

	Positive	Negative	Balanced/Mixed	Neutral
News Story	1	1	5	2
News Analysis	0	0	1	0
Column	2	1	1	0
Editorial	3	0	1	0
Total	6	2	8	2

CONCLUSION

While the historical perception in regards to the successes and failures of the Kennedy White House may always be somewhat distorted as a result of the assassination in November 1963, most scholars agree that

Kennedy was a definite trailblazer in his use of the news media and in his overall communication strategy. Televised press conferences, while no longer as novel to the American public now as they were in 1961, still remain an important public strategy for presidents. And, while Kennedy may have "gone public" much less often than his successors, it is still his example of style and public presence that presidents try to emulate. Like all presidents, Kennedy's leadership style can be praised and/or criticized from many angles. Accordingly, the case studies provided in this chapter provide an analysis of how the Kennedy administration used different communication strategies on two key domestic issues, achieving very different results, not only in legislative outcomes, but in press coverage as well.

Overall, the amount of media coverage for both policies studied is consistent with Kennedy's amount of public activities. At that time, unlike with later presidents, the White House did not stage media events to gain coverage of presidential policies; therefore, most news coverage was generated by congressional and/or interest group activity. Clearly, the Kennedy administration had learned an important lesson from its defeat on Aid to Education in 1961. While the proposed tax cut was a higher political priority, since the national economic picture always plays a key role in a presidential election, the political strategy behind the proposed tax cut seemed more organized and focused by late 1962 and early 1963, compared to earlier legislative efforts. At least when comparing these two policies, Kennedy seemed to benefit from a learning curve with the time he had spent in the White House, and he began to develop a firmer grasp of his leadership style, as well as a better understanding of his relationship with both Congress and the American public.

ENDNOTES

1. While Kennedy is widely recognized as the first "television" president, it is important to note that Dwight Eisenhower was the first president to rely on such media strategies as taped press conferences for later television broadcast, televised cabinet meetings, televised "fireside chats," and various other television photo opportunities. See Craig Allen, *Eisenhower and the Mass Media* (Chapel Hill, NC: University of North Carolina Press, 1993). Allen argues that Eisenhower's contribution to the way presidents communicate during the television age is often overlooked, and that Eisenhower and his advisors developed a highly effective communication strategy that fit perfectly with the rapid expansion of television during the 1950s.

2. Memo to Sorensen from Salinger, 4/17/61, in White House Staff Files of Pierre Salinger, John Fitzgerald Kennedy Library.
3. Arthur M. Schlesinger, Jr., *A Thousand Days: John F. Kennedy in the White House* (New York: Fawcett Premier, 1965), 655-6.
4. Charles Roberts, "Kennedy and the Press: Image and Reality," in *The Kennedy Presidency: Seventeen Intimate Perspectives of John F. Kennedy*, Ed. Kenneth W. Thompson (Lanham, MD: University Press of America, 1985), 178.
5. Pierre Salinger, recorded interview by Theodore White, August 10, 1965, pp. 108-9, John F. Kennedy Library Oral History Program.
6. Ibid., 100.
7. Ibid., 106-7.
8. Memo to Sorensen from Salinger, 4/17/61, in White House Staff Files of Pierre Salinger, John Fitzgerald Kennedy Library.
9. Michael Emery and Edwin Emery, *The Press and America: An Interpretive History of the Mass Media*, 8th ed. (Needham Heights, MA: Simon & Schuster, 1996), 399-401.
10. John Tebbel and Sarah Miles Watts, *The Press and the Presidency: From George Washington to Ronald Reagan* (New York: Oxford University Press, 1985), 479.
11. Document written by Salinger defining his role as press secretary, not dated, in the White House Staff Files of Pierre Salinger, John Fitzgerald Kennedy Library.
12. See Richard Reeves, *President Kennedy: Profile of Power* (New York: Simon & Schuster, 1993), 278-80; and Theodore C. Sorensen, *Kennedy* (New York: Harper and Row Publishers, 1965), 318-22.
13. Pierre Salinger, recorded interview by Theodore White, August 10, 1965, pp. 142-3, John F. Kennedy Library Oral History Program.
14. Charles Roberts, "JFK and the Press," in *Ten Presidents and the Press*, Ed. Kenneth Thompson (Washington, DC: University Press of America, 1983), 70.
15. James N. Giglio, *The Presidency of John F. Kennedy* (Lawrence, KS: University Press of Kansas, 1991), 255.
16. For discussions on Kennedy's voracious reading habits of newspapers and magazines while in the White House, as well as his friendships with members of the press, see Sorensen, 310-8; and Pierre Salinger, *With Kennedy* (New York: Doubleday, 1966), 116-20.
17. Salinger, 118-9.
18. Michael Baruch Grossman and Martha Joynt Kumar, *Portraying the President: The White House and the News Media* (Baltimore: Johns Hopkins University Press, 1981), 164.
19. Letter from Paul Martin to Pierre Salinger, 1/25/62, in White House Staff Files of Pierre Salinger, John Fitzgerald Kennedy Library.

20. Pierre Salinger, recorded interview by Theodore White, August 10, 1965, pp. 146-7, John F. Kennedy Library Oral History Program.

21. Benjamin C. Bradlee, *Conversations With Kennedy* (New York: W.W. Norton & Company, 1975), 154.

22. Emery and Emery, 401-2; and Giglio, 267.

23. Schlesinger, 660.

24. Giglio, 1.

25. Paul Brace and Barbara Hinckley, *Follow the Leader: Opinion Polls and the Modern Presidents* (New York: HarperCollins Publishers, 1992), 35-6.

26. Ibid., 121-2.

27. Vito N. Silvestri, "John Fitzgerald Kennedy," in *U.S. Presidents as Orators: A Bio-Critical Sourcebook*, Ed. Halford Ryan (Westport, CT: Greenwood Press, 1995), 223-4.

28. Steven R. Goldzwig and George N. Dionisopoulos, *"In a Perilous Hour:" The Public Addresses of John F. Kennedy* (Westport, CT: Greenwood Press, 1995), 9-10.

29. Ibid., 11-3. However, Sorensen maintains that Kennedy "played a major role in every major speech, selecting subject matter and themes, arguments and conclusions, quotations and phrases." See *"Let the Word Go Forth:" The Speeches, Statements, and Writings of John F. Kennedy*, Ed. Theodore C. Sorensen (New York: Delacorte Press, 1988), 2.

30. Ibid., 145.

31. Compiled from *The Public Papers of the Presidents of the United States: John F. Kennedy, 1961-1963* (Washington, DC: Government Printing Office, 1962-64).

32. Silvestri, 225. Most of Kennedy's speeches were also brief, lasting only 20 to 25 minutes in length. See Sorensen, *"Let the Word Go Forth,"* 4.

33. Goldzwig and Dionisopoulos, 16.

34. Compiled from *The Public Papers of the Presidents of the United States: John F. Kennedy, 1961-1963* (Washington, DC: Government Printing Office, 1962-64).

35. Policy issues under the Environment/Land Management/ Energy category also ranked higher in 1963, but this can be attributed to a tour of the Western United States that Kennedy took during that fall, during which he gave several policy addresses in more rural settings where conservation was an appropriate topic.

36. See Larry Berman, *The New American Presidency* (Boston: Little Brown and Company, 1987), 239; and Jeff Fishel, *Presidents & Promises: From Campaign Pledge to Presidential Performance* (Washington, DC: CQ Press, 1985), 195.

37. *Congressional Quarterly Almanac*, 1964, Vol. XX (Washington, DC: Congressional Quarterly Service, 1965), 525.

38. Paul C. Light, *The President's Agenda: Domestic Policy Choice From Kennedy to Reagan* (Baltimore: Johns Hopkins University Press, 1991), 139-40.

39. Theodore Sorensen, recorded interview by Carl Kaysen, May 20, 1964, p. 151, John F. Kennedy Library Oral History Program.

40. Memorandum from Sorensen to Kennedy, 7/12/62, in the President's Office Files, John Fitzgerald Kennedy Library.

41. Memorandum from Walter Heller to Kennedy, 7/31/62, in the President's Office Files, John Fitzgerald Kennedy Library.

42. Theodore Sorensen, recorded interview by Carl Kaysen, May 20, 1964, p. 156, John F. Kennedy Library Oral History Program.

43. Walter W. Heller, "Why We Must Cut Taxes," *Nation's Business* (November 1962): 281-4.

44. Memo from Heller to Kennedy, 12/15/62, in the President's Office Files, John Fitzgerald Kennedy Library.

45. Theodore Sorensen, recorded interview by Carl Kaysen, May 20, 1964, p. 156, John F. Kennedy Library Oral History Program.

46. *Congressional Quarterly Almanac*, 1964, 525.

47. From *Public Papers of the Presidents of the United States: John F. Kennedy, 1963* (Washington, DC: Government Printing Office, 1964).

48. Theodore Sorensen, recorded interview by Carl Kaysen, May 20, 1964, p. 157, John F. Kennedy Library Oral History Program.

49. *Congressional Quarterly Almanac*, 1964, 518.

50. William T. O'Hara, *John F. Kennedy on Education* (New York: Teachers College Press, 1966), 1-15.

51. *Public Papers of the Presidents of the United States: John F. Kennedy, 1961* (Washington, DC: Government Printing Office, 1962), 22.

52. *Congressional Quarterly Almanac*, 1961, Vol. XVII (Washington, DC: Congressional Quarterly Service, 1962), 213.

53. See Schlesinger, 651, and Light, 106.

54. Barbara Kellerman, *The Political Presidency: Practice of Leadership* (New York: Oxford University Press, 1984), 80-1.

55. Ibid., 84-5.

56. *Congressional Quarterly Almanac*, 1961, 213.

57. Memo dated 12/29/61 from White House Staff Files of Theodore Sorensen, Box 32, John Fitzgerald Kennedy Library.

3

Johnson and Nixon: Playing Ball in the Kennedys' Court

Following the communicative successes of the Kennedy years, especially the image building through the increasingly powerful medium of television, presidential advisors to both Lyndon Johnson and Richard Nixon would face a daunting task. The stage had been set for the White House to continue to present both the president and his policy agenda in such a way as to meet the demands and expectations of the news media as well as the public. The 1960s witnessed tremendous growth for the public leadership aspect of the presidency, in which Johnson, as well as the political issues of the day, played a critical role. After Kennedy's assassination in November 1963, the task of leading a grieving nation fell to Johnson. However, upon first taking office, Johnson was handicapped by a public that, despite his three decades of public service, did not recognize him as a well established political leader. Nonetheless, he would quickly develop a vast and diverse policy agenda to promote his vision for a "Great Society," a domestic plan which would ultimately be hindered by the continuing American military involvement in Vietnam. Nixon won the presidential election in 1968, one of the most tumultuous years in American politics, due in part to his promises to end the Vietnam War. But just as it was for Johnson, that task proved elusive, and the continued American involvement in Southeast

Asia would hamper Nixon's policy efforts on the domestic front. Nixon also did not enjoy a good relationship with the press and was quite inaccessible, both to the Washington press corps and to the public. Both Johnson and Nixon were credited with widening the credibility gap between the public, the press, and the presidency while in office, due mostly to Vietnam and then to Nixon's involvement in Watergate. And, in terms of their communication strategies, both would suffer from trying to live up to the public expectations of leadership during the new television age that had been set by the Kennedy administration.

JOHNSON AND THE PRESS

James H. Rowe, Jr., a longtime Democratic presidential advisor and one-time advisor to Franklin Roosevelt, once commented on the difference between the presidencies of Kennedy and Johnson: "I used to say that Roosevelt was a man of style and substance, Kennedy had style, and Lyndon Johnson had substance."[1] Despite serving as Kennedy's vice president, Johnson differed from Kennedy, both personally and politically as president, in almost every way imaginable. However, Johnson would work hard during his five-plus years in office to emulate Kennedy's success at dealing with the press and presenting an image as a strong leader to the American public. Johnson's public strategies were different than Kennedy's, as was his public style. Johnson's relationship with the press was also a paradox—enjoying a fairly good personal relationship with the White House press corps while the credibility gap widened tremendously due to Vietnam. He knew how to court the press, and he would routinely call White House regulars into the Oval Office to ply them with food and answer their questions. When first taking office, he preferred an informal relationship with key members of the Washington press corps. He held barbecues for reporters at the LBJ Ranch, swam with them in the pool, and walked with them through the White House gardens. He held slightly more press conferences than Kennedy, and he would also develop a television strategy that included speaking directly to the American people about important issues, including Vietnam.[2]

From his early days as President, Johnson believed that he had to seduce the press and sell them on his extensive political agenda. Success, he believed, was not possible without the support of public opinion, and that could be cultivated in part through positive coverage by the "opinion-makers"—the three television networks, as well as the *New York Times, Washington Post, Time, Newsweek,* and *U.S. News and World Report.* According to George Christian, the last in the succession of Johnson's four press secretaries, serving from 1966-1969, Johnson took charge of much of his own press relations, which actually benefited the press: "He was accessible. He was quotable. He made a ton of news any time he wanted to, and sometimes when he didn't. His achievements were monumental and his mistakes also took on such proportions."[3] While Johnson liked many of the reporters within the White House press corps, he was suspicious of and disliked just as many others. He also complained frequently about an anti-Texas bias by the "eastern-establishment" press, and was convinced, especially as America became more involved in Vietnam after 1965, that many in the press were out to bring down his presidency.[4] Christian believed that to some extent, Johnson's suspicions of the press were well founded:

> A few of the White House reporters plain didn't like the President. They were after him from the minute he came into office, practically. These were difficult guys to deal with. They might be perfectly decent people in some respects, but they had a real hang-up on Lyndon Johnson. As a result, they questioned everything he said. They questioned the credibility of the whole government and, particularly, him on almost every issue. They might be outspoken critics of the war, or of the Dominican intervention, or something else. They just generally, were antagonistic reporters.[5]

Johnson knew that he would have a difficult time living up to the legacy that Kennedy had left with the Washington press corps, especially since Kennedy had been personal friends with many journalists. Pierre Salinger, a holdover from the Kennedy administration as press secretary until he resigned in 1964, acknowledged that Johnson was more accessible to the press and spent more time with newspapermen than Kennedy did as president. The difference, however, was that Johnson respected journalists and their opinions much less:

> There [was] a very, very clear difference. The difference [was] that Kennedy listened to the questions and tried to answer them, and Johnson [gave] a monologue. In other words, when a newspaperman [went] to interview Johnson for an hour, he may end up listening to Johnson's speech for fifty-nine minutes on a subject which he doesn't give a God damn about and ask him one question.[6]

Johnson would never develop the kind of rapport or sense of ease in communicating with reporters that Kennedy had, nor would he trust them. According to Robert Kintner, former president of NBC and a special assistant to Johnson from 1966-1967, only a select few members of the press gained even a hint of Johnson's trust:

I think he has always been very wary of the press, as the press. I think, on the other hand, he enjoyed talking alone with individual members of the press, whom he, quote, "semi-trusted," end quote, such as Drew Pearson, such as myself, such as the AP and UP people covering the Senate.[7]

Access for the press was not a problem during the Johnson years in the White House, since the President viewed journalists as members of a special interest group that needed to be bargained with and courted.[8] As early as his first press conference on December 7, 1963, Johnson made a point to let the White House press corps know that he would be accessible:

I want to communicate with the American people, and I want to maintain accessibility, and I want there to be a free flow of information to the extent possible, and limited only by security, and I should like, of course, after the period of mourning, to try to determine just what would be the most effective way, with your counsel and cooperation.[9]

Following the 1964 election, as the focus of the Johnson communication strategy began to shift to more policy concerns and away from the campaign, Philip Potter of the *Baltimore Sun* urged Johnson to maintain the accessibility that had existed in the early months of the administration, especially informal opportunities, such as a walk through the White House grounds, to talk with the President:

While covering the Korean War in 1950, I came to the conclusion our military owed the press only three things: 1. Accessibility to the battlefields, so we could gather the essential information for the people back home. 2. Such logistic facilities as made it possible for us to live in the theater. 3. Means of communication to get our files out to our papers. In my judgment, the military owed us nothing more, and were to be judged only by the above standards. In essence, I think this is what the White House owes the Press.[10]

However, many of his advisors would later acknowledge that Johnson made a grave error in not only giving too much access to the press, but treating them in the same manner as he had as Senate Majority Leader. The White House press corps was not a group that could be bullied into submission like the dozen or so Capitol Hill reporters that had relied on him for inside information on the workings of the Senate. As President, Johnson needed the reporters more than they needed him, since they also had alternative sources to rely on, such as White House staff members and executive agencies. Also, news on Johnson as Senate Majority Leader consisted mostly of policy and political maneuverings, while news on Johnson as President was much more personal in nature. Johnson had given the White House press corps virtually free access to the Oval Office and he was never far from their view, even when he would return to the LBJ Ranch in Texas for time away from Washington.[11] Christian recalled that too much access caused a problem in Johnson's overall relationship with the press:

> I always thought sometimes our relationships with the press were a little too close and a little too familiar. There was no great mystique about President Johnson as far as the press was concerned. They knew him too well. He had been in the Senate. A lot of them knew him there. . . . In a way public officials are better off when they're a bit removed from the herd, you know. If you can develop a mystique that you're a little bit removed from the ordinary person and that you're a little insulated, and a little distant, and unfamiliar, and maybe treat them at arms length, sometimes I think your press relations are better. . . . He was in the arena a little too much. . . . The familiarity itself became somewhat of a problem. There was very darned little that Lyndon Johnson said, did, thought, that the press wasn't aware of. He talked with them a good deal privately or publicly. He made a lot of appearances where they could see him a great deal. He just generally became such a familiar President to them that they may have treated him a little too familiarly. He wasn't the king.[12]

Columnist Drew Pearson also acknowledged to Press Secretary Bill Moyers, who served from 1965-1966, that as early as the summer of 1965, Johnson was suffering from overexposure to the press. His numerous off-the-record meetings with newspapermen, according to Pearson, were beginning to undermine his image and credibility among the White House press corps, as well as take up too much of the President's time:

> [This] is a drain on his time [and] these guys go out and blab. There is an old saying that intimacy breeds contempt. . . . I have heard various newsmen who have seen the President talk privately not merely about what he said but about his mannerisms, his alleged Texas corn, his alleged determination to influence the press through these personal interviews. They consider him a little too eager, a little too friendly, a little too self-revealing. Most of these guys will not go out and write about what the President said because they recognize the seal of confidence. But they will go out and talk to their colleagues. . . . In my opinion Eisenhower was the most do-nothing President we have had

in years. Yet his press relations were amazingly good . . . because Jim Hagerty was smart enough to create an aura of mystery around Eisenhower. He never saw any newspapermen. Because he was aloof, because he only appeared at certain intervals, the press and the public got the impression that he was doing important things. Actually he was playing golf and bridge. But the aura of mystery and importance continued right up to the end.[13]

Johnson also exhibited an obsession with any news concerning his presidency. Three television sets were installed in the Oval Office for Johnson to monitor coverage on all three major networks, which supplemented AP and UPI tickers for up-to-the-minute news reports. Johnson would routinely begin his mornings, usually at 5:00 or 5:30 a.m., by reading half a dozen major newspapers and watching all three morning network news shows. Johnson rarely missed the Sunday interview shows such as *Meet the Press* and *Face the Nation*, and he would also monitor any breaking stories on CBS radio news.[14] According to Christian, Johnson's obsession with the news sometimes gave an advantage to members of the press, who knew how to get a rise out of him:

> He read the newspapers and listened to the radio better than anybody else at the White House, or anybody else in Washington. He knew more what was going on than anybody else, and he got a lot of his information by just being well informed through the papers and everything. Well, exposure to that much news copy became sort of an albatross, in a way, because the press knew it. The press knew it could antagonize him if they wanted to.[15]

Kintner believed that Johnson worried excessively about every word that was written or spoken about him in the press, and he often tried to convince the President that his energy on the matter was greatly misplaced:

> You could never convince President Johnson that a sentence or two of critical comment about him really meant nothing. Number one, at that point newspapers had very little influence in the country. As far as information, it had all passed to radio and television. And, two, people really don't read articles sentence by sentence. And, three, if they read something derogatory, they're just as apt to forget it as something in praise; it's an overall impression . . . [and] it wasn't important in the way history would judge him or it wasn't important in the way the voters would react. Particularly in relation to the newspapers. But you could not get that out of his mind. I mean, he would get early editions of the *Washington Post*, and get on the telephone, call Kay Graham . . . [He'd] call the reporter in question,

accuse them of trying to get him, of printing inaccuracies. I think it was one of his weaknesses as president, the attention he paid to what was said about him, and in the minute detail that he paid attention, and in addition, the time he spent in angry exchanges with members of the press either over the telephone or personally or in press conferences.[16]

Potter also warned Johnson about how his colleagues in the press treat presidents, and that Johnson should be prepared to be constantly misinterpreted and inaccurately quoted, among other things:

> Some are going to tell you the course you ought to be pursuing. Some are going to strive to create divisions between you and your cabinet members, your staff and other subordinates or associates. There are going to be attempts to create rifts between you and the vice president; between you and those in the legislative branch; between you and Senator [Robert] Kennedy, particularly. There is no way on earth you or your staff can guard against some of these things . . . all you can do is submit as gracefully as may be to the errors. . . . As you well know, corrections, although necessary, never catch up to allegations and charges. Thus, my first suggestion is for you to do what you can to curb sensitivity to press criticism and error. It will only give you ulcers.[17]

Perhaps the greatest challenge in developing a communication strategy during the Johnson years was the inevitable comparisons to the Kennedy image. Not only did Johnson have to face the public's memory of the young and eloquent fallen President, but he had to contend with the rising political star of Robert Kennedy, the heir apparent to the Kennedy dynasty, as well. While many advisors urged Johnson to be more himself around the reporters, the results did not always receive good press. Images of Johnson showing off his scar from gall bladder surgery or lifting his pet beagles up by the ears were not the finest moments of the public aspect of his presidency. Perhaps the most famous story of Johnson's antics with members of the press was the 85-90 m.p.h drive that several reporters took with Johnson across the LBJ Ranch in his Lincoln Continental, his cowboy hat hiding the speedometer and his cup of beer on the dashboard. Even a *GQ* cover story in March 1966 showing Johnson on the front porch of his ranch wearing a "Kennedyesque" two-button suit, or any other photo opportunity as part of the Johnson public relations strategy, could not compete with the public's enduring memory of the Kennedy family sailing or playing touch football. As a result, Johnson was convinced that "Kennedy press zealots" had created a conspiracy against him—that once President Kennedy had died, despite

Johnson's extensive Great Society policy agenda, the press automatically shifted its attention to Bobby to carry on the legacy.[18]

Kintner recalled Johnson's paranoia that some members of the press were pro-Kennedy and thus anti-Johnson, but he disagreed that the assessment was true:

> [Johnson had] two deep-rooted and wrong impressions. He thought anybody who was ever associated with the Kennedys was against him. That's in a broad term, but I think it's almost literally true. I think that was incorrect. . . . He felt that located in Georgetown were a group of columnists and Kennedy followers who were out to get him.[19]

Kintner also disagreed with the President's belief that people viewed him as less presidential than Kennedy since he was a Texas native:

> I think he was wrong that people characterized him as the uncouth Texan who couldn't compare to the smooth Kennedy graduate of the Harvard Ivy League schools. That was always in his mind, both his method of dress, his method of talking, and the regard that people felt for him. I think the President felt there was a conspiracy, not in the sense of a planned conspiracy, against him on the part of people who had gone to eastern schools and been educated differently than he was, who weren't from states like Texas . . . I'm sure that he felt they looked down on him and Mrs. Johnson.[20]

Even the Johnson staff was not immune from comparisons to the Kennedy administration. In March 1966, Presidential Aide Harry McPherson lamented to Bill Moyers that the press considered the Johnson staff "humorless" drones who were afraid to have any fun, unlike the fun-loving Kennedy staff, which made good copy for the administration:

> This view of the White House is of course directly related to the image of the Kennedy staff—young, vibrant, light-hearted, Finding Government Fun. I don't know what the prescription is, or even whether there should be one. But I do think the press—a cynical crowd who would rather destroy a stuffed shirt than eat—will continue to sneer so long as we show thin skins, fear, and the kind of sanctimony people display who never enjoy themselves.[21]

The Kennedy legacy even haunted Johnson in his use of press conferences. Aides urged Johnson to follow Kennedy's lead in using live televised press conferences, which the press had come to expect as formal events held in the State Department auditorium. However, the limitations of press conferences as an effective public relations tool for Johnson were recognized early on, since they had evolved into "a performance in which neither questions nor answers can be as concise and concrete as they once were. The reporter is made into an unpaid actor for television." Additional means of communicating with the press, namely informal sessions held by Johnson in the Oval Office, were used as opposed to making sweeping changes to the formal press conferences.[22] Johnson preferred these more informal meetings with the press, and despite holding more total press conferences than Kennedy, he rarely held formal televised events.[23] Presidential aide Jack Valenti urged Johnson to do more live press conferences, but Johnson recoiled at the idea:

> I really don't know why. Maybe he felt that that Kennedy phantom which ran down every corridor in that White House all the years we were there would come alive like Banquo's ghost at every one of these press conferences and they would compare him unfavorably with Kennedy.[24]

Kintner would later urge Johnson to limit his use of informal sessions with reporters in the Oval Office, despite the success that Franklin Roosevelt had enjoyed with this type of session, since having Johnson sit behind a desk while answering important policy questions did not take advantage of his commanding presence.[25] Kintner continued to urge Johnson to use more formal press conferences "at which he [was] good and have them televised so that he can get directly to the public with his own words."[26]

In the give and take of the presidential/press relationship, Johnson enjoyed maintaining unpredictability with the White House press corps in announcing his travel and speaking schedule. While Johnson believed this helped in controlling the flow of news, it mostly served to annoy members of the press throughout the Johnson years. As late as December 1967, members of the press were still complaining about the lack of advance notice for press events, and aides were still trying to persuade Johnson that it was a serious problem. Christian urged Johnson for the need to develop a better pattern to which the press could become accustomed, since the "irritations of travel . . . remains our sorest spot with the White House regulars. They claim they had little trouble with Eisenhower's travel, more with Kennedy's and much more with ours."[27] The scheduling of press conferences was also unpredictable in the Johnson White House. Whenever possible, Johnson avoided the formal sessions that would be scheduled in advance, preferring to deliberately announce them at the last minute and to hold them on weekends. This served an important purpose: to avoid difficult policy questions from reporters who would otherwise have time to do some research on a subject if informed of the press conference well in advance. He also opened press conferences with a lengthy statement, which would often take up to half of the time allotted, thus minimizing time for questions, which he would then often dodge or answer indirectly.[28]

If Johnson's performance at press conferences did not live up to the Kennedy standard in the eyes of the press, neither did his overall communication style. He was often criticized for his public speaking style, which represented a dramatic difference from his personal style when not on the public stage. Remembered as a highly effective and persuasive communicator in a one-on-one or small group setting, when on television or in front of a large public group, Johnson was terrified of slipping into his usual, colorful and profanity-laced style of speaking. As a result, he insisted on reading from formal texts, which projected an image of "feigned propriety, dullness, and dishonesty." He also relied on a "monstrous" podium, which reporters nicknamed "mother"

> because it encompassed the orating President with enormous sound-sensitive arms. Teleprompters rose from the top but the microphones themselves remained invisible. Johnson took 'mother' with him wherever he went, carefully wrapped in furniture padding. Without his podium, Johnson felt lost.[29]

Johnson always considered the use of television to be an effective communication tool, and as a result, had a theater built within the White House in 1964 from which he could broadcast a message to the American people whenever he wished. However, technical problems with the theater, including the improper use of lighting, camera positions, and until 1967, the lack of color broadcasts, often "proved to be something less than the ideal arrangement."[30]

Aides constantly tried to improve Johnson's image and performance on television. Valenti often tried to convince Johnson to develop a different strategy for using television, especially in terms of the content of his public messages. Valenti believed that Johnson would be more effective using television as an information and educational medium, and less as a crisis medium to update the nation on events in Vietnam or other crucial domestic matters, with "the President teaching the people, guiding the people as to what was important." He also wanted Johnson to abandon the use of the teleprompter and rely on notes, but Johnson refused:

The whole business of his communication with the people I think affected him. You know the old cliché, but it was true, that in a small room with a hundred people or ten people Johnson was magnificent—the most persuasive man I have ever met. But when he went before television, something happened. He took on a presidential air, he fused a kind of a new Johnson which wasn't the real Johnson. He became kind of stiff and foreboding.[31]

Kintner, who was brought to the White House for his public relations expertise, also attempted to alter the President's persona and image on television, and he used people he still knew at NBC to improve Johnson's make-up and lighting, and to attempt to make his television appearances more professional in general. In October 1966, Kintner received approval to hire Walter O'Mara, "the best lighting expert in television," to improve the lighting in an attempt to show Johnson "at his best."[32] Kintner also advised Johnson on other image details, such as the need to wear his glasses on all television appearances "and keep them on. Lots of people wear glasses, and it would make you more at ease."[33] But ultimately, Kintner recalled, Johnson would always back away from any real discussion of his weakness on television:

No matter how much he was told or how much television was explained to him, he could never acclimate himself to the new media. He treated it like an old time southern orator, rather than Jack Kennedy's conversational treatment, rather than the new Nixon style of conversation. I was personally very involved in this, because when I was in the White House, I attempted three things which he would do for a short period of time and then would drop. One was that he spend some time really on his television talks before he got on the air; and two that he talk naturally, the way that he would talk to somebody in that little office of his; and three, drop all those political physical gestures that orators of the days before television used; and that in his press conference, he stop filibustering with a whole set of inconsequential announcements and respond to questions during the whole period, but respond not with anger or not with emotion, but respond the way he would talk to someone in his small office. He was terribly effective alone with a reporter, a banker, a farmer, a political leader. He was one of the most persuasive talkers, but he had an inability to translate that. . . . He listened, discussed it, and he tried to change. Then he would drop it because he was not at ease apparently with it. But I think it's one of the factors that made him so unpopular.[34]

While television remained a large part of the Johnson communication strategy, aides also focused on other areas of press relations and presidential communication. Efforts were made to maximize positive coverage in regional newspapers. As Moyers reported to Johnson in August 1965: "I try to spend a little time each day helping some of the non-Washington, non-New York reporters. Over a period of time, their material is just as important to us, especially their ability to get our story out to the hinterlands."[35] Positive coverage in the regional press was also sought through the use of strategic speaking locales outside of Washington. Following positive coverage in the regional press after a speaking event in Missouri in January 1966, Moyers reported to Johnson that such appearances would be important for cultivating support of administration policies, particularly Vietnam:

> When the President chooses a locale outside of Washington to talk about world affairs or domestic issues, the regional newspapers give it extra play. The President has favored them by making his pronouncements in their area, and whatever he says is bound to be accepted much more favorably. Regional pride affects these papers deeply.[36]

Moyers also believed that the Washington press corps, on whom the White House relied to tell its daily story, were "out of touch with the mood of America" and "jaded" in their opinions. Coverage in regional newspapers from smaller cities across the country, on the other hand, would offer the administration a better opportunity to promote its policies in a favorable manner. Moyers urged Johnson to hold a one-on-one interview with Daniel Dwyer, general manager of the *Union-Gazette* in Port Jervis, New York:

> They supported you strongly in 1964 and still do. And Dwyer feels that it is papers like his and towns like his who give you real support in your Vietnam policy. His story would be a good one. And we can move it nationally. And it would be a unique grass-roots opinion from Washington.[37]

Other communication strategies included regular reports to Johnson by key aides on press coverage of the administration, as well as their contacts with members of the press. Domestic policy advisor Joseph Califano included a daily news summary in his reports to Johnson (a practice that would be greatly expanded during the Nixon administration), while Christian and McPherson reported regularly to the President (Christian almost daily while press secretary) by memo about press contacts.[38] A concerted effort was also made for coordination between agencies and the White House on press announcements, especially news on foreign policy.[39] In February 1965, Presidential Aide Horace Busby urged better coordination of press releases between the White House and departments and agencies. Departmental releases without White House assistance tended to be too factual, which produced "news stories lacking any flavor of the Presidential personality." Representatives from departments and agencies would begin meeting with key aides in charge of presidential communications to develop "better communication, not just more publicity."[40] Too much news coming from the White House was also considered a problem at times. Johnson insisted that all major news flow from the White House, but this made many Americans associate the President with all of the nation's problems—instead of department and agency heads, who were more responsible for the implementation of specific policies.[41] However, success in the area of press coordination and the ability of the administration to speak in one voice (a strategy that would later be mastered by the Reagan administration) proved to be somewhat elusive for Johnson's aides. By July 1968, with only six months remaining in Johnson's term, attention was still being paid to the issue by staff members. The weekly staff meeting was suggested as the venue in which to correct the problem, to

> provide the full staff with what it now lacks: a control point to plug everyone in to the media opportunities that best serve the President. We all know the problems of moving on our separate tracks— Appointments, Speeches, Press, Programs, Congress, Departments, etc. We also know how often we move the train out, bound for collision with one of our own headlines, a Department story, or just leaving the press standing behind in the station.[42]

The much-discussed "credibility gap" will perhaps always remain the most enduring legacy of Johnson's relationship with the press. American military involvement in the Vietnam War negatively impacted Johnson's attempt to create a Great Society and ultimately his own political credibility. Inaccurate White House reports to the press and the American public about Vietnam began, during the Johnson administration, in August 1964 with the Gulf of Tonkin Resolution. The details of the incident, which allegedly involved North Vietnamese torpedo boats firing on the U.S. destroyer *Maddox*, are still in dispute. Yet, it marked the real U.S. entry into the Vietnam War, as Congress gave Johnson the authority to unilaterally take action against any such military attacks. His promises during the 1964 presidential campaign to not send American troops to fight a war in Southeast Asia soon became a dim memory as U.S. military involvement dramatically escalated by early 1965. The suspicion among the press corps that they were not receiving the entire truth or the full story from Johnson and his advisors also escalated. The image making of America's involvement in Vietnam had actually begun during the Kennedy years, but Johnson's obsession with secrecy and his propensity to give half-truths to the press about Vietnam and other policies had created a public relations nightmare for the White House.[43]

George Reedy, a longtime Johnson aide who became press secretary following Salinger's departure, often warned Johnson about the dangers of relying too heavily on public relations and not viewing the press as a service institution that could aid the President in the proper flow of communicating information to the public. Johnson disagreed, and instead viewed the press as the means for presidential publicity. Johnson often withheld information from Reedy in order to save announcements for public relations events, while Reedy wanted timely and factual news to present to the press. The two men could never reconcile their views of the role of a press secretary within the White House, and Reedy would resign from the post in July 1965.[44] In an undated memo sent to Johnson at some point during Reedy's tenure as press secretary, he urged the President to move away from using public relations activities to solve the "problem of press relations in the White House," which had been created, in Reedy's opinion, by too many staged events and not enough straight answers to the press about foreign and domestic policy concerns:

> The function of the Press Office should be to assist the press in obtaining access to the news under conditions in which it can be handled. For the time being, propaganda activities should be suspended completely and every effort should be spent on restoring the confidence of the working newsmen in the integrity of the White House. . . . It should be recognized that from the President's standpoint the real objective of a press operation *is to reach the public, and not just reach the press.* Nothing is accomplished by winning the favor of news correspondents unless those correspondents can present the public with balanced, timely accounts of what they are doing. . . . It is essential that the press relations of the White House have an air of spontaneity rather than appear to be a series of announcements and news stories forced down the correspondents' throats. *The White House really does not have to have 'announcements' to make news since any White House response to a question is news.* Finally, efforts must be made to exploit the greatest White House asset—*the ability to capture the front page of any newspaper at any time.* The front page is captured only by *on-the-record announcements made at the proper times*—not by backgrounders and indirect means of communication in which we have indulged so much that we have taken on an appearance of furtiveness.[45]

Even some of Johnson's supporters in the press, like Potter of the *Baltimore Sun*, warned Johnson about his growing credibility problem by relying too heavily on public relations, suggesting that, to "maintain credibility, [give] us the real news, not trying to contrive or manufacture news when there is none."[46] But ultimately, information coming from both the White House and the Pentagon on Vietnam would remain the largest culprit in widening the credibility gap between Johnson and the press, and eventually the press and the American public. The military not only knowingly provided false information to the press about the day-to-day operation in Vietnam, but it also would withhold information that would be detrimental to public opinion concerning the ability of America to win the war. Many members of the press disputed the official information coming from the government, and when television reports began to show the American public graphic scenes from the front, opinion about the war became divided, and support for Johnson and his Vietnam policy began to wane. His many Great Society programs in the areas of social security, welfare, education, and civil rights among others, for which he had received a sweeping mandate during the 1964 presidential election, also began to suffer from a lack of Congressional funding due to the expense of the war. One of the most memorable and dramatic television reports on Vietnam came from Morley Safer at CBS News in August 1965, titled "The Burning of the Village Cam Ne," which showed U.S. Marines leveling a 150-home village in retaliation for a Viet Cong attack.[47] The report prompted Senator George Smathers to write a letter to Johnson about his concern over news reports that seemed to cast U.S. involvement in Vietnam in "its worst possible light," including the Safer report:

If the program had been carefully planned and staged by the Chinese communists, it could not have served their purpose better. A reporter with a name like "Morrie Safer" made the Marine effort to flush out the Viet Cong look ridiculous and futile. He showed pictures of them rounding up a few old men and women and setting fire to thatched huts. He said these people (the Vietnamese) "will not understand Johnson's flimsy promises of help" when they see American troops destroying their homes. He did not show the Marines wounded in the action nor any shots of the sniper fire. He made it look as if we are spending billions of dollars out there, burning down thatched huts and bravely capturing helpless women and old men. Such propaganda will of course hurt the war effort immeasurably. I do not recall this sort of coverage emanating from the Korean theater of war, and I strongly recommend that you consider putting some sort of restrictions on what is unfortunately all too often either a prejudiced or an irresponsible coverage in Viet Nam.[48]

As Johnson's credibility and image continued to suffer, Reedy once again attempted to provide his former boss with advice on how to handle press relations in January 1967. Convinced that the manipulation of news through public relations was the administration's biggest problem with the press, Reedy believed that a "normal press operation" would give Johnson "the elbow room" to resolve "overwhelming facts of history" such as Vietnam. To Reedy, a normal press operation meant one that was "quiet and orderly," provided "straight answers" to the press that were believable, and that provided the "establishment of a reasonable routine in regard to briefings, travel and press conferences." He concluded that

> the overglamourization of the press office which began with Roosevelt has, in my judgment, been harmful to every president. It gives the impression that the White House is interested first in publicity and has only a secondary concern about the needs of the nation. The American people still dislike publicity agents, however much the press may like them. The face of the White House should be the face of the President—not of an assistant whose sole function is to handle press matters that are essentially routine despite the overglamourization.[49]

Later that year, Moyers, who had by then left the administration, urged Johnson to rely on an informal television appearance to "talk things over" with the American people about Vietnam, such as a "Conversation with the President" that Johnson had used effectively during the spring of 1964:

> You have never done as well since you did then on television, not in making headlines but in providing the people with a sense of relief. . . . There is an uneasiness in the land that could be arrested to a considerable degree by a reassuring talk from you. . . . The dissenters will not retreat, but the great majority of the middle will be reassured that the dark road ahead can be safely traversed. It is a question of purpose not popularity, of strength not safety, and only the President can reaffirm purpose and provide strength. I believe that such a conversation would help not only the country but you as well.[50]

Johnson did appear on television for another "Conversation with the President" to discuss Vietnam, as well as other domestic and international issues, which ran on all three networks on December 19, 1967. But despite several television appearances by Johnson, both formal and informal, he could not stop the widening of the credibility gap, and his press relations on the issue of Vietnam could not stop the erosion of public support for his policies or his presidency. By 1968, Johnson had become increasingly antagonistic towards the press, as many reporters and columnists rebelled against the continued efforts of the White House to manage the news in its favor. Members of the White House staff had also become frustrated with the press tactics, as evidenced in a February 1968 memo from McPherson to Christian on the subject:

> For a long time I've been troubled by the President's frequent public references to the press's credibility gap, and by other contemptuous asides that revealed his rage with reporters. I thought that this must be galling to them, and that even though the present situation— press attacks President—is one-sided and hence unfair, making it two-sided is unwise. It violates [Georgia] Senator [Richard] Russell's cardinal rule, "Never get into a p-ing contest with a polecat." I hope you can persuade the President that these public attacks not only do no good; they do positive *bad*.[51]

From the start, Johnson had good intentions to provide what he believed to be adequate access to the press. He courted reporters, wined and dined them, and wanted to out-do Kennedy in both public relations and his overall relationship with the Washington press corps. While Kennedy had been the perfect president to usher the White House into the television age, Johnson was ultimately betrayed by the medium he and his advisors tried so hard to master. Johnson's image on television could never live up to Kennedy's, and the reporting of events in Vietnam on television, which brought the war into the living rooms of Americans on a nightly basis, was the beginning of the end of Johnson's credibility with both the press and the public. Perhaps no communication strategy could have altered Johnson's fate as president because of the many outside political factors during the 1960s; Johnson's personality and desire for both control and secrecy involving information proved to be detrimental to his relationship with both the press and members of his staff. Those same issues would aid in the downfall of Johnson's immediate successor in the White House, while success in the use of public relations as a White House communication strategy would not come until the 1980s.

JOHNSON'S PUBLIC ACTIVITIES

As president, Johnson's speeches often reflected his idealism towards both his domestic agenda and what America could achieve abroad, particularly by a defeat of communism in Vietnam. Throughout his long political career, Johnson relied on many staff members and other advisors to write a majority of his speeches. By early 1964, a "brain trust" had been developed within the White House to write Johnson's speeches. During the early years of the administration, Ted Sorensen and Richard Goodwin, two of Kennedy's premiere speechwriters, remained in the White House. Various other aides served as speechwriters, including Cater, McPherson, Harry Middleton, and occasionally Moyers, Valenti, and Christian, among others. Johnson would also rely on Democratic leaders of Congress, his cabinet members, and various members of the business community for advice on his speech drafts. Johnson was always involved in the process as well, and the goal of his speechwriters was to prepare a draft that would match his personal style.[52]

Valenti often worked with younger speechwriters in the White House in an attempt to capture Johnson's style. He was always concerned with prose, the meter and the rhythm of the sentence, ". . . and aware of the fact that the President wanted a newsworthy item in every speech, not just a lot of blather and rhetoric, but there ought to be some pungent specific fact that was worthy of recounting by a newspaper later on." However, tailoring a speech to Johnson's style was not always an easy task: "The people who [were] writing it [tried] to keep it within his style, although the President had great admiration for sort of a spare eloquence that Goodwin was very good at." Throughout the process, according to Valenti, Johnson would read through the speech several times, making it his speech, and doing a lot of the rewriting himself. But Valenti often played an important role in the coordination of the process:

> Yes, I wrote some of the speeches, but mainly it was a question of making sure the speech got written because we were turning out lots of written prose. If it was a major speech we worked on it for weeks. If it were a Rose Garden type speech with the President making a presentation or meeting a group, that could be done within twenty-four hours. But it was on the important speeches, say, like the Howard University speech that Dick Goodwin did most of the work on—I sat with Dick and he brought in Pat Moynihan for the statistical background. That speech would go through ten or fifteen drafts with Dick and myself working, I worked with him, and then getting the speech to the President and the President making notations on it, changes, back to myself, back to Goodwin, and this round-trip operation continuing on.[53]

Kintner recalled that Johnson never thought his speechwriters were doing a good job, and he refused to spend time with them before a speech, which made the job more difficult.

He always felt they were inferior to Kennedy's. Now, Kennedy was a different type of speaker. He had a very intimate relation with his ghost writer. He did not assign his speeches to a lot of people. But Johnson always felt that his writers didn't write interestingly enough. I've never known him to be satisfied with a speech, either before, after, or at any point.[54]

However, Johnson would meet with prominent people outside of the White House, sometimes even members of the press, for the opportunity to experience the free association of ideas. According to Robert Hunter, a speechwriting assistant to Cater in 1964-1965, the job of the speechwriting department was to develop a draft that was symbiotic and in tune with the President's thinking on issues. Johnson was very focused on developing the policy message he wanted to present in his speeches, and he would adapt speeches to his own speech pattern, which was very slow and deliberate. The Kennedy legacy both hurt and helped Johnson in this area, since from a policy standpoint, especially in 1964, Johnson

> took the Kennedy legacy and turned it into reality. Carrying on Kennedy's legacy gave Johnson a great capacity [in his speeches]. His speeches touched different people than Kennedy's did. He had no eloquence, but much better depth. He spoke to a different class of people.[55]

The Johnson style is evident in his use of public activities. He frequently used "pseudo events" to garner media attention, since whatever a president did was considered newsworthy: "Because the Presidency is the object of unrelenting attention and mandatory 'coverage,' Johnson was able to use routine procedures as political instruments."[56] Johnson also relied heavily on Rose Garden speeches, which were often brief remarks to talk about a specific policy to various groups gathered at the White House. The job of the speechwriters was to make sure that such remarks "always had a joke and a proposal."[57] Johnson's public activities were at their peak during his first 13 months in office, due in part to his reelection efforts in 1964 (see Table 3.1). By 1965, much of the administration's effort was focused on strategic television appearances, either longer addresses about Vietnam or shorter announcements about specific policies. Policy addresses were not a top priority; Johnson's remarks at these events were usually brief and did not include detailed or specific discussions about issues. Most of Johnson's longer, detailed addresses were used on the campaign trail, either for his own candidacy or those of fellow Democrats in Congress. He also relied on using an opening statement at most press conferences to announce news on policy matters and various White House appointments; these state-

Table 3.1. Johnson— Public Activities.[58]

	1963-64	1965	1966	1967	1968-69
National Addresses	13	3	1	3	7
Policy Addresses	41	12	9	14	18
Press Conferences	36	16	40	22	20
Radio Addresses	0	0	0	0	0
Brief Statements/Nonpolicy Remarks	285	166	206	183	215
Partisan Remarks/Campaign Speeches	88	3	11	8	12
Press Conferences with Foreign Dignitaries	0	0	1	0	0
Signing Ceremonies	36	48	39	18	43
Teleconference Remarks	2	2	1	3	0
Roundtable Discussions	0	0	0	0	0
Town Meetings/Q&A Sessions	1	0	0	0	0
Remarks to/Exchanges with Reporters	5	6	10	16	17
Total	507	256	318	267	332
Daily Average	1.25	0.7	0.87	0.73	0.86

ments were often long and quite detailed about policy issues, much more so than most of his policy addresses. To go along with his expansive policy agenda, Johnson also increased the frequency of public signing ceremonies at the White House to promote his policies when signed into law, at times elaborate public forums which "brought to an end a legislative process that had begun with the preparation of a presidential message. Another program had come home from the Congress to the White House."[59] In total, Johnson participated in 1,680 public activities between November 22, 1963, and January 20, 1969.

THE JOHNSON POLICY AGENDA

Johnson's presidency could perhaps be viewed as beginning and ending with a Kennedy assassination. As the Senate majority Leader in 1960, he was denied the Democratic presidential nomination, instead working hard as Kennedy's running mate to ensure a slim victory over Nixon. Three years later, he would become president in a manner that no one could have predicted. Despite 30 years of public service in Congress, Johnson was still widely unknown nationally. He needed to establish his own right to govern, and he worked hard to push through unfinished business from the Kennedy agenda, including civil rights laws, the 1964 tax cut, Medicare, and voting rights. On the issue of civil rights, Johnson told the nation that "no memorial oration or eulogy could more eloquently honor President Kennedy's memory than the earliest possible passage of the civil rights bill." Many African Americans were concerned about having a new president from the South, but Johnson's skills on Capitol Hill worked in his favor, and when the bill passed, he was endeared to the nation's liberals.[60] Following his convincing electoral mandate in 1964, Johnson's agenda was dominated by his plans for a Great Society, which included the War on Poverty, Medicare and Medicaid, Head Start, various urban, education, and environmental bills, the creation of the departments of Housing and Urban Development and of Transportation, and a long list of other bills that would be signed into law. Most programs, however, would suffer because of the ensuing quagmire in Vietnam, which limited the availability of congressional funding for various domestic programs. Unable to have both a war in Vietnam and a Great Society, Johnson left office in 1969 with much of his domestic agenda incomplete.[61]

The public agenda that Johnson presented to Americans in his major addresses throughout his tenure in the White House focused mostly on Vietnam, and occasionally other foreign policy issues, more often than any other policy on his agenda (see Table 3.2). The Diplomatic/Military policy category clearly outpaced any other during each year of the Johnson administration, followed by the Domestic Fiscal/Monetary policy category every year but 1965, when the Political Reform (due to the Voting Rights bill) and Education categories ranked second and third, respectively. Despite Johnson's vast domestic agenda, he rarely used major addresses to promote his plans for a Great Society. These occasions, instead, were used to discuss foreign policy and economic issues. Johnson began to discuss Vietnam in 1964, and he also promoted remaining items on the Kennedy agenda, including a tax cut, a civil rights bill, and the building of a strong defense. During the presidential campaign, he also introduced various plans to end poverty in America, but offered few specific details.

After decisively winning the presidency in his own right, Johnson's public agenda continued to focus greatly on Vietnam in 1965 as American military involvement in Southeast Asia escalated; he also used major addresses to discuss American interest in the political unrest and attempts to maintain democracy in the Dominican Republic. Vietnam continued to dominate Johnson's public agenda from 1966 until he left office in January 1969, as well as other U.S. foreign policy matters, including relations with the Soviet Union, the Middle East, Latin America and the Alliance for Progress, and Africa. Economic matters also became a topic in major addresses in 1966, as Johnson urged the continuation of a strong economy through preventative measures to

Table 3.2. Johnson's Public Agenda (Major Public Addresses).[62]

	1963-64	1965	1966	1967	1968-69
Domestic					
Education	97 - 3%	145 - 8%	54 - 3%	113 - 6%	72 - 3%
Health Care	22 - <1%	11 - <1%	12 - <1%	19 - 1%	104 - 5%
Welfare/Entitlements	226 - 7%	56 - 3%	50 - 3%	92 - 4%	118 - 6%
Anticrime	33 - <1%	6 - <1%	117 - 7%	358 - 17%	63 - 3%
Political Reform	223 - 6%	165 - 9%	23 - 1%	10 - <1%	44 - 2%
Science/Technology/Transportation	43 - 1%	39 - 2%	10 - <1%	8 - <1%	2 - <1%
Environment/Energy/Land Management	56 - 2%	24 - 1%	4 - <1%	12 - 1%	27 - 1%
Defense	281 - 8%	17 - 1%	27 - 2%	10 - <1%	11 - 1%
International					
Diplomatic/Military	1179 - 32%	975 - 56%	898 - 51%	846 - 41%	1030 - 49%
Trade/Economic	151 - 4%	96 - 5%	43 - 2%	55 - 3%	178 - 8%
Economic					
Domestic Fiscal/Monetary	718 - 20%	82 - 5%	474 - 27%	479 - 23%	276 - 13%
Unemployment/Jobs	597 - 16%	130 - 7%	37 - 2%	47 - 2%	193 - 9%
Total	N = 3666	N = 1746	N = 1749	N = 2049	N = 2118

control recession and inflation. In 1967 and early 1968, he also placed anticrime on his public agenda, in part by introducing the Safe Streets Act and the Gun Control Act for consideration by Congress, and also because of civil unrest in cities such as Detroit, and his public responses to the 1968 assassinations of Dr. Martin Luther King, Jr. and Robert Kennedy. On March 31, 1968, Johnson announced during a televised address to the nation that he would not seek reelection, and following that, his public agenda focused on his attempts to bring a peaceful settlement to the war in Vietnam and on reviewing his policy accomplishments while in office.

THE FIRST TIER: MEDICARE-1965

The Issue and White House Strategy

By the time Johnson signed the Medicare bill into law in July 1965, 30 years had passed since Franklin Roosevelt had first considered such an addition to the original Social Security Act of 1935. Harry Truman had also supported a federal plan to provide medical coverage to the nation's elderly, but he had met fierce opposition from, among other groups, the American Medical Association. Following the anti-Medicare Eisenhower years, the Kennedy administration worked hard to place Medicare supporters on the House Ways and Means Committee, under which the jurisdiction for the plan fell. However, support in Congress for the plan had remained elusive, even in the early months of the Johnson administration. Medicare had only passed once in the Senate, by a narrow margin in 1964, and had never made it out of committee in the House, thanks to the committee chairman, Democrat Wilbur Mills of Arkansas.[63] A fiscal conservative, Mills did not want to back an issue that so bitterly divided the parties if it would only pass by a small margin. He also feared large federal deficits resulting from the program, and was sympathetic to the AMA's argument that Medicare represented socialized medicine. However, following the sweeping Democratic victory in 1964, which gave the party a two-thirds majority in the House, Mills realized that he could no longer ignore public opinion and the support of his more liberal-leaning colleagues on the Ways and Means Committee. After the defeat of Medicare in late 1964, one of Johnson's only legislative defeats that year, the President publicly vowed to make Medicare one of his top priorities in 1965. Soon after, Mills publicly acknowledged that with a sound financing plan, his committee would be able to work with the White House in achieving passage of Medicare.[64]

Following Mills' announcement, as well as after viewing several polls that showed public support for Medicare, Johnson became convinced that passage of the plan was inevitable. He used his State of the Union address on January 4 to outline the importance of the bill, and sent a detailed message on Medicare to the Congress on January 7. Johnson's legislative strategy on most domestic bills could be summed up as "pass now, ask questions later." Medicare was no exception, and it represented "an urgent need exacerbated by decades of inaction, a ringing presidential challenge, and a rush of well-funded legislation."[65] A key component of his Great Society program, Johnson relied on his connections on Capitol Hill to achieve consensus on Medicare. While he often gave the task of dealing with policy details to others within the administration, Johnson "made the key decisions about which program ideas to initiate and then orchestrated the politics of passage." When Johnson knew that he had the votes in Congress for a particular measure, especially in 1965 with 295 House Democrats to support Medicare, he focused his political skills of persuasion on small groups of people rather than on the American public; "he had the votes in Congress; there was no need to return to the well of public opinion."[66]

As a result, Johnson's strategy in passing Medicare focused more on winning congressional approval and less on convincing the American public about the merits of the proposal. Following the State of the Union address, Johnson rarely spoke about Medicare during public appearances. In his remarks to the President's Council on Aging in February 1965, Johnson recalled how public support had become stronger for Medicare in recent years:

> President Kennedy and I went into most of the 50 States in 1960 talking about it. I listened to the recordings of my appearances throughout this nation in 1960 and the deafening applause, if there ever was any deafening applause to anything I said, always came when I talked about a program to provide medical care under social security for the aged. So make no mistake about it. The people are ahead of us in this field. They want this program. They will support this program. They are going to have this program. The question now is just its timing.[67]

Johnson would only discuss Medicare in scheduled public settings on three other occasions prior to signing the legislation into law.[68] Assured of public support, Johnson's toughest opposition on Medicare would come from the AMA and conservative Republicans, who would each present an alternate, more conservative, plan to the administration's proposal. The AMA had spent millions of dollars over the years in its opposition to Medicare, and as Johnson would recall later, by 1965 the

powerful lobby was still pouring millions into its campaign of opposition. But . . . the times had caught up with the idea. The cost of ill-
ness in old age had become a matter of national concern. Spiraling
medical costs struck fear not only in the senior citizens themselves
but also in their sons and daughters, who often had to pay stagger-
ing hospital bills for elderly relatives while they were struggling to
rear their own families.[69]

But Johnson also had powerful and influential backers of the plan.
Pending final approval of the bill in Congress in June 1965, Moyers
updated the President on the public relations strategy for Medicare,
which would receive Johnson's approval:

> The AMA has bought one half hour on national TV news next week
> to present its case against Medicare. The AFL-CIO would like to buy
> time the next night to present the Administration's views—with
> Clint Anderson, Wilbur Mills and Hubert Humphrey comprising a
> panel for our viewpoint. Is this OK with you?[70]

In the end, Johnson had been a persuasive and effective communicator with the AMA, with whom he met just days prior to signing the
bill due to the possibilities of a much-rumored AMA boycott once
Medicare was enacted.[71] Johnson had also used television to his advantage while meeting with members of Congress soon after the bill had
been introduced. Not having informed them that television cameras
would be waiting for them following the meeting, Johnson was able to
use the occasion to gain a public commitment on the importance and
priority of Medicare from Senate Finance Committee Chairman Harry
Byrd, who had sidetracked similar legislation in the past.[72] Johnson
would ultimately get his legislative victory on Medicare, and he would
sign the bill into law in Independence, Missouri, at the Truman Library,
with the former President in attendance on July 30, 1965. However,
many within the Johnson administration advised against a trip outside
of Washington for the signing ceremony. Busby stated his adamant
opposition to the signing in Independence, which is his view was "inad-
visable" and would damage Johnson's public image:

> The association of the present legislation with President Truman's
> 1945 proposal would be grotesque distortion with unhappy and
> impolitic overtones. President Truman requested medical coverage
> for all the population, regardless of age—a close parallel to Great
> Britain's "socialized medicine." The connotation of a signing at
> Independence would be not that Truman's work had been complet-
> ed, but that President Johnson next intended to enlarge Medicare to

meet Truman's objectives. The results [would] be more unfavorable than favorable reaction, a boycott and denunciation of the ceremony by leaders of the AMA with whom we are now attempting to work and most likely some distasteful remarks by President Truman himself about the medical profession. . . . August 15 is the anniversary of the original Social Security Act [and] it would be fitting to sign the Bill at Hyde Park on Saturday, August 14—if such a ceremony is desired. My own strong inclination is against dramatizing the Bill by a trip out of Washington. Inevitably, this will turn into a circus. Such a dramatization in a quest for publicity might unhappily coincide with somber decisions or news relative to Viet Nam. . . . My opinion is that the Bill Signing needs very little gingerbread to make it newsworthy and historic. I doubt the wisdom of the President "playing FDR" at the particular time in history—it will add credence to the adverse images of vanity, self-centeredness, etc.[73]

Nonetheless, Johnson would have the signing ceremony on July 30 in Independence with Truman, which he believed was befitting for such a monumental piece of legislation:

[Truman] has started it all, so many years before. I wanted him to know that America remembered. It was a proud day for all of us, and President Truman said that no single honor ever paid him had touched him more deeply.[74]

Press Coverage

Considering the importance of Medicare and the extensive changes that it would create in the area of health insurance for the aged, the *New York Times* provided extensive coverage for the policy between November 1964 and July 1965 with a news item appearing, on average, slightly less often than once every other day. However, most stories were generated by either congressional or interest group activity on Medicare; only 11 percent of the coverage was generated by presidential activity, while 53 percent of the coverage originated with Congress and 36 percent from interest group activities (see Table 3.3). These numbers remain consistent with Johnson's public strategy, which was limited in the number of public statements made by the President. Many of the stories generated by Congress focused on Republican attempts to introduce an alternate plan to Medicare, and nearly all of the interest group stories focused on the AMA's campaign to defeat the bill.

Of the stories generated by Johnson, the tone of coverage was mostly either positive or neutral (see Table 3.4). With such a large Democratic margin in both the House and the Senate, coverage of the

Table 3.3. Amount and Type of *New York Times* Coverage of Medicare (November 1964-July 1965).

	White House	Congress	Interest Group/Other
News Story	10	52	39
News Analysis	1	0	2
Column	1	1	1
Editorial	2	12	2
Total	14 - (11%)	65 - (53%)	44 - (36%)

Table 3.4. Tone of *New York Times* Coverage of Presidential Activities on Medicare (November 1964-July 1965).

	Positive	Negative	Balanced/Mixed	Neutral
News Story	4	0	1	5
News Analysis	0	0	1	0
Column	1	0	0	0
Editorial	1	1	0	0
Total	6	1	2	5

issue seemed to reflect Johnson's optimism for passage of the bill. Only two editorials appearing in the *Times* about Medicare focused on the President's role in the policymaking process. The first editorial on December 6, 1964, criticized Johnson for a Medicare proposal that was too "modest." The *Times* urged Johnson to take full advantage of the mandate that he had been given by the voters in 1964, and to promote a much fuller domestic agenda than he had been willing to introduce at that point. Since Medicare was only one of a handful of initiatives that Johnson had yet to discuss publicly, the paper suggested that Johnson might not be willing to seize such a golden opportunity for a president to pursue his agenda. However, the second editorial on the issue, appearing on April 9, 1965, was much more complimentary to Johnson, stating that the passage of the bill in the House marked a "historic triumph in a long struggle" for three Democratic presidents: Truman, Kennedy, and Johnson. The *Times* approved of Medicare and the direction that such a plan would take in caring for the nation's elderly.

THE SECOND TIER: THE SAFE STREETS AND CRIME CONTROL ACT OF 1968

The Issue and White House Strategy

Following the passage of numerous domestic programs as part of his Great Society in 1965 and 1966, one of the issues that Johnson turned his attention to in 1967 was the increase of crime in America. In October 1966, in a speech to the Conference of State Committees on Criminal Administration, Johnson linked the issue of crime to his legislative War on Poverty: "Poverty. This is the real enemy. Strike poverty down tonight and much of the crime will fall down with it." And as a preview of his Safe Streets Act to be introduced in early 1967, Johnson also discussed a five-point strategy to combat crime: an increased understanding of crime; more help for police (including better pay); a more efficient and equitable system of criminal justice; better prisoner rehabilitation; and the search for social reform as well as criminal reform. He also criticized the press for not paying attention to his public appeals to fight crime:

> I was quite disappointed that I made a statement very much of this same general tenor to three meetings of Governors that came here to meet with the President and I didn't see the press recognize it, although if we make a mistake in Vietnam it gets adequate attention. If we make a mistake other places we have no difficulties. But recording the President's appeal to all the Governors of the States of the Union to come in now and take the leadership in helping us to reverse this trend did not waken excitement or did not really come to the public interest.[75]

In 1965, Johnson had formed the President's Commission on Law Enforcement and the Administration of Justice to produce a comprehensive study on crime and law enforcement in the United States. That study, along with an Interagency Task Force under the Chairmanship of the Attorney General, was used to develop Johnson's crime program for 1967. The objectives of the program included federal support, both financial and technical, for local law enforcement and criminal justice systems in the areas of education and training, comprehensive planning, research, equipment, information systems, and programmatic support.[76]

Feeling the need to identify himself with a strong anticrime policy, which he viewed as "essential politics" due to the increased public outcries about crime, Johnson introduced the Safe Streets and Crime Control Act in his State of the Union address in January 1967, and he outlined the specifics of the plan in a special message to Congress on crime the following month.[77] Throughout 1967, Johnson continued to publicly discuss the need to fight crime, addressing the issue in remarks to the National Conference on Crime Control in March, the Lawyers Conference on Crime Control in May, and the Meeting of the International Association of Chiefs of Police in September. With public opinion increasingly divided over the continued U.S. involvement in Vietnam, as well as several urban riots across the nation, Johnson's aides viewed his new anticrime stance as good for the presidential image. Presidential aide Tom Johnson urged the President to continue speeches to groups outside of Washington, like the one to the Chiefs of Police, which had been portrayed positively in the press:

> I am more convinced now than ever before that we have to get the President back into the arena swinging with both fists for the programs we believe in and the policies we think are right. . . . the President was fighting for what he thought was right. He denounced those who preach crime and violence in no uncertain terms. The people I talked with in the South said, well thank God, the real Lyndon Johnson is still alive and genuine. Everybody has known the President over the years as a fighter—a man who never would turn his back on a fight. They like that. They admire a fighter. To make strong speeches which have significant impact on the public requires getting out of Washington. . . . That was why [the Chiefs of Police speech], with the law enforcement audience and a hard-hitting crime speech, hit the headlines big all over the country.[78]

Despite Johnson's attention to the increase in crime and urban civil unrest during his public appearances, Congress was not moving quickly on the Safe Streets bill. The House passed the bill in August, but they had rewritten major portions of it due to the desire of Republicans and Southern Democrats to allocate funds in the form of block grants to states, as opposed to the administration's plan for direct grants to local authorities. Still waiting for the Senate to move on the bill, Johnson would again request action for the federal government to become involved in the fight against crime in a 1968 message to Congress; however, the Senate would not pass a version of the bill until May 1968. Along the way, the basic provisions of the bill changed dramatically from the original bill proposed by Johnson. The Senate, like the House, also favored federal funding in the form of block grants. The final version of the bill also contained controversial provisions not supported by the administration that allowed local police broad authority in wiretapping and attempted to overturn Supreme Court decisions on the rights of defendants (including *Miranda v. Arizona*, 1966). It also included a gun control provision (a ban on interstate shipments of pistols and revolvers) that was much weaker than the one Johnson had requested.[79]

Many congressional liberals urged Johnson to veto the final version of the bill that he would receive in June 1968 because, as many argued, the gun control efforts were too weak and the wiretapping provision was unconstitutional. However, with the assassinations of Martin Luther King, Jr. and Robert Kennedy fresh in the minds of the public, and wanting to provide the financial assistance to local law enforcement officials, Johnson signed the bill into law on June 20, 1968, stating: "I have decided that this measure contains more good than bad and that I should sign it into law."[80] Overall, the passage of the bill was seen as a defeat for Johnson; Republicans had worked hard to make sure that a Democratic president did not take away an issue they had been championing for years. Johnson would recall his disappointment over the wiretapping provision, which he considered "a grave danger to our constitutional rights. Privacy is among the most basic rights of the individual and is too precious to be violated by electronic snooping."[81] But Johnson's desire to establish a program of federal assistance for fighting crime at the local level won out in the end:

> Some of my advisers were so concerned about the wiretapping provision that they urged me to veto the Safe Streets Act, but I did not accept this counsel. We desperately needed immediate assistance for our local police forces, for our courts, and for our correctional system. I signed the bill, confident that we had finally launched an intelligent national attack on the problem of crime.[82]

Press Coverage

Coverage in the *Times* for the Safe Streets and Crime Control Act did not equal that of the more expansive Medicare program. In spite of the long congressional battles for the bill, the issue received coverage that included a news item appearing, on average, only once every seven days. However, like with Medicare, most stories were generated by either congressional or interest group activity; only 22 percent of the coverage was generated by presidential activity, while 53 percent of the coverage originated with Congress and 25 percent from interest group activities (see Table 3.5). In comparison to Medicare, these numbers are a bit inconsistent with Johnson's public strategy since the President spoke more often publicly about the Safe Streets Act. Yet, the issue was not as high a priority as Medicare was in 1965, which might explain the smaller amount of coverage. The bill also took much longer to become a law from start to finish, which might have decreased the intensity of coverage as well.

Table 3.5. Amount and Type of *New York Times* **Coverage of the Safe Streets and Crime Control Act (January 1967-June 1968).**

	White House	Congress	Interest Group/Other
News Story	10	30	18
News Analysis	0	2	0
Column	2	2	0
Editorial	6	9	2
Total	18 - (22%)	43 - (53%)	20 - (25%)

Many of the stories on the Safe Streets Act which were generated by Congress focused on the controversial aspects of the bill, such as the wiretapping provision, as well as the many changes that were made while being considered in both houses. Many of the interest group stories focused on support for the bill from various law enforcement groups.

Of the stories generated by Johnson, the tone of coverage was predominantly balanced, with most news stories representing both the Democratic and Republican stands on major provisions of the bill (see Table 3.6). A total of six editorials appeared in the *Times* that focused on Johnson and the Safe Streets Act. Five of the editorials were coded as balanced/mixed, while one was coded as negative. The *Times* never seemed pleased with the substance of the bill as introduced by Johnson. On February 9, 1967, an editorial stated that, in general, such a crime bill was a step in the right direction, but that many aspects of the bill, especially the gun control provision, was too weak, with no "top level dispo-

Table 3.6. Tone of *New York Times* **Coverage of Presidential Activities on the Safe Streets and Crime Control Act (January 1967-June 1968).**

	Positive	Negative	Balanced/Mixed	Neutral
News Story	0	0	8	2
News Analysis	0	0	0	0
Column	0	2	0	0
Editorial	0	1	5	0
Total	0	3	13	2

sition to tackle the lobby that keeps open this highroad to murder and armed assault." Nearly a year later in the legislative process, after Johnson had reintroduced the need for passage of a crime bill during his 1968 State of the Union address, the *Times* remained only somewhat supportive in a January 19 editorial. Johnson's address had provided them with little inspiration, and gave evidence to the negative effects in many areas of Vietnam:

> The huge American involvement in one tiny corner of Southeast Asia has taken precedence over every other aspect of American policy, both foreign and domestic, over the lives of citizens, the economy of the country and the very thought processes of Administration and Government.

On June 14, 1968, only days after Congress submitted the bill for Johnson's approval, the *Times* urged the President to exercise his veto power, which would force Congress to consider a tougher antigun law than the bill contained. The paper was most critical of Johnson when he did sign the bill into law, which it claimed on June 21, 1968, was "more a surrender to public hysteria over crime in the streets than it is an expression of conviction that the bill represents a sound contribution to the defense of law and order." The *Times* vehemently disagreed with Johnson's contention that the bill contained more good than bad.

NIXON AND THE PRESS

Perhaps no president has had as complicated a relationship with the press as Richard Nixon, who raised the adversarial relationship between the president and the press to new heights during his tenure in the White House. Any scholar wishing to broach the subject is faced with a daunting task and must ask, "Where to start?" Nixon's political career spanned several decades, as did his tumultuous relationship with members of the American press. Early on, Nixon earned a reputation as a dogged and tough campaigner, and at times even a ruthless one, first running for the House of Representatives and then for the Senate, representing his native California. He was also seen as controversial, especially during his involvement in the House of Representatives investigation of suspected spy Alger Hiss. Press coverage of the trial allowed Nixon, who had found incriminating documents on Hiss, to become a national political figure practically overnight. However, the Hiss trial was just the beginning of Nixon's well-documented ups and downs with the press. Soon after accepting the Republican vice-presidential nomination in 1952, he gave the famous "Checkers" speech, where an embattled Nixon took to the airwaves to refute charges of corruption from an alleged campaign slush fund.

Rarely was there ever a middle-of-the-road between Nixon and the press; either Nixon seemed to be working the press to his advantage, or the press seemed to be working against Nixon. Incidents falling into the former category include the "Checkers" speech that secured his position on the Eisenhower ticket; coverage of his confrontation of Nikita Kruschev in the famous 1959 "Kitchen Debate," which received a positive public response; or the "New Nixon," better able to control the press, that emerged during the 1968 presidential campaign. Those in the latter category include the televised debates with Kennedy during the 1960 presidential election; Nixon's premature farewell to the press after losing the 1962 California gubernatorial race; the attempt to stop publication of the *New York Times* and *Washington Post* during the 1971 Pentagon Papers case; and, of course, the role played by the press in Watergate.[83]

In later years, Nixon would recall that, while his "battles with the media have been so well publicized, it may surprise people to learn of the good relations I have had with many members of the press in years past."[84] But the legend of Nixon's hatred and paranoia of the press has yet to fade. Noted Washington correspondent Lou Cannon recalls that the animosity was much stronger on Nixon's part than on that of the press: "Nixon hated us. It was reciprocated in some ways, but not as much as he thought."[85] It was Nixon's long history of battling the press since the start of his political career, not an overtly anti-Nixon bias in the press, that defined the relationship; Nixon resented criticism by the press, and "while he tried hard at times to be conciliatory, he was never able to relax with the press, or any other group for that matter, or to work effectively with the press."[86]

During the Nixon years in the White House, the President and his aides essentially declared war on the press, and spent much of their time strategizing against the "enemy." Nixon was friendly towards many of the top publishers around the country, but he despised most reporters, convinced that they were against him. Presidential aide and speechwriter William Safire recalled hearing Nixon say "the press is the enemy" on several occasions, which served as encouragement to the White House staff to "do battle with what he was certain was an ideological bias against nonliberals combined with a personal bias against him."[87] Efforts were constantly made to either harass the press, or make them acquiesce to the President's views. Vice President Spiro Agnew was instrumental in these efforts, most notably by making several speeches to publicly criticize the press for its biased and negative stories. The *New York Times* and *Washington Post* were at the top of Nixon's media hit list, as were *Time* and *Newsweek*, and were often criticized for their "Eastern establishment," traditionally Democratic, bias. The administration also employed a technique, though not always success-ful, of cutting off access to information sources within the White House to prominent newspapers, especially the *Times* and the *Post*. Television networks also were threatened with the nonrenewal of broadcasting licenses for important affiliates by the Federal Communication Commission, a nonpartisan agency, in an attempt to gain more favorable coverage for Nixon's policies.[88]

Early in Nixon's first term, key White House staffers began work on an extensive system of evaluating the President's coverage by many members of the national press. The goal of the "covert" operation was to determine which members of the press were friends of the administration, and more importantly, which were enemies. Television commentators were always of particular interest to the White House, which wanted to know where coverage fell into one of three categories: Generally For Us, Generally Objective, or Generally Against Us. Not only was the project high priority and top secret within the White House, but the attempts to gain detailed profiles on television commen-tators were extensive, including scouring through correspondents' Secret Service files, which were necessary to obtain a White House press pass. As Press Secretary Ronald Ziegler reported to Chief of Staff H.R. Haldeman in November 1969, the project was somewhat precarious:

> We have exhaustedly explored ways in which we could obtain this background without the possibility of a leak that we were undertak-ing such a project. . . . If we were to pursue information such as where these individuals were previously employed, what their gen-eral background is, I am very concerned in the light of the Vice President's recent addresses a serious problem could be caused. As we go along we will attempt to compile such information in person-al conversations, etc., but this will take some time.[89]

Among the television notables on the list were White House favorite Howard K. Smith of ABC, one of only three in the Generally For Us category; Dan Rather of CBS, categorized as Generally Objective; and then, on the Generally Against Us hit list, such broadcast heavyweights as Frank Reynolds and Sam Donaldson of ABC, Eric Sevareid and Roger Mudd of CBS, and David Brinkley and Sander Vanocur of NBC.[90] Further analysis less than two weeks later provided Nixon with several additional assessments of television anchors and commentators: Rather, a presumed Democrat, nonetheless "generally covers the news fairly"; Sevareid takes an "intellectual pose" and is therefore "unpredictable;" John Chancellor of NBC, who generally sides "with the liberals" and is "tricky;" Brinkley, a "Kennedy Democrat and his cynicism shows through frequently with sarcasm;" Chet Huntley, Brinkley's coanchor at NBC, who "at one time at least was an independent Republican, although not all of his comments would indicate this . . . he is less provocative of the two-some on his show and probably more fair;" and finally, Walter Cronkite of CBS, who is objective and "doesn't have the tendency to be snide, which is noted in some of the others."[91]

By mid-1970, White House staffers had compiled an extensive list of more than 200 journalists from television, radio, and print, and placed each into one of six categories: Friendly to Administration, Balanced to Favorable, Balanced, Unpredictable, Usually Negative, and Always Hostile. Not surprisingly, those considered to be leaning more in favor of the administration came from traditionally more conservative publications, such as *U.S. News and World Report, Business Week,* and the *Chicago Tribune,* while many of those considered negative or hostile were from traditionally more liberal publications, such as the *New York Times,* the *Washington Post,* and the *Boston Globe.*[92] Those within the good graces of the administration included syndicated columnists William F. Buckley and Joe Alsop, while those viewed unfavorably included Tom Wicker and James Reston of the *New York Times,* David Broder of the *Washington Post,* syndicated columnists Jack Anderson and the writing team of Rowland Evans and Robert Novak, Morton Kondracke of the *Chicago Sun-Times,* Hugh Sidey of *Life,* and Marvin Kalb of CBS.[93]

Friendly members of the press, it was often suggested by White House advisors, should be rewarded for their efforts. For example, backgrounders with the President, or special invitations or other perks could be given to those reporters providing favorable coverage. According to Haldeman, a good strategy involved attempts "to do more in-depth discussion between friendly members of the press and the President. . . . We need to develop a plan for working with friendly or potentially favorable members of the press, and also for dividing the hostile working press."[94] The monitoring system was even suggested, at one point, to include keeping tabs on television talk shows such as the *Smothers Brothers* on CBS, where Nixon was the frequent butt of jokes, and *The Tonight Show with Johnny Carson* on NBC, since Nixon was often the subject during the opening monologue. The theory was to have supporters write letters to the producers to object to the anti-Nixon comments, and also to rely on the FCC's Equal Time rule for reply from the White House.[95] According to Richard Moore in the Attorney General's office:

> If we simply develop an efficient monitoring system, we probably will find something every night that entitles us to time to reply. And soon the negative comments will become rarer and rarer. . . . I would

like to see a week's output of anti-administration material—I think it
would knock our hats off—and would come from surprising
sources, not just from politicians, but entertainment personalities
and various kinds of celebrities generally.[96]

In addition to the monitoring system, another strategy of track-
ing coverage of the administration in the national press was the inception of the daily news summary, which included the "ideas and opinions contained in a cross-section of news reports, editorials, columns,
and articles" from more than 50 newspapers, 30 magazines, and the
Associated Press and *United Press International* wire services.[97] The administration received numerous requests from many sources to receive a
copy of the news summary, but all were turned down since the summary was "strictly an internal document prepared for the President and the
White House staff."[98] Mort Allin, a staff assistant to Nixon, described the
summary as including a representative sample of columns, editorials,
news analyses, and cartoons from newspapers and magazines, all con-
densed to reflect the "central theme as well as a quote or two to give the
flavor of the piece." The goal, according to Allin, was to keep the
President informed of the views and opinions of the nation:

> The President is interested not only in comment and reaction to his
> programs but he also wants to keep abreast of the daily develop-
> ments which are going on across the nation and affect every citi-
> zen—developments which may well be more important to the coun-
> try than some piece of legislation. By keeping an eye on stories
> reported in all the media, the President maintains an excellent feel of
> the nation's pulse.[99]

Safire would later refute the notion that the news summary was a form
of "sinister" monitoring of the press, calling it instead "the most sincere
compliment" paid to the press to be read so carefully on a daily basis by
the White House, and a way of providing ideas for policies and projects
that Nixon would later pursue.[100]

Another innovation involving the news that emerged during the
Nixon administration was the creation of the White House Office of
Communications in 1969. A separate entity from the White House Press
Office, the Office of Communications was designed to handle long-term
public relations for the administration. Specific actions included rela-
tions with local media outlets and generating letters to the editor, among
others, to build support and interest in the President's programs.[101]
Nixon also approved the construction of a new pressroom for
Washington correspondents, moving them out of the old, cramped
pressroom that had been established by Theodore Roosevelt. While the

reporters may have appreciated the new work area in the West Wing of the White House, their new location was also disadvantageous in that they could no longer view the comings and goings of presidential visitors to the Oval Office. Reporters would have to stand outside, just as they had at the turn of the century, to see who was visiting the President: "Now, nearly seventy years later, they were back out in the weather, outside the West Wing, the only differences being that they were a hundred feet farther up the driveway."[102]

Just as with the Kennedy and Johnson administrations, Nixon's use of television remained a top priority among White House media strategists. Following his defeat by Kennedy in the 1960 presidential election, and then his defeat in the 1962 gubernatorial race in California, Nixon spent a great deal of time and effort studying his mistakes with the news media prior to his presidential bid in 1968. As a result, voters that year saw a skillful Nixon appearing on television, but only before controlled audiences asking filtered questions. Once elected, Nixon continued to keep a tight control over press access to him, giving one of the lowest number of press conferences per year of any president during the twentieth century. He averaged 11 press conferences each year during his first two years in office, but that number dropped in subsequent years, and when he left office in 1974, he had only held a total of 38 press conferences, an average of seven per year. Nixon did, however, learn how to use prime time television to deliver important messages to the public. Adopting a strategy utilized by Johnson to discuss the Vietnam War, Nixon would request time on network television during the evening hours to make brief statements about his policies or other events. This occurred 37 times while Nixon was in office, a higher average than any other president.[103]

Also in keeping with the tradition inaugurated by Kennedy, press conferences were televised, and White House advisors continually weighed the pros and cons of using the specific forum for a discussion of particular issues. For example, in April 1971, where top news stories focused on Vietnam, the Middle East, China, and arms reduction talks with the Soviet Union, speechwriter and advisor Pat Buchanan reminded Nixon of the advantages of a press conference where he could "[stand] firm in the midst of a week of turmoil talking about what is going on in the street." However, Buchanan believed the press conference would only benefit the administration if Nixon had some new insights to pass on to the American people on key issues

which the nation has seen discussed night in and night out; day in and day out. . . . But if this is to be just another press conference, for exposure—would recommend that RN not do it live, but make his points with headlines; rather than intruding upon the prime time of folks.[104]

However, Nixon's press conferences were routinely lacking in hard news, as were Ziegler's briefings with the press, where he would deny that anything of significance was occurring.[105] Nixon himself later recalled his move to hold fewer press conferences as a prudent political strategy:

> A politician should not assume that the more press conferences he has, the better. It is important not to cheapen the currency by becoming too available. He should have a press conference only when he is well prepared and when there are subjects worth discussing. I did not have as many press conferences as I should have. But on the other hand, I doubt if having more would have helped with my relationship with the press, particularly when the big issues were Vietnam and then Watergate, where the lines were drawn and no quarter given on either side.[106]

Another strategy of having Nixon and his views reach the American public through television, and therefore not filtered through the print press, was to allow one-on-one interviews with network personalities. White House documents from early 1971 show how intense the White House strategy was on this issue, including extensive research on Nielsen ratings on various nights of the week to determine when best to have the President appear in a one-on-one with Howard K. Smith on ABC. Different time slots were considered so as to work around some of the most popular television shows at the time, including *Gunsmoke, Lucy,* and *Laugh-In.*[107] The one-on-one format was considered a good idea for Nixon, since an earlier interview with Barbara Walters on NBC had been effective, by "creating a relaxed and warm atmosphere within which the President appears comfortable and completely at ease."[108] However, ratings for Nixon's one-on-one with Smith on March 22, 1971, were disappointing, with the White House earning only an 11 share, while a movie on NBC earned a 42 share, and Doris Day and Carol Burnett on CBS earned a 25 and 32 share, respectively, for the 9:30-10:30 p.m. time slot. Charles Colson, special counsel to Nixon, lamented that he was

> personally astonished by these figures, if they are accurate. . . . In my opinion, the President was the best last night that I have ever seen him. Maybe if it only reached 9 to 10 million we should consider some means for rebroadcasting the interview. We also might consider in future one-on-one's whether we can't have it carried on over three networks simultaneously. I know this is something the networks don't want to do, but perhaps we could force it. In any event we should insist on more promotion.[109]

Ultimately, the overall press strategy in the Nixon White House seemed to center on the concept of limiting Nixon's accessibility to the press, whether through the infrequent use of press conferences, making televised appearances where no questioning by reporters was allowed, or by having Nixon fade from public view for a time, only to reappear with a dramatic policy announcement. Interviews were also infrequent, and usually were only given to those trusted and "friendly" members of the White House press corps.[110] The Nixon press team was often criticized for its attempts to sell the President through a public relations strategy, and by keeping him from full view, thus creating an "isolated president." Speechwriter Jim Keogh expressed concern to Haldeman in June 1970 that the administration was relying too much on "gimmicks" to promote the President's agenda:

> Too many people are spending too much time drawing up too many game plans. . . . Let's face a few facts. Most of the working media people are 1) against us, and 2) suspicious of us. In the main, they are hard to fool. . . . It is very difficult for us to put anything over on them; it is practically impossible for us to subvert them. If they were for us we could do these things; since they are not, we can't. When we try a gimmick they usually are waiting at the entrance to the alley and they wind up making us look more devious than we are. This gives us a credibility problem. The results often turn out to be counter productive. And the media wind up being more suspicious of us than ever.[111]

While Nixon worked hard at trying to convince the public that he did not care about his image, he was constantly involved in directing the "PR Group" within the White House to develop a strong presidential image of him doing a good job as the chief executive.[112] The "PR Campaign," as it was called within the White House, became a tactical concern in May 1971 when news stories started appearing on the subject, including a network news profile on "image makers" in the White House. Buchanan suggested to Nixon that the administration ease up on emphasizing "color anecdotes" about the President, instead relying on a message based on policy accomplishments since, "if there is anything that turns off Middle America, it is Madison Avenue."[113] Nixon would recall his own philosophy on media exposure as not being able to "go to the well too often. Only on a major issue of universal concern should a president try to reach the people directly to avoid having his views filtered through the press."[114] Key staffers like Buchanan agreed with this philosophy, and suggested that it was the job of the White House staff to limit Nixon's public appearances:

The President's greatest political asset is the Presidency—part of the power of that asset adheres in the *distance* between the Presidency and the people. Harry Truman as Harry Truman is a clown—as President, he fills the shoes of Lincoln, Wilson, etc. The more we show of RN the individual in front of a camera, the more in my judgment we diminish some of the mystery, aloofness that surrounds the office. We make the President too "familiar" a figure— and not in the best sense of that word. . . . I have never been convinced that Richard Nixon, Good Guy, is our long suit; to me we are simply not going to charm the American people; we are not going to win it on "style" and we ought to forget playing ball in the Kennedys' Court.[115]

Many scholars have documented that the Nixon administration was consumed with trying to control and manipulate the press. Nixon clearly hated the press, which he believed held all the cards when it came to controlling the political agenda. Nixon prepared for the battle with the White House press corps everyday since he believed that "the media are far more powerful than the President in creating public awareness and shaping public opinion."[116] Despite his obsession with attacking the press, Nixon experienced strong support from the press during his reelection campaign in 1972. He received the endorsement of 753 out of 809 American newspapers, and he also gained positive coverage that year for his trips to Peking and Moscow. Nonetheless, Nixon never discounted the power of the press while in office, going farther than any other president to manipulate media coverage.[117] The Nixon administration raised the art of media manipulation to new heights, adopting a strategy based on appeasement, evasion, and intimidation to garner public support.[118] Anyone who doubts that Nixon and his White House staff had virtually declared war on the American press need look no further than the words of Buchanan, just weeks after Nixon's landslide reelection in 1972, where he outlines the "Attack Operation" against many members of the national press corps:

Vitally important for the credibility of this Administration that neither the *Post* nor CBS get away scot-free with what they did in the campaign. Should they do so, then any hostile media institution can consider us a paper tiger, and the word will go forth for networks to carve up the more conservative candidate—two weeks before an election—and nothing will happen. We need a strategy of how to deal with CBS, and that should go into the final product. We need a strategy for dealing with the problems raised by the PBS situation, and public broadcasting in general. . . . We need a listing—not extended—of perhaps the 10-20 most serious media problems we face—in terms of hostile TV reporters, commentators, columnists and their counterparts in the writing press. And this memorandum should name them—and include specific measures which the White House Staff can and will take to deny these individuals materials to use against us. A black-out is one tactic and could be enforced in the present environment, for example, by firing the first guy in the bureaucracy found talking to Daniel Schorr. But, unless there is a campaign to specifically deny privileged access to our adversaries, then any strategy is something of a joke.[119]

NIXON'S PUBLIC ACTIVITIES

Nixon may not be remembered as the greatest orator who ever occupied the White House, but speeches were a vital part of his overall leadership strategy. On the subject of public speaking, Nixon credits early debating experience as a child in school as preparation for his later political debates. Throughout his political career, he always stayed closely involved with the writing of his speeches, even writing all of them while Vice President. Nixon believed that, in order to give a successful speech, the speaker had to make it his own, even if it were written by someone else, by adding key ideas and phrases. Nixon practiced that philosophy in tandem with his belief in not taking his message to the American people too often. Writing a good speech, he believed, was "useless unless the speaker has a message. If you don't have something worthwhile to say, it is best not to make a speech at all."[120]

The process of writing a speech in the Nixon White House began with a draft from a member of the speechwriting team, which Nixon would then dictate into a tape recorder to work out the rhythm and language of the speech to make it his own. Keogh headed the team during the first term, and senior writers included the conservative Buchanan, who provided hard-hitting rhetoric on issues; Raymond K. Price, Jr., who helped Nixon with "vision and compassion" in his speeches; and Safire, who aided with economic issues and provided Nixon with occasional humor. Price took over as head of the team during the second term, with David Gergen as an assistant. Nixon usually worked with just one writer on each speech, depending on the topic and slant of the address. Nixon's speeches are remembered most for their simplicity in message: "He meant his words to be understood by an immediate audience not to be admired by future generations."[121]

Keogh recalls the care that Nixon took in writing his own speeches, including extensive editing and rewriting to make the speech fit his speaking style exactly. Nixon's public events were also enhanced by a love of reading and his ability to store information for later use. According to Keogh, Nixon was a master at giving "mini speeches," such as a toast at a State dinner. He would receive suggested remarks, about a page and a half in length, along with briefing papers from key departments. He would usually combine all of the information with his own knowledge on the subject, and then give extemporaneous remarks that resembled a complete, albeit brief, speech:

> [T]he little mini speech without a text was his most remarkable talent. . . . All of that came right out of his head. His mind—I've never encountered a mind of that kind—had the capacity to store all this, organize it, and then spin it out. I used to go to some of these things and sit there and listen to him, marveling how he did it.[122]

When looking at Nixon's public activities (see Table 3.7), the amount is somewhat similar to that of Kennedy's. Nixon chose to pursue public activities infrequently, especially when compared to some of his successors in the White House. And holding true to the efforts of the White House staff, Nixon became more isolated with each passing year. Public activities steadily dropped off each year, which is surprising especially in 1970, a midterm election year, and 1972, Nixon's own reelection campaign year. While much of Nixon's public strategy focused on television events like primetime addresses to the nation, press conferences did not play a key role in the administration's game plan. During his first term, Nixon held a total of 30 press conferences, averaging only 8 per year. Nixon, like Kennedy, did not hold many on-the-record exchanges with reporters, but again, that total does not reflect off-the-record exchanges or interviews. Clearly, the administration did not rely on question-and-answer type forums, and Nixon also gave few policy addresses. Interestingly, he gave the most policy addresses in 1971, an off-election year. Some White House advisors continually urged Nixon to give a series of radio addresses on specific policy topics as early as 1969. Presidential documents show that the idea was considered sound by various advisors, but the actual events continued to be postponed. Eventually Nixon would give four radio addresses during his first term, as well as a series of paid radio addresses on key policies during the fall of 1972 as part of his reelection campaign efforts.[123] A series of radio addresses finally materialized during 1973 and 1974; a series of six such addresses substituted for a State of the Union Address to the nation in 1973. Between January and March 1973, Nixon gave radio addresses on six aspects of the State of the Union message that he submitted to Congress, including the federal budget, the environment, the economy, human resources, community development, and law enforcement and drug abuse prevention. By early 1973, with the Watergate investigation consuming more and more public attention and White

Table 3.7. Nixon—Public Activities.[124]

	1969	1970	1971	1972	1973	1974
National Addresses	6	8	8	7	8	7
Policy Addresses	17	8	23	6	7	8
Press Conferences	8	6	9	7	7	2
Radio Addresses	0	0	3	1	9	10
Brief Statements/						
Nonpolicy Remarks	219	145	108	83	98	59
Partisan Remarks/						
Campaign Speeches	8	29	4	38	1	5
Press Conferences with						
Foreign Dignitaries	0	0	0	0	0	0
Signing Ceremonies	4	12	5	7	3	9
Teleconference Remarks	0	0	1	0	0	0
Roundtable Discussions	0	0	0	0	0	0
Town Meetings/Q&A Sessions	0	0	2	1	1	2
Remarks to/Exchanges with Reporters	4	22	7	6	4	1
Total	266	230	170	156	138	103
Daily Average	0.77	0.63	0.47	0.43	0.38	0.47

House preoccupation, radio addresses allowed Nixon to communicate with the public on domestic policy issues without making public appearances. In total, Nixon participated in 1,063 public events between his inauguration on January 20, 1969 and his resignation from office on August 8, 1974.

THE NIXON POLICY AGENDA

Nixon took office following one of the most tumultuous political years in the nation's history; 1968 had seen two prominent national figures, Robert Kennedy and Martin Luther King, Jr., assassinated; rioting in the streets of Chicago during the Democratic National Convention; and massive student protests nationwide over the continuing American involvement in the Vietnam War. Also, the economic picture in the United States began to decline, with lower productivity of American industries, inflation, and slower economic growth; Nixon had also inherited Johnson's War on Poverty domestic programs, enacted without a tax increase, as well as the continued financial drain of Vietnam.[125] Nixon focused most of his attention on foreign policy, not only dealing with Vietnam, but "revel[ing] in the glow of his role as international statesman" in his diplomatic efforts involving détente with the Soviet Union, his trip to China, and tensions in the Middle East. However, while Nixon stayed involved with the development of domestic policy in some areas, like welfare, crime, and taxes, he did not pay much attention to other issues on the domestic agenda, like the environment, campus unrest, or health issues, but rather delegated the job of pursuing policy initiatives in these areas to others within the White House.[126]

In 1969, Nixon was slow to present his domestic agenda to both Congress and the American public. However, cues were given to key members of Congress, suggesting that the President's legislative priorities on the domestic agenda included welfare reform, revenue sharing, crime, and the environment, among others.[127] By 1971, Nixon did a better job of outlining his policy goals in his State of the Union address; the "Six Great Goals" for his "New American Revolution" included welfare reform, revenue sharing, health insurance reform, environmental initiatives, government reorganization, and full employment. Most of the issues required legislative approval for implementation, and most were stalled in the Democratic Congress that was not overly sympathetic to Nixon's policy agenda. Upon election in 1968, Nixon was without a mandate to govern, becoming the first president since 1848 to not carry at least one house from his own party into power. Nixon had also gotten off to an inauspicious start with Congress when the Senate defeated his first two nominations to the U.S. Supreme Court. As a result, Nixon realized that ". . . he would get little support from the legislative branch and that he would have to use the prerogative powers of the presidency to affect pubic policy."[128] John Ehrlichman, assistant to the President for domestic affairs, recalls that many of the administration's policy efforts were hurt by the fact that Nixon did not want to be bothered with building congressional coalitions. Nonetheless, enough moderate and conservative coalitions were formed on various issues to achieve legislative victories in some areas: ". . . Nixon simply didn't want to spend the kind of time that was required to cultivate these folks. . . . On balance, his legislative record was pretty decent considering what we had stacked up against us."[129]

When looking at the Nixon agenda as presented in his major public addresses during the first term (see Table 3.8), it becomes clear that foreign policy issues routinely dominated his speeches. Nixon talked frequently about the ongoing war in Vietnam, especially in primetime televised addresses to the nation. The Soviet Union was also discussed, but the "Cold Warrior" rhetoric of the Kennedy era had shifted more to Nixon's view of détente as a strategy to deal with the threat of communism. A clear gap exists between the percentages in the

Table 3.8. Nixon's Public Agenda (Major Public Addresses).[130]

	1969	1970	1971	1972	1973	1974
Domestic						
Education	24 - 2%	13 - 1%	4 - <1%	28 - 2%	9 - <1%	76 - 6%
Health Care	1 - <1%	2 - <1%	135 - 7%	1 - <1%	10 - <1%	178 - 13%
Welfare/Entitlements	102 - 8%	46 - 4%	160 - 8%	4 - <1%	35 - 3%	28 - 2%
Anticrime	12 - 1%	98 - 8%	119 - 6%	3 - <1%	112 - 9%	10 - <1%
Political Reform	2 - <1%	23 - 2%	287 - 15%	136 - 12%	5 - <1%	64 - 5%
Science/Technology/ Transportation	18 - 1%	3 - <1%	0 - 0%	7 - 1%	18 - 1%	142 - 10%
Environment/Energy/ Land Management	14 - 1%	104 - 9%	43 - 2%	5 - <1%	316 - 24%	168 - 12%
Defense	74 - 6%	15 - 1%	16 - 1%	66 - 6%	38 - 3%	69 - 5%
International						
Diplomatic/Military	692 - 57%	537 - 45%	574 - 30%	754 - 65%	298 - 23%	225 - 16%
Trade/Economic	58 - 5%	2 - <1%	109 - 6%	103 - 9%	71 - 5%	96 - 7%
Economic						
Domestic Fiscal/Monetary	143 - 12%	187 - 16%	120 - 6%	13 - 1%	343 - 26%	274 - 20%
Unemployment/Jobs	71 - 6%	153 - 13%	318 - 17%	43 - 4%	56 - 4%	40 - 3%
Total	N = 1212	N = 1183	N = 1885	N = 1163	N = 1311	N = 1370

Diplomatic/Military category and other categories for all four years during the first term. Economic issues, as they are with most presidents,
came next on the list in all years but 1972. The category of Domestic
Fiscal/Monetary ranked second in priority during 1969 and 1970, as
Nixon pushed for wage and price standards in an effort to fight inflation, and the Unemployment/Jobs category ranked second in 1971. By
1973, however, Diplomatic/Military issues received less attention in
Nixon's speeches, as he began to focus more on the faltering economy
and the energy crisis. The economy would continue to remain at the top
of Nixon's policy agenda during 1974 as well. Another pattern that
seems to emerge from the Nixon policy agenda between 1969 and 1972
is that most domestic issues ranked near the bottom of the administration's priority list, with some getting next to no public attention from the
President. However, by his last year and a half in office, Nixon began
focusing much more on domestic issues in his major addresses, including health care, transportation, and anticrime programs.

THE FIRST TIER: WELFARE REFORM IN 1971-1972

The Issue and White House Strategy

The Nixon administration proclaimed as early as 1969 that reform of the
welfare system was a top priority, as participation in welfare programs
nationwide continued to escalate. Using a national televised address in
August 1969, Nixon announced his Family Assistance Plan, which
would guarantee a minimum income for poor families, insisting that the
program was more "workfare" than welfare. The House passed a version of the bill in April 1970, but due to partisan wrangling in the Senate
over additions and compromises to the bill, including a filibuster in
December 1970, the issue was dropped for the 91st Congress. In 1971,
Nixon again put welfare reform at the top of his priority list, naming it
as one of his "Six Great Goals" in his State of the Union address. The
administration soon learned, however, that the 92nd Congress would be
no easier to work with on the issue. Once again, the House passed a version of the bill in June 1971, which included Nixon's Family Assistance
Plan with a higher minimum income, as well as changes in Social
Security, Medicare, and Medicaid. It would take nearly 16 months
before the Senate would debate the bill in September 1972, but when a
version of the bill passed three weeks later, the welfare reform provisions had been deleted. Opposed by several liberal Senators as not providing adequate assistance, Nixon's Family Assistance Plan had become

"a lost priority and a political hot potato as the President and the Congress prepared to confront voters in the national election."[131]

From the start, Nixon portrayed his ambitious and somewhat radical proposal for overhauling the welfare system as a conservative "workfare" program. And while those on the left saw FAP as not providing enough assistance to the poor, those on the right could not agree with what they saw as an overly generous and expansive welfare program. Not only did the "odd coalition" created by the issue lead to its ultimate demise, but Nixon also hurt himself with his "sporadic support" of the bill. Since introducing the plan in 1969, Nixon seemed at times apathetic about the proposal; he "let it drift in Congress and did not seem anxious to spend his political capital on pushing FAP through the legislative process."[132] Nixon also did not provide much truth in his own advertising about the bill, downplaying its radical nature, and relying on a "specialized vocabulary for the complexities of welfare that misleads everyone."[133]

By 1971, Nixon was not willing to back up the claim that FAP was a top priority for his administration with public action. Following the State of the Union address that January, he only briefly mentioned welfare reform in a handful of major addresses during the rest of the year, never devoting the majority of an address to the issue. In 1972, no mention of welfare appeared in any major address,[134] which then seems to beg the question, was Nixon truly committed to his own plan? In terms of strategy, Nixon had failed to "seize the day," and he never created "a climate hospitable to his highest domestic priority." The White House also relied on a bad packaging strategy, lumping welfare reform in with other reforms, such as that of the federal government and the draft. And when Nixon did talk about welfare reform, he failed to court the liberal base in Congress needed for passage of the bill, emphasizing work requirements and de-emphasizing the provision for a guaranteed income.[135]

The upcoming presidential election in 1972 also played a role in White House strategy on welfare reform. In December 1971, when it appeared that Congress was close to passing a bill, the administration began contemplating Nixon's response to the compromise package in terms of political assets and liabilities. Nixon was better off signing welfare reform legislation, even with an increase over his proposed minimum income, since the bill would also include "workfare" requirements. As Buchanan argued, a veto would show Nixon as soft on "workfare" and would leave him "vulnerable on perhaps the most sensitive of domestic national issues" prior to the election year. A chance to sign the legislation, Buchanan continued, would provide a "golden opportunity" for Nixon to issue a major signing message, where he "would assume credit for all the tough, work-requirement elements of this legislation. We could claim credit for them and take what is clearly the popular side of the welfare reform question."[136] Welfare reform was also seen as a potential "fissure" on which to divide the Democrats during the election. According to White House "research" on the issue, Nixon should focus on his support for lower-income workers, therefore dividing the issue between "the loafing classes (welfare, students) and the working classes":

> Since taking office, the President has increased by 500 percent—from $400 million to $2 billion—the food stamp and food assistance funds; and he still gets it in the neck for "starving the poor." Methinks there would have been more gratitude and greater rewards if those funds had been directed to the President's potential friends in the working class, and their interests. If the President would become the visible and outspoken champion of the Forgotten American, the working people of this country—and assert that the welfare types have been taken care of for years; it would force a division within the Democratic Party, would align the media against us—but methinks it both divides them and assists us.[137]

Campaign strategy aside, Nixon lost interest in welfare reform in 1972 as the campaign progressed, which contributed to its congressional defeat that year. While it is believed that Nixon still wanted to reform the nation's welfare programs, he did not speak publicly about the issue again until 1974. But by then, due to Watergate, his message did not carry much weight.[138]

Press Coverage

The *New York Times* provided extensive coverage of Nixon's welfare reform proposal between January 1971 and October 1972, with a news item appearing, on average, slightly less than once every other day. However, most stories were generated by either congressional or interest group activity on welfare reform; only 14 percent of the coverage was generated by presidential activity (see Table 3.9). Of the stories generated by Nixon, the tone of coverage was mixed. Most news stories were coded as neutral, that is, presenting a descriptive discussion of events from the previous day. Nixon did, however, receive news story coverage that portrayed his policy and actions in a positive light. While the totals for the tone of all news items show a balanced picture overall for coverage on this policy, with Nixon receiving just as many positive as negative news items, editorials and columns on welfare reform were generally critical of the President's proposal (see Table 3.10). From the start in January 1971, coverage for Nixon's revamped welfare reform

Table 3.9. Amount and Type of *New York Times* **Coverage of the Welfare Reform Proposal (January 1971-October 1972).**

	White House	Congress	Interest Group/Other
News Story	26	111	85
News Analysis	1	4	0
Column	6	11	4
Editorial	8	22	3
Total	41 - (14%)	148 - (53%)	92 - (33%)

Table 3.10. Tone of *New York Times* **Coverage of Presidential Activities on the Welfare Reform Proposal (January 1971-October 1972).**

	Positive	Negative	Balanced/Mixed	Neutral
News Story	7	3	3	13
News Analysis	1	0	0	0
Column	1	3	2	0
Editorial	2	5	1	0
Total	11	11	6	13

package seemed to reflect a willingness to give the President a chance to take action. But as the political process became drawn out, and as the White House and Congress became involved in partisan maneuvering, the coverage in the *Times*, especially on the op-ed pages, reflected a frustration with not only Nixon, but with Congress as well, for politicizing the issue of welfare reform.

THE SECOND TIER:
ENVIRONMENTAL PROTECTION IN 1970

The Issue and White House Strategy

Before he became president, and even during the 1968 presidential election, the environment was not a high priority issue on Nixon's agenda, and he had no record in dealing with environmental issues. Only as environmental protection became an increasingly important issue to the public, as shown through public opinion polls in the late 1960s, did the Nixon administration begin to recognize the environmental "crisis" as an important component of the domestic agenda.[139] Sensing the public mood, in a 1969 book on environmental issues, the newly elected President wrote:

> Perhaps no single goal will be more important in our future efforts to pursue the public happiness than that of improving our environment. This goal, I believe, is one that will help define a new spirit for the Seventies, a new expression of our idealism, a new challenge that will test our ingenuity. I am confident that this goal can be met, but only if we give it the same priority Theodore Roosevelt did when he described the conservation and proper use of natural resources as "the fundamental problem which underlies almost every other problem of our national life."[140]

As the environmental movement began to grow across the country, Nixon began to feel pressure to take action. As the nation prepared to celebrate the first Earth Day on April 22, 1970, calls were made publicly for increased federal regulations and spending on environmental cleanups and other related projects. In an attempt to remain both pro-business and pro-environment, Nixon began a pattern of "bold rhetoric and mild actions," talking tough but supporting only mild changes to existing policies for fear of alienating his support within the business community.[141] As a result, 1970 became Nixon's year to deal with the public's concern, at least as much as he was willing to, over the environment. On January 1, 1970, Nixon signed into law the National Environmental Policy Act, which received front-page headlines around the country due to the slow news days over the New Year's holiday weekend. Nixon, attempting control over the political agenda on the environment, called the signing a fitting start to the new decade of the 1970s and declared environmental protection a "now or never" issue of extreme importance.[142] He also promised in his State of the Union address later that month that his administration would take charge on ensuring environmental protection through programs implemented by the federal government, outlining a plan to clean up the pollution that was threatening America.[143]

While giving few major addresses overall in 1970 (see Table 3.8), Nixon did discuss the environment several times publicly although, after the State of the Union, never in great detail. Behind the scenes, however, Nixon had never set a clear policy agenda for his administration in dealing with environmental issues. Other agencies within the executive branch, such as the Department of the Interior and the Council on Environmental Quality, were often responsible for discussing the administration's views on the environment, but even these agencies did not always agree on the public message they were conveying.[144] For the most part, Nixon remained out of the loop on discussions by his staff on how to handle the environment, and unlike with issues such as welfare reform, he did not participate in the development of policy. His main concern was to stay "out of trouble on environmental issues," showing concern, but careful not to take any action that would harm the economy.[145]

In spite of his hands-off approach to environmental policies, Nixon did create the Environmental Protection Agency in July 1970. As part of several executive reorganization plans submitted to and accepted by Congress, the EPA was created as an agency independent of other Cabinet departments by consolidating other major programs that were responsible for fighting pollution. These included, among others, the Federal Water Quality Administration from the Interior Department; the National Air Pollution Control Administration and sections of the Environmental Control Administration (dealing with solid waste management, water hygiene and radiological health), and the Food and Drug Administration (dealing with pesticides) from the Department of Health, Education and Welfare; functions of registration and licensing for pesticides from the Department of Agriculture; and radiation protection standards from the Atomic Energy Commission.[146]

The environment would remain a concern of the Nixon administration throughout the first term, most notably from the standpoint of political implications for the President, especially when Senator Edmund Muskie, a strong environmental proponent, was considered the Democratic frontrunner for the 1972 presidential election. In September 1971, Nixon was advised by John Whitaker, a White House advisor on environmental issues, to avoid giving a speech that had been prepared, entitled "The Eco-Crusader and the Strategy of Quality." Political polarization on the environment, Whitaker argued, would cause irreparable damage to Nixon publicly. Demonstrating real leadership on a complex issue, not labeling those concerned with the environment as radical and crusading zealots, would better serve Nixon's reelection efforts:

It is my firm conviction, backed up by all the polling data available, that the backbone of those concerned over the environment is white, middle-class, suburban America and that housewives are a major component. To equate this group with a sort of wild-eyed radicalism is erroneous and politically harmful. There *are* zealots in the movement. They are *not* calling the tune, and they are a small, though highly vocal, minority. The best way to insure more influence for them is for you to attack them.[147]

Press Coverage

Environmental protection was not a top priority for the Nixon administration, nor did it receive extensive coverage in the *Times*, at least not from a political standpoint. Only 70 news items appeared during the ten-month period between January and October 1970, which suggests that media coverage was only beginning to focus on the environment as a story-generating issue, and that the federal government was just beginning its action in dealing with the environment. On average, a news item appeared in the *Times* once every four days during the time period studied. And unlike the Nixon welfare reform proposal, where most coverage was generated by Congressional and interest group activity, stories on environmental protection during 1970 were most often generated by the White House (see Table 3.11). This is best explained by the fact that Nixon used his executive powers to reorganize several agencies to create the EPA, which did not require approval of legislation by Congress. Therefore, less partisan wrangling over the issue meant fewer stories originating from Capitol Hill. In terms of the tone of coverage on this issue, a majority of the news items were balanced, providing a good assessment of both Nixon's environmental plans and the views of his political opponents (see Table 3.12). Of the editorials written on this policy, all were either positive or balanced in tone. All seemed to approve of Nixon's discussions on how to protect the environment and his creation of the EPA. On the other hand, most were skeptical as to whether or not Nixon would really go through with his plans, given that he was a Republican, pro-business president. Coverage seemed also to recognize that the Nixon White House was controlling the legislative agenda where the environment was concerned, and items on the op-ed pages encouraged Nixon to take a bold stand in supporting environmental protection. In July, a *Times* editorial referred to Nixon's creation of the EPA as a "statesman-like move," but as the Nixon record on the environment shows, the *Times* was perhaps correct to assume that the White House was pushing political rhetoric over political action.[148]

Table 3.11. Amount and Type of *New York Times* Coverage of Environmental Protection Proposals (January 1970-October 1970).

	White House	Congress	Interest Group/Other
News Story	14	19	16
News Analysis	2	0	1
Column	6	0	3
Editorial	7	1	1
Total	29 - (41%)	20 - (29%)	21 - (30%)

Table 3.12. Tone of *New York Times* Coverage of Presidential Activities on Environmental Protection Proposals (January 1970-October 1970).

	Positive	Negative	Balanced/Mixed	Neutral
News Story	0	0	9	5
News Analysis	0	1	1	0
Column	1	0	4	1
Editorial	1	0	6	0
Total	2	1	20	6

CONCLUSION

In many respects, especially in the area of White House communication strategies, both the Johnson and Nixon presidencies could never completely emerge from the overwhelming shadow of the Kennedy legacy. Both presidencies also left their own legacies; however, they would mostly be negative ones for the presidential/press relationship. Johnson was obsessed with television, which was a vastly expanding medium during the 1960s, but it would ultimately become his undoing. Not only could he never quite master television to present a strong and appealing image of himself as president, but the daily news coverage on television about Vietnam only served to refute White House claims of success on the battlefields. As a result, the credibility gap grew tremendously during the Johnson years, and the effects are still being felt today in the presidential/press relationship.

The strength of Johnson's communication skills came not in his public activities, but in his ability to persuade members of Congress, his cabinet, and other influential people in Washington who were important to the policymaking process behind the scenes. This was certainly evident in the passage of Medicare, a policy for which he did not need to rally public support in 1965. Most of his legislative successes came during his first two years in office, and he masterfully used the circumstances of Kennedy's death to push through many items on the domestic agenda. However, by 1967 Johnson, due to Vietnam, had lost much of his political clout and the opportunity to continue the expansion of his Great Society. He had also lost several Democratic seats in Congress in 1966, which made passage of his version of the Safe Streets Act difficult. Coverage in the *Times* of both issues seems to suggest that the nation's leading newspaper was much more inclined to support Johnson when he was in control of his liberal agenda, with items such as Medicare, and not supportive when he was forced to compromise with conservative members of Congress, as he did with the Safe Streets Act.

Johnson, who like many presidents wanted to have control over the political agenda, also wanted to control his coverage in the press. He may not have achieved the latter, but it was not for a lack of understanding by him and his advisors about how the press operated. On April 1, 1968, the morning after he had announced in a televised address to the nation his intention to not seek reelection, Johnson spoke to the National Association of Broadcasters in Chicago. He shared with the audience both his frustration with and understanding of the news media, particularly television, and its relationship to his presidency:

> Certainly, it is more "dramatic" to show policemen and rioters locked in combat than to show men trying to cooperate with one another. The face of hatred and of bigotry comes through much more clearly—no matter what its color. The face of tolerance, I seem to find, is rarely "newsworthy." Progress—whether it is a man being trained for a job or millions being trained or whether it is a child in Head Start learning to read or an older person of 72 in adult education or being cared for in Medicare—rarely makes the news, although more than 20 million of them are affected by it. Perhaps this is because tolerance and progress are not dynamic events—such as riots and conflicts are events. Peace, in the news sense, is a "condition." War is an "event."[149]

Like the Johnson administration, the Nixon years were marked by changes in both the presidential/press relationship and the development of White House communication strategies. The Nixon administration can be credited with the growth of the White House press operation due to the creation of the Office of Communications, as well as the formal implementation of a daily news summary for use by presidential advisors. But perhaps more importantly, the Nixon White House is remembered best for its paranoia about the press, as well as the attempts it made to declare war on many press freedoms. In his writings following his resignation from the White House in 1974, Nixon did admit that he did not have the best relationship with the press, nor did he feel that he was covered fairly much of the time, especially after leaving Washington. And while it remains difficult to analyze the Nixon administration beyond the ever-present cloud of Watergate, documents from key Nixon staffers seem to corroborate the tale of extensive White House maneuvers to not only monitor the press, but to counterattack almost every move that was made, especially by the liberal journalists who belonged to the "Eastern establishment press." Nixon may have had one of the worst relationships with the press of any modern president, but as much of the animosity came from within the White House as was generated by the White House press corps. However, Nixon, like Johnson, was influential in not only increasing the credibility gap between journalists and the government, but also helped to set the stage for future presidents in their attempts at controlling the press. Many aspects of the Nixon presidency will live in infamy for decades to come, and among those, it will certainly be remembered for providing a fascinating case study on presidential/press relations.

However, as the later part of this chapter shows, Nixon did not do much to help his own cause. The amount of his public activities decreased each year he was in office, which limited his ability to get his message out to not only the press, but to the American people as well. Often, his press strategy seemed to rely on avoidance, and his rhetorical strategies to promote the policies examined here showed a willingness to make grand statements, but a failure to follow up with activities that would win the support of the press, public, or Congress. While Nixon may have believed a liberal bias existed in much of the American press, the tone of the coverage he received on the two policies examined here seem to suggest that any bias that may have existed in the *Times* came from a policy perspective, not a personal one. Most often, the coverage turned negative only when Nixon failed to follow through politically with his own initiatives. At least during his first term, prior to the onslaught of media coverage of Watergate in 1973 and 1974, Nixon's coverage seemed no better or worse than any other president during the modern era, especially for a president who seemed unwilling to accommodate the press by being accessible. Both Johnson and Nixon would provide important lessons about communication strategies for their successors in the White House; however, the effects of the credibility gap would limit, in one way or another, the communicative successes of each future president.

ENDNOTES

1.   Panel discussion with James H. Rowe, Jr., "Perspectives From the White House on Leadership," in *Twenty Years of Papers on the Presidency*, Ed. Kenneth W. Thompson (Lanham, MD: University Press of America, 1995), 42.

2.   Michael Emery and Edwin Emery, *The Press and America: An Interpretive History of the Mass Media*, 8th ed. (Boston: Allyn and Bacon, 1996), 418-9.

3.   George Christian, "Another Perspective," in *The Johnson Presidency: Twenty Intimate Perspectives of Lyndon B. Johnson*, Ed. Kenneth W. Thompson (Lanham, MD: University Press of America, 1986), 121.

4.   Robert Dallek, *Flawed Giant: Lyndon Johnson and His Times 1961-1973* (New York: Oxford University Press, 1998), 368-9, 592-3.

5.   Oral history interview of George Christian by Joe Frantz, 12/4/69, Interview II, p. 7, Lyndon Baines Johnson Library.

6.   Oral history interview of Pierre Salinger by Theodore White, July 19, 1965, p. 51, John Fitzgerald Kennedy Library.

7.   Oral history interview of Robert Kintner by Joe Frantz, 7/13/72, p. 6, Lyndon Baines Johnson Library.

8.   Doris Kearns, *Lyndon Johnson and the American Dream* (New York: Harper & Row, 1976), 247.

9.   *The Public Papers of the Presidents of the United States: Lyndon B. Johnson, 1963-64* (Washington, DC: Government Printing Office, 1965).

10. Letter from Philip Potter to Lyndon Johnson, 12/5/64, PR 18, WHCF, Box 356, Lyndon Baines Johnson Library.

11. Ibid., 302-3, and John Tebbel and Sarah Miles Watts, *The Press and the Presidency: From George Washington to Ronald Reagan* (New York: Oxford University Press, 1985), 490-1.

12. Oral history interview of George Christian by Joe Frantz, 12/4/69, Interview II, pp. 14-5, Lyndon Baines Johnson Library.

13. Letter from Drew Pearson to Bill Moyers, 7/9/1965, PR 18, WHCF, Box 357, Lyndon Baines Johnson Library.

14. Christian, "Another Perspective," 121.

15. Oral history interview of George Christian by Joe Frantz, 12/4/69, Interview II, p. 19, Lyndon Baines Johnson Library.

16. Oral history interview of Robert Kintner by Joe Frantz, 7/13/72, pp. 7-8, Lyndon Baines Johnson Library.

17. Letter from Philip Potter to Lyndon Johnson, 12/5/64, PR 18, WHCF, Box 356, Lyndon Baines Johnson Library.

18. Jeff Shesol, *Mutual Contempt: Lyndon Johnson, Robert Kennedy, and the Feud That Defined a Decade* (New York: W.W. Norton & Company, 1997), 310-6.

19. Oral history interview of Robert Kintner by Joe Frantz, 7/13/72, p. 25, Lyndon Baines Johnson Library.

20. Ibid., 32.

21. Memo from McPherson to Moyers, 3/8/66, PR 18, WHCF, Box 358, Lyndon Baines Johnson Library.

22. Memo from Douglass Cater to Moyers, 12/6/63, Office Files of Bill Moyers, Box 51, Lyndon Baines Johnson Library.

23. In June 1966, Kintner wrote a confidential memorandum to Johnson comparing the number of press conferences during the same time period given by Johnson and Kennedy. The memo goes into great detail about the methodology used in tallying the number of press conferences; after 942 days in office, using Kintner's counting scheme, Johnson had held 65, while Kennedy had held only 59. Memo from Kintner to Johnson, 6/20/66, Office Files of Robert Kintner, Box 8, Lyndon Baines Johnson Library.

24. Oral history interview of Jack Valenti by Joe Frantz, 7/12/72, Interview V, p. 27, Lyndon Baines Johnson Library.

25. Memo from Kintner to Johnson, 6/3/66, Office Files of Robert Kintner, Box 7, Lyndon Baines Johnson Library.

26. Memo from Kintner to Moyers, 4/30/66, Office Files of Robert Kintner, Box 7, Lyndon Baines Johnson Library.

27. Memo from Christian to Johnson, 12/7/67, EX PR 18, WHCF, Box 360, Lyndon Baines Johnson Library.

28. Kearns, 248.

29. Ibid., 303.

30. Memo from Jack McNulty to Christian, 7/27/67, PR 18-1, WHCF, Box 368, Lyndon Baines Johnson Library. McNulty, a staff assistant to the President, acknowledged to Christian that Johnson's image on television was still a problem even after nearly four years in office: "I am told that you and Tom Johnson have opened the door for ideas and suggestions. I will contribute an obvious one. Something should be done to make the President look better on television." He urged White House coordination with the networks, but to keep the President's best interest, and not that of the networks, "foremost in mind."

31. Oral history interview of Jack Valenti by Joe Frantz, 7/12/72, Interview V, pp. 27-9, Lyndon Baines Johnson Library.

32. Memo from Kintner to Johnson, 10/13/66, PR 18-1, WHCF, Box 368, Lyndon Baines Johnson Library.

33. Memo from Kintner to Johnson, 10/6/66, PR 18-1, WHCF, Box 368, Lyndon Baines Johnson Library.

34. Oral history interview of Robert Kintner by Joe Frantz, 7/13/72, pp. 14-5, Lyndon Baines Johnson Library.

35. Memo from Moyers to Johnson, 8/10/65, Office Files of Bill Moyers, Box 11, Lyndon Baines Johnson Library.

36. Memo from Moyers to Johnson, 1/25/66, Office Files of Bill Moyers, Box 11, Lyndon Baines Johnson Library.

37. Memo from Moyers to Johnson, 7/14/66, Office Files of Bill Moyers, Box 11, Lyndon Baines Johnson Library.
38. Various memos detailing press contact reports can be found in the Office Files of George Christian, Box 3, Lyndon Baines Johnson Library.
39. Oral history interview of George Christian by Joe Frantz, 12/4/69, Interview II, pp. 21-2, Lyndon Baines Johnson Library.
40. Memo from Busby to Johnson, February 1965, Office Files of Horace Busby, Box 52, Lyndon Baines Johnson Library.
41. Memo from Tom Johnson to Johnson, 12/9/66, PR 18, WHCF, Box 358, Lyndon Baines Johnson Library.
42. Memo from Charles Maguire to Jim Jones, Sherwin Markman, Tom Johnson, and Larry Levinson, 7/26/68, EX PR 18, WHCF, Box 361, Lyndon Baines Johnson Library.
43. Tebbel and Watts, 496-7.
44. Ibid., 494.
45. Memo from Reedy to Johnson, not dated, Office Files of Bill Moyers, Box 7, Lyndon Baines Johnson Library.
46. Letter from Potter to Johnson, 12/5/64, PR 18, WHCF, Box 356, Lyndon Baines Johnson Library.
47. Emery and Emery, 418-9.
48. Letter from Smathers to Johnson, 8/6/65, PR 18, WHCF, Box 357, Lyndon Baines Johnson Library.
49. Letter from Reedy to Johnson, 1/3/67, EX PR 18, WHCF, Box 359, Lyndon Baines Johnson Library.
50. Letter from Moyers to Johnson, 5/1/67, PR 18-1, WHCF, Box 368, Lyndon Baines Johnson Library.
51. Memo from McPherson to Christian, 2/29/68, EX PR 18, WHCF, Box 361, Lyndon Baines Johnson Library.
52. Kenneth S. Zagacki, "Lyndon Baines Johnson," in *U.S. Presidents as Orators: A Bio-Critical Sourcebook*, Ed. Halford Ryan (Westport, CT: Greenwood Press, 1995), 231-2.
53. Oral history interview of Jack Valenti by Joe Frantz, 3/3/71, Interview IV, pp. 31-3, Lyndon Baines Johnson Library. Johnson delivered the Howard University commencement speech, entitled "To fulfill these rights," on June 4, 1965. The speech focused on improving the social and economic conditions of all African Americans.
54. Oral history interview of Robert Kintner by Joe Frantz, 7/13/72, p. 29, Lyndon Baines Johnson Library.
55. Interview with Robert E. Hunter, February 16, 1999.
56. Kearns, 247.
57. Interview with Robert E. Hunter, February 16, 1999.
58. Kearns, 249.
59. Larry Berman, *The New American Presidency* (Boston: Little Brown and Company, 1987), 248-9.

60. Compiled from the *Public Papers of the Presidents of the United States: Lyndon B. Johnson, 1963-69* (Washington, DC: Government Printing Office, 1965-71).

61. Ibid., 251-3.

62. Compiled from the *Public Papers of the Presidents of the United States: Lyndon B. Johnson, 1963-69* (Washington, DC: Government Printing Office, 1965-71).

63. *Congressional Quarterly Almanac*, 1965, Vol. XXI (Washington, DC: Congressional Quarterly Service, 1966), 236.

64. Dallek, 206.

65. Shesol, 239-40.

66. Erwin C. Hargrove, *The President as Leader: Appealing to the Better Angels of Our Nature* (Lawrence, KS: University Press of Kansas, 1998), 118-9.

67. Remarks to the President's Council on Aging, 2/16/65, *Public Papers of the Presidents: Lyndon B. Johnson, 1965* (Washington, DC: Government Printing Office, 1966).

68. According to the texts of public appearances as recorded in the *Public Papers of the Presidents*, the three instances included Remarks to the Press Following a Meeting With Congressional Leaders to Discuss Medical Care Legislation on 3/26/65, Remarks at the Democratic Congressional Dinner in the Washington Hilton Hotel on 6/24/65, and Remarks at the Democratic Congressional Dinner in the D.C. Armory, also on 6/24/65.

69. Lyndon Baines Johnson, *The Vantage Point: Perspectives of the Presidency 1963-1969* (New York: Holt, Rinehart and Winston, 1971), 213.

70. Memo from Moyers to Johnson, 6/8/65, Office Files of Bill Moyers, Box 11, Lyndon Baines Johnson Library.

71. Hargrove, *The President as Leader*, 119.

72. Johnson, 216, and Dallek, 208.

73. Memo from Busby to Valenti, Cater, Moyers, and Watson, 7/22/65, Office Files of Horace Busby, Box 18, Lyndon Baines Johnson Library.

74. Johnson, 219.

75. Remarks to the Delegates to the Conference of State Committees on Criminal Administration, 10/15/66, *Public Papers of the Presidents: Lyndon Baines Johnson, 1966* (Washington, DC: Government Printing Office, 1967).

76. Memo written by James Gaither, "Summary Description of the Safe Streets and Crime Control Act of 1968," 11/15/68, Presidential Task Forces Files of James Gaither, Box 5, Lyndon Baines Johnson Library.

77. Dallek, 406-7.

78. Memo from Tom Johnson to Christian, 9/21/67, EX PR 18, WHCF, Box 360, Lyndon Baines Johnson Library.

79. *Congressional Quarterly Almanac,* 1968, Vol. XXIV (Washington, DC: Congressional Quarterly Service, 1969), 225-6.

80. Statement by the President Upon Signing the Omnibus Crime Control and Safe Streets Act of 1968, *Public Papers of the Presidents: Lyndon Baines Johnson, 1968-69* (Washington, DC: Government Printing Office, 1970).

81. Johnson, 335. There is great irony in this statement, since Johnson secretly taperecorded more than 10,000 conversations in the Oval Office while President. For a discussion on this topic, see Dallek, 407-9.

82. Johnson, 335.

83. For a brief yet thorough discussion of Nixon's long relationship with the press, see Michael A. Genovese, *The Nixon Presidency: Power and Politics in Turbulent Times* (New York: Greenwood Press, 1990), 48-56; and Tebbel and Watts, 500-15.

84. Richard Nixon, *In the Arena: A Memoir of Victory, Defeat and Renewal* (New York: Pocket Books, 1990), 293.

85. Lou Cannon, "The Press and the Nixon Presidency," in *The Nixon Presidency: Twenty-Two Intimate Perspectives of Richard M. Nixon,* Ed. Kenneth Thompson (Lanham, MD: University Press of America, 1987), 196.

86. See *Ten Presidents and the Press,* Ed. Kenneth W. Thompson (Washington, DC: University Press of America, 1983), 81.

87. William Safire, *Before the Fall: An Inside View of the Pre-Watergate White House* (New York: Da Capo Press, 1975), 104, 342.

88. George C. Edwards, *The Public Presidency: The Pursuit of Popular Support* (New York: St. Martin's Press, 1983), 128-32.

89. Memo from Ziegler to Haldeman, 11/25/69, in White House Special Files: Staff Member and Office Files of H.R. Haldeman, Box 124, Richard M. Nixon Presidential Materials Staff, National Archives at College Park, Maryland.

90. Ibid.

91. Memo from Herbert G. Klein to Nixon, 12/5/69, in White House Special Files: Staff Member and Office Files of H.R. Haldeman, Box 124, Richard M. Nixon Presidential Materials Staff, National Archives at College Park, Maryland.

92. Memo from Mort Allin to Haldeman, 7/22/70, in White House Special Files: Staff Member and Office Files of H.R. Haldeman, Box 124, Richard M. Nixon Presidential Materials Staff, National Archives at College Park, Maryland. For a discussion of the ideological leanings of major newspapers, see Emery and Emery, *The Press and America,* 537-70.

93. Ibid., Memo from Allin to Haldeman.

94. Memo from Haldeman to Klein and Ziegler, 11/30/70, in White House Special Files: Staff Member and Office Files of H.R. Haldeman, Box 124, Richard M. Nixon Presidential Materials Staff, National Archives at College Park, Maryland.

95. Stanley I. Kutler, *The Wars of Watergate: The Last Crisis of Richard Nixon* (New York: Alfred A. Knopf, 1990), 168.
96. Memo from Moore to Haldeman, 6/24/70, in White House Special Files: Staff Member and Office Files of H.R. Haldeman, Box 124, Richard M. Nixon Presidential Materials Staff, National Archives at College Park, Maryland.
97. Tebbel and Watts, 504.
98. Letter by Mort Allin to Richard Britton, 1/8/71, in White House Special Files: Staff Member and Office Files of Patrick J. Buchanan, Box 3, Richard M. Nixon Presidential Materials Staff, National Archives at College Park, Maryland. Extensive documentation on the daily news summaries can be found in the Buchanan files, Boxes 1-8.
99. Letter by Mort Allin to Alice Plato, 1/29/71, in White House Special Files: Staff Member and Office Files of Patrick J. Buchanan, Box 3, Richard M. Nixon Presidential Materials Staff, National Archives at College Park, Maryland.
100. Safire, 342-3.
101. For an extensive analysis of the evolution of the Office of Communications, see John Anthony Maltese, *Spin Control: The White House Office of Communications and the Management of Presidential News* (Chapel Hill: University of North Carolina Press, 1994).
102. Tebbel and Watts, 505.
103. Emery and Emery, 441-3.
104. Memo from Buchanan to Nixon, 4/23/71, in White House Special Files: Staff Member and Office Files of Patrick J. Buchanan, Box 3, Richard M. Nixon Presidential Materials Staff, National Archives at College Park, Maryland.
105. Tebbel and Watts, 505.
106. Nixon, *In the Arena*, 301.
107. Memo from Mark Goode to Dwight Chapin, 2/23/71; and memo from Goode to Ziegler, 3/8/71; both in White House Special Files: Staff Member and Office Files of H.R. Haldeman, Box 124, Richard M. Nixon Presidential Materials Staff, National Archives at College Park, Maryland.
108. Memo from Goode to Haldeman, 3/15/71, in White House Special Files: Staff Member and Office Files of H.R. Haldeman, Box 124, Richard M. Nixon Presidential Materials Staff, National Archives at College Park, Maryland.
109. Memo from Colson to Haldeman, 3/23/71, in White House Special Files: Staff Member and Office Files of H.R. Haldeman, Box 124, Richard M. Nixon Presidential Materials Staff, National Archives at College Park, Maryland.
110. Tebbel and Watts, 506.
111. Memo from Keogh to Haldeman, 6/24/70, in White House Special Files: Staff Member and Office Files of H.R. Haldeman,

Box 124, Richard M. Nixon Presidential Materials Staff, National Archives at College Park, Maryland.

112. Kutler, 167-8.

113. Memo from Buchanan to Nixon, 5/3/71, in White House Special Files: Staff Member and Office Files of Patrick J. Buchanan, Box 3, Richard M. Nixon Presidential Materials Staff, National Archives at College Park, Maryland.

114. Nixon, *In the Arena*, 302.

115. Memo from Buchanan to Nixon, 9/17/71, in White House Special Files: Staff Member and Office Files of Patrick J. Buchanan, Box 3, Richard M. Nixon Presidential Materials Staff, National Archives at College Park, Maryland.

116. For example, see Stephen E. Ambrose, *Nixon: The Triumph of a Politician 1962-1972* (New York: Simon & Schuster, 1989), 229.

117. Ibid., 659.

118. Joseph C. Spear, *Presidents and the Press: The Nixon Legacy* (Cambridge, MA: MIT Press, 1984), 31.

119. Memo from Buchanan to Ziegler, 12/14/72, in White House Special Files: Staff Member and Office Files of Patrick J. Buchanan, Box 3, Richard M. Nixon Presidential Materials Staff, National Archives at College Park, Maryland.

120. Nixon, *In the Arena*, 242-51.

121. Hal W. Bochin, "Richard Milhous Nixon," in *U.S. Presidents as Orators: A Bio-Critical Sourcebook*, Ed. Halford Ryan (Westport, CT: Greenwood Press, 1995), 253-4.

122. James Keogh, "Nixon, The Press and the White House," in *The Nixon Presidency: Twenty-Two Intimate Perspectives of Richard M. Nixon*, Ed. Kenneth Thompson (Lanham, MD: University Press of America, 1987), 205-6.

123. Several memos detailing plans for radio addresses, including suggested topics, can be found in the White House Special Files: Staff Member and Office Files of H.R. Haldeman and Dwight Chapin, Richard M. Nixon Presidential Materials Staff, National Archives at College Park, Maryland. For example, in a memo from Safire to Chapin dated 10/6/69, Safire states: "I've been pushing for a series of radio addresses for so long now, I've given up." By 1971, topics such as Vietnam, the elderly, economic growth, and government reform were suggested, but were postponed, and were eventually covered in the campaign radio addresses paid for by the Committee to Re-Elect the President.

124. Compiled from *The Public Papers of the Presidents of the United States: Richard M. Nixon, 1969-74* (Washington, DC: Government Printing Office, 1971-75).

125. Genovese, 61-2.

126. Ibid., 72.

127. Paul C. Light, *The President's Agenda: Domestic Policy Choice From Kennedy to Reagan* (Baltimore: Johns Hopkins University Press, 1991), 159.

128. Berman, 259-61.

129. John Ehrlichman, "The White House and Policy-Making," in *The Nixon Presidency: Twenty-Two Intimate Perspectives of Richard M. Nixon*, Ed. Kenneth Thompson (Lanham, MD: University Press of America, 1987), 133.

130. Compiled from *The Public Papers of the Presidents of the United States: Richard M. Nixon, 1969-74* (Washington, DC: Government Printing Office, 1971-75).

131. *Congressional Quarterly Almanac, 1972*, Vol. XXVIII (Washington, DC: Congressional Quarterly Service, 1973), 899-900.

132. Genovese, 78-80.

133. Vincent J. Burke and Vee Burke, *Nixon's Good Deed: Welfare Reform* (New York: Columbia University Press, 1974), 3.

134. This does not include campaign speeches, which are not counted as major addresses in this study.

135. Barbara Kellerman, *The Political Presidency: Practice of Leadership* (New York: Oxford University Press, 1984), 149-50.

136. Memo from Buchanan to Nixon per John Ehrlichman, 12/15/71, in White House Special Files: Staff Member and Office Files of John Ehrlichman, Box 38, Richard M. Nixon Presidential Materials Staff, National Archives at College Park, Maryland.

137. Memo from "Research" to Haldeman, 10/5/71, in White House Special Files: Staff Member and Office Files of H.R. Haldeman, Box 124, Richard M. Nixon Presidential Materials Staff, National Archives at College Park, Maryland.

138. Joan Hoff, *Nixon Reconsidered* (New York: HarperCollins Publishers, 1994), 132.

139. Ibid., 21.

140. Richard M. Nixon, "A Statement from President Nixon" in *The Environment: A National Mission for the Seventies*, by the Editors of Fortune (New York: Harper & Row Publishers, 1970), 12.

141. Genovese, 90-1.

142. John C. Whitaker, *Striking A Balance: Environment and Natural Resources Policy in the Nixon-Ford Years* (Washington, DC: American Enterprise Institute for Public Policy Research, 1976), 50.

143. Genovese, 91.

144. Joe Browder, "Decision-Making in the White House," in *Nixon and the Environment: The Politics of Devastation*, Ed. James Rathlesberger (New York: The Village Voice, 1972), 261.

145. Hoff, 23.

146. *Congressional Quarterly Almanac, 1970*, Vol. XXVI (Washington, DC: Congressional Quarterly Service, 1971), 465.

147. Memo from Whitaker to Nixon through Ehrlichman, 11/21/71, in White House Special Files: Staff Member and Office Files of

John D. Ehrlichman, Box 21, Richard M. Nixon Presidential Materials Staff, National Archives at College Park, Maryland.

148. "Plan for the Environment," *New York Times*, July 12, 1970, IV-12.
149. Remarks in Chicago Before the National Association of Broadcasters, 4/1/68, *Public Papers of the Presidents: Lyndon Baines Johnson, 1968-69* (Washington, DC: Government Printing Office, 1970).

4

Ford and Carter:
The Aftermath of Watergate

Richard Nixon's resignation from office on August 9, 1974 did not bring the Watergate saga to an end. His Vice President and successor in the White House, Gerald Ford, may have declared in his inaugural address that the nation's "long national nightmare is over," but Nixon's political scandal would continue to haunt the occupants of the Oval Office for the next six and a half years. Despite their differing party affiliations, the presidencies of Gerald Ford and Jimmy Carter would share many similarities. Both came to the White House as a result, direct in the case of Ford and indirect in the case of Carter, of Watergate. Both would lose their bids for reelection due to the nagging feeling among the American public that each was a mediocre leader and that a change was needed in Washington. Both Ford, the House Republican Minority Leader prior to becoming Vice President after Spiro Agnew's resignation in 1973, and Carter, a former one-term Democratic Georgia governor, were viewed as down to earth, honest, and moral men. They attempted to mold their public images while president as "regular guys" who downplayed the trappings of the office. Each also had the daunting task of restoring credibility to the White House after the years of the so-called imperial presidencies of Nixon and his predecessor Lyndon Johnson. Unfortunately, they would suffer from lackluster communication skills, poor relations with Congress, and tough economic times for the nation that would

111

limit many opportunities for effective leadership. However, each left a positive, if not overwhelming, legacy by repairing some of the damage Nixon had done to the presidency. Ford showed strong moral leadership at a time when the nation desperately needed it, and he "reset the nation's ethical compass and put the ship of state on a course that avoided disaster."[1] Carter continued the effort and "lost no time in trying to continue where Ford left off in encouraging faith in the nation's cherished [political] institutions."[2]

FORD AND THE PRESS

When Ford assumed the office of the presidency in August 1974, one of his first presidential statements was a reassurance to Americans that under the constitutional system of government, the people rule. He took office during the final stages of America's withdrawal from Vietnam, with a sagging economy due to high inflation, and with "a higher degree of public cynicism about politicians" than perhaps any modern president had faced before. During his first month in office, Ford gained the respect and praise of a beleaguered and battered White House press corps that had endured nearly six years of the Nixon administration. However, the honeymoon ended for Ford on September 8, 1974, when he granted Nixon a full presidential pardon for any offenses he may have committed in connection with Watergate. Ford's press secretary, Jerald terHorst, resigned in protest, and the President was soon faced with extensive public criticism and "a press corps whose skepticism had been quickly revived."[3]

Ford's public image was both an asset and a detriment to his presidency. Following the imperial presidencies of Johnson and Nixon, Vietnam, and Watergate, the American public saw Ford as an ordinary man with an ordinary family. During the first month of his administration, prior to the Nixon pardon, Ford enjoyed a good relationship with the press, which "fawned over the new president." Following the months of negative stories about Nixon and Watergate, Ford initially provided the press with nicer images, like retrieving his own morning paper while still in his pajamas on the front porch of his Alexandria, Virginia home. "People wanted to believe that the Ford administration could heal America."[4] Ford was considered an "unpretentious, unassuming man," an image that America discovered during the first month of his presidency.[5] Unlike Nixon, Ford also sought to restore the public's accessibility to the president and worked hard at developing an "open presidency" with the press, telling reporters after taking office that he would be "as open and candid as possible."[6] Just 11 days after Ford

assumed the presidency, terHorst received a letter of both encouragement and praise for a "splendid beginning" from NBC's John
Chancellor:

> Today, we watched the President announce [Nelson Rockefeller as
> Vice President] in the Oval Office, and there was something in my
> subconscious which nagged at me much of the day. I now know
> what it was. It was *informal* television. No Royal Family stuff. No
> holding a picture of the regal seal; no shots designed to keep the
> President smack in the middle of the picture, all the time. I liked it
> very much, and if I can make a McLuhanesque guess, I'll bet a lot of
> people liked it without knowing why. Since Kennedy, I suppose,
> television directors and producers on the White House staff have
> worked very hard to show the boss in shots and angles which are
> not only flattering, but which tended, in the end, to be so damned
> *monarchical.* And I think those kinds of shots create a void between a
> President and the other people in the room with him. What I saw
> today was the Administration, the leaders—the government, of
> which Mr. Ford was a part. There were some shots which didn't
> show the President at all. How long has it been since we saw that?
> Today's ceremony had a fine, plain, honest look about it. If it was
> hastily arranged by amateurs, I think you should *stick* with those
> amateurs. And I think you should consider these matters when you
> get around to hiring TV types to handle your coverage.[7]

terHorst also received a detailed memo from Nixon advisor Pat
Buchanan on how to maximize the potential of his position as press secretary. While differences in communication strategies would certainly
exist between Nixon and Ford, Buchanan pointed out how truly powerful the press office could be for any president:

> You start off your post with the two commodities which are truly
> sine qua non. First—total access to The Man; second, the confidence
> of the press. With these assets in place, you should consider the
> office as a place of opportunity, not simply to provide information,
> and a regular "news flow", but to explain and educate the country
> through the press, to articulate and argue the positions and policies
> of the President. The customary Cabinet Office has the devil's time
> of it making the evening news or page one. You can make any of
> them any day of the week. With this capability, you should, there-
> fore, have at least the substance and issues backup of a Cabinet
> Officer. By that I mean research and writing support so that your
> daily appearances out there can enable you each day to make not
> only hard news, but to provide the philosophical, political and prac-
> tical grounding of Presidential decisions.[8]

Buchanan also offered advice on how to communicate the President's message should the honeymoon with the press end. The Office of Communications, created during the Nixon administration and headed then by Herb Klein, would be crucial in dealing with a hostile press:

> Herb's role was basically to carry the message to the country, to editorial conferences, city-by-city and state-by-state. He served a most valuable role—as sort of a roving ambassador to the press outside of D.C. The current White House—like the Nixon White House in the last two years—has nothing like this. But, should the honeymoon suddenly fade away, you should keep in mind the possibility of enlisting this kind of surrogate, who can get daily press and wire coverage moving around the country, taking the President's case directly into the editorial offices.[9]

No one in the Ford administration expected the honeymoon to end so abruptly. Following the pardon, which came with little warning despite much discussion among both his advisors and the press, Ford's image in the press changed drastically. Reporters were no longer amused by this "regular guy" who ate English muffins in the White House, and following Ford's drop in public approval (from 70 to about 50 percent), they began to criticize Ford from every angle. His presidency had initially been romanticized, but was now at the mercy of the same press corps that had been lied to on a regular basis by Johnson and Nixon. The shadow cast by Nixon was a difficult one for Ford to escape, especially with the press. After the pardon, the press began to speculate on Ford possibly brokering a deal with Nixon over his resignation (a controversy that has yet to be completely put to rest), as well as writing stories associating Ford with Watergate and accusing him of being no different than his predecessors in dealing with the press and public.[10] Ron Nessen, who would replace terHorst as press secretary, recalled the difficulties he and others in the White House experienced with the press due to the broken trust between the President and the press after Watergate:

> I had hanging in my White House office a framed quotation from a column by Jerry Greene in the *New York Daily News*: "Watergate is harder to wash away than the spray of a skunk." The specter of Richard Nixon haunted the Ford White House from the first day to the last. The White House press corps, particularly, remained obsessed with Nixon. It was difficult for many journalists to come down from the high of Watergate. They were addicted. Lies! Tapes! Exposures! Drama! Officials caught, disgraced, jailed! A president driven from office! The valiant press vindicated! Its wicked accusers

discredited! Who could be happy again covering mundane matters like budgets, energy and legislative proposals?[11]

The departure of terHorst as press secretary was also costly for the Ford administration. A long-time friend of Ford's from Michigan, terHorst was a former reporter with international experience, a syndicated columnist in Washington, and a well-respected man among Washington reporters. Nessen, an experienced reporter himself even at the early age of 40, would only exacerbate the already tense relationship between the President and the press. Nessen was well-known for his quick temper and thin skin, and he was also considered "prickly, to say the least." The mood in the pressroom also returned to one of contention between the White House and reporters with confrontations occurring on a regular basis.[12] Nessen was given tremendous access to information within the White House, including attendance at most staff meetings, and he assured Ford that he had no problem with not discussing all that he knew during press briefings with his former colleagues. However, he did not enjoy a friendly relationship with the press, who had grown accustomed to little presidential access during the Nixon years. Nessen often criticized the press for being suspicious and cynical, yet they also considered him to be suspicious, due in part to the fact that he knew much more about what went on in the White House than he was permitted to discuss publicly. Also, the barrage of questions from the press corps about Ford's many mishaps, such as bumping his head on a helicopter or tripping down stairs, would lead to "open confrontation" between Nessen and many reporters. Since the press had been lied to before about the health of presidents, reporters persisted with questions about Ford's public stumblings and whether or not they were health-related. Nessen did not consider the overkill of coverage about Ford's mishaps to be legitimate news copy.[13]

Nessen's credibility with the press would also be hurt by his "tendency to magnify everything [Ford] did in a way that sounded like aggressive press agentry."[14] An example, which Nessen himself recalls in his memoirs, was when he stated that an agreement Ford had made with Soviet leaders on SALT II arms control negotiations was one of the most significant developments in American diplomacy since World War II. As he told reporters, "It was something Nixon couldn't do in five years. But Ford did it in three months." Nessen's proclamation was much exaggerated since negotiations would eventually break down, and Ford would not sign a SALT II treaty. Afterwards, both Nessen and the reporters knew that the statement had gone a bit too far, but the damage to the relationship had already been done. The comments became a lead news item during the following few days, and several news organizations were preparing stories on Nessen's poor performance during the trip to Vladivostok. Nessen tried to mend his relationship with reporters by a meeting over drinks in his office, but to little avail:

> By the end of the meeting, much of the heat had been let out of the press complaints and the critical stories were softened somewhat. But the trip ended whatever honeymoon I had with the press. After that I was never able to recover fully the lost opportunity to build a relationship of mutual respect and friendship with the White House press corps.[15]

After the meeting, Nessen received critical advice from John Osborne, Associate Editor at *The New Republic*, on how to deal with the tense environment in the pressroom that had been created:

> 1) I don't understand why you and your staff are as upset as you seem to be about the Far East Trip. . . . It seemed to me to go about as well as such a tightly scheduled trip could go and has gone in the past. 2) All the talk from us at your meeting about having the President schedule his trips for the media's convenience is crap, in my opinion. It's our business to adjust to his needs, not his to adjust to ours. *Vide* what happened during and after Mr. Nixon's China trip. I among others ridiculed him and his staff for making the trip a gigantic TV show—which he did. 3) You are right to be worried about the press-room attitude toward you. The consensus is unfavorable. I think you are capable of working it out and hope you will. I have suggestions. Quit apologizing. Get from the President, if you don't already have it, assurance that he understands your difficulties and is not about to sacrifice you. Only that, I should imagine, can restore the confidence you started out with and that remains essential. Quit blaming Ziegler; forget him and the "poison" he bequeathed. It was the period, not Ziegler, that fundamentally poisoned the press-room atmosphere. He didn't help, of course. But from the start of his tenure he did have one great virtue, one that I mentioned as a requirement for any successful press secretary last night. He reflected his President. His lies were Nixon's lies. . . . When he was angry, irritated, pleased at the podium, one could be reasonably sure that Nixon was (or Haldeman was—same thing, in those circumstances). Example of the latter point: never do things like reflecting upon Nixon as a negotiator unless the President wishes you to. I have a right to assume, for instance, that you didn't do that in this case without sensing or knowing that it was the President's view, too. I make a point of it in my trip story; a story that won't do you any good, I fear, but in my view is completely justified and is straight reporting. 4) Drop your line about "partnership," "friends with friends," etc., both from your remarks and from your mind. I've always thought the line that presidential press secretaries serve two

masters, the President and the media, is bunk. Press secretaries serve and have one master, their President. You serve him by informing us, true. But there is and should be a built-in conflict in interest—conflict between us and you is inevitable. You are right in expecting and asking for courtesy in our communication with and demands upon you. The Watergate aftermath aside, a few boors in our company help to make—do make—this press room the meanest, nastiest, and from your side the most difficult one in my memory. On the other hand, it's our right and duty to be demanding, insistent to the point of insult at times. It's bound to happen. Don't blame yourself for that, assuming of course that you have handled your end with reasonable competence and grace.[16]

In June 1975, the press office staff held a retreat at Camp David to discuss how to improve its relationship with the press and overall communication strategy. Topics for discussion about areas needing improvement included inconsistencies in scheduling daily press briefings, too much time spent by Nessen in preparing for briefings (which omitted the option of Nessen saying he needed to check with the President before answering a question), an increase in the availability of radio actualities and audiotaped briefings for use by the broadcast press, and an improvement in the coordination between the press office and other departmental spokesmen, among others.[17] Also discussed was the criticism directed at Nessen's attitude and his relationship with the White House press corps:

It is felt that Ron questions the news judgment of the correspondents. When they ask Ron a question, and it is felt that sometimes he does not have the answers to all/most of the questions, instead of answering the question, he asks the reporter why he would ask such a question. The reporters feel that these briefings are held to obtain news, not Ron's heated feelings on current issues. They feel that he should answer in facts only. When asked a question, he should answer as direct as possible. If he does not know the answer, write the question down. And, come back the next day and say, "Mr. X., in answer to your question yesterday . . . ." By doing this, he will not only answer the questions of the reporters, but let them know that he is trying to keep them as informed as possible. . . . Because of the Watergate cover-up, the reporters feel that it is their "duty" to probe into unanswered questions. This does not reflect on Ron's ability to answer the questions. . . . They feel that President Ford has the best relationship with reporters—better than the past two/three presidents. He is open, honest, and realizes the problems of the press. Ron is not doing the President a service by trying to cover-up unanswered questions, or with his attitude toward the press.[18]

The tone of Ford's coverage was also hurt by the President's image as an inept leader. Despite the nice guy image, Ford was viewed as not "presidential" by the press when he first became Vice President in 1973. The press also placed high expectations on Ford once he assumed the presidency, hoping we would unite the country after Watergate and work effectively with Congress by passing essential legislation to get the country "moving again," which was a tall order given both the slumping economy and the political environment Ford had inherited.[19] Ford may have been viewed by the American public and the press as normal and nice, but three negative aspects of his image also emerged. The first, that he was "athletically graceless" and a klutz, was driven home on a weekly basis by Chevy Chase's parodies on NBC's *Saturday Night Live*. Second, Ford had earned a reputation for lacking "intellectual grit," an issue that was clearly raised during one of his 1976 presidential debates with Carter, when he stated that Poland was not under Soviet domination. Finally, Ford's competence as president was routinely questioned, with many Americans doubting that "he was up to the job." The press coverage of Ford only perpetuated the negatives of his image, and while reports of his falls and stumbles made for good copy, "whether or not it was an important story is open to debate."[20]

The tone of Ford's coverage was at least partially due to Watergate, and in many respects, out of the control of the White House staff. Following the *Washington Post* stories by Bob Woodward and Carl Bernstein that contributed to Nixon's downfall, two reporters who were not members of the White House press corps, other reporters who spent their days at the White House became more aggressive about seeking out stories, whether legitimate or not. According to John Carlson, Assistant Press Secretary, some of the coverage was inevitable:

> I'm not sure what else we could have done. After Watergate, Vietnam, big headlines, Ford comes in. And what kind of news can you write? "Ford bumps head on the helicopter"? That's the kind of stuff they based their news on. One day we were going to announce a major farm program. And Ford was to announce it at the Iowa state fair. Where better to do it than in middle America. And we wrote all these great press releases. We had the Secretary of Agriculture ready to do some in-depth press briefings. And we were going to about 10 different cities in four days. And the big announcement was set for the Iowa state fair. And we got out there and President Ford said "I'm so delighted to be here today to announce our $6.8 billion farm aid program here at the *Ohio* state fair." Well, of course, nobody talked about the farm bill that night on the evening news. Instead they talked about "Ford fatigued," "Ford screws up." That's the kind of stuff that really hurts.[21]

As the White House began to prepare for the 1976 presidential election in late 1975, Ford's advisors began to discuss how to handle the "klutz" issue. In a memo to Nessen, Jim Shuman, a staff member in the press office, declared two major issues involving image that needed to be addressed as the campaign approached. The primary issue would be to articulate Ford's philosophy about the role of the federal government in society. The other would be Ford's image as a klutz:

> The secondary issue, which may remain unspoken, is the competency of Gerald Ford. Is he, as John Chancellor said at Yale Sunday, merely an "amiable Midwestern conservative—a kind of a klutz"? . . . . The "klutz" image—which actually may not be all that bad (people do feel affection toward a klutz—but which we *must* dissipate, can be dealt with through two methods. One is high quality staff work. This will counter the incorrect image some have of a "lack-luster staff." It should include a Press Office and other offices that operate smoothly, with all parts coordinated, and no preventable mistakes.[22]

Negative press coverage of Ford continued throughout the 1976 campaign, and staff members continued to work at preventing stories that portrayed their president in a bad light. A July 1976 memo about mistakes made during the primary season urged better coordination to avoid negative press throughout the general election campaign. A total of 21 stories were highlighted in the memo as reflecting negatively on Ford, most of which covered events which were preventable by better staff work. Among the stories Ford endured:

> *Ft. Lauderdale*—motorcycle policeman falls off cycle on motorcade route (front page of Sunday *Washington Post*). *Miami*—wreck on freeway en route drop-by involving pile-up of cars. *West Palm Beach to Ft. Lauderdale*—rain on the President's motorcade. *Senland Farm Mishap*—cows soil President's suit. *Vail, Colorado*—ski fall on *second* press day. *South Lawn*—hitting head on helicopter. *Charlotte, North Carolina*—Future Homemaker's speech and resulting story regarding the weakness of the speech writing staff. Telling the press that the President plans to be Presidential this week. Each one of these items has one thing in common: they all reflect negatively on the President. . . . It must be kept in mind that the response of the viewer is not to the man but to the image. Therefore, it becomes absolute necessity that some one person or group maintain a constant vigil over the image and over the response. We have control over the candidate; we have partial control over the media. We have used neither of these elements of control to our advantage.[23]

Another problem with Ford's image, according to advisors, was difficulty in having him look presidential, especially during the campaign. More control and coordination was also stressed in this area:

> The problem with this situation is two-fold. One, you lose control when you step out of the White House, and you lose the most powerful tool which we possess, the incumbency. Two, the video of the President on the road looks no different from the video of Jimmy Carter or Ronald Reagan or Mo Udall. When edited together in three or four minute packages on the nightly news, the President's video playing next to Reagan's video bears little or no difference save the Presidential Seal or Air Force One in the background. In media terms the power of the Presidency or the power of the incumbency has been squandered in the primary process. Since that time we have appeared more Presidential with the aid of the Bicentennial and [Queen Elizabeth's] visit. Similar Presidential type settings of this nature should be constructed now for September and October, strategically programmed and marketed so as to provide a constant backdrop unavailable to anyone but the President of the United States.[24]

Several problems and solutions were identified that included bad camera angles, poor lighting, and scenes of chaos at airport arrivals around the country. Others included:

> *Problem*: The President looks non-Presidential when he wears hats and jackets presented to him.
> *Solution*: Have him hold up the hat or jacket for the cameras, but never should he put them on.

> *Problem*: Current rule of thumb: "Well we've got two hours here, what can we find to do with him."
> *Solution*: This attitude has led to the President attending too many meaningless events. His events should be carefully chosen, and again coordinated with the image-maker to allow for maximum exposure. Few advancemen think in terms of the 20 million or so viewers who will see the coverage, and, as a result, too often decisions are made to placate the locals at the expense of the press and the President's image.

> *Problem*: Another rule of thumb: The more exposure the better. Maximum exposure!
> *Solution*: This problem begs for the overall coordination of marketing of the image. The Nixon people were very good at this. The President has been hurt by over-exposure. The best way to control this is by keeping him in the White House and bringing the media to

him, then having him come out at strategic times achieving the desired effect. But, the travel blitz and indiscriminate choosing of things for the President to do adversely affected his image. The President's schedule on the road should be coordinated for maximum media effect. We should know after a pre-advance what picture we want to float. We should know the type of story that should float. If we have no picture, we should then depend on a good and newsworthy speech.[25]

Ford also had difficulty in articulating policy themes and an overriding vision for the nation. Advisors often wondered whether to promote Ford as merely a "caretaker" of the Constitution, especially following Watergate, or to promote him as a leader with a clear vision to take the country into the next decade. Ford's voting record in Congress, and many of his vetoes as President, reflected that of a traditional conservative Republican opposed to a large and intrusive federal government. Developing a better theme in Ford's speeches and his press coverage was discussed at the June 1975 retreat at Camp David by the press office, and staff members were urged to "get out the line" about Ford's leadership and political vision:

We need to give attention to a series of vetoes which were sustained in Congress which portray the President as a strong leader; however they are portrayed by the President's opponents negatively, as the President being against people, against jobs, etc. . . . We have a chance to communicate the philosophy of government which is limited which realizes it can't do everything for everybody. In daily contact with press, if you can present this in a subtle way, it doesn't make the President look like a 1930s Republican. Someone has to put this in rhetoric. It has to be said in a number of ways—planted to columnists. One problem is that the President is giving speeches and has nothing to say.[26]

A plan of action was developed by Shuman in August 1975 regarding the creation and articulation of Ford's vision, christened "Responsible Individualism," which represented the "strong reversal of the two-hundred year-long trend toward big and centralized government." A three-stage approach would be utilized to carry Ford through the 1976 presidential election:

Stage I: Recognition and Learning. This stage would have the President acknowledging, probably in a speech, that much has changed in the United States during the past decade. He would then set out to learn about it, through on-site tours, meetings, confer-

ences; posturing himself as a leader concerned about his people and
desirous of finding out how they are positively and successfully
attacking problems—and virtually all of our national problems fit
under the overall schematology of "Responsible Individualism."
Stage II: Reflective. This period would also last three to four months
while programs were developed. During it the President would continue to make speeches and do other Presidential-type activities.
There would be no public announcements of new policies, but the
President in Bicentennial speeches could articulate the basic premis-
es of "Responsible Individualism." Stage III: Implementation. This
would coincide with the election campaign, it would follow the traditional political pattern of a campaign, but would be well in tune
with what the voters were thinking, and it would be offering fresh
solutions.[27]

Unfortunately for Ford's election efforts, by May 1976 his staff
was still struggling with the development of a clearly articulated agenda
and vision. While Ford was traveling extensively around the country and
participating in various townhall meetings, talking about "Responsible
Individualism in his speeches," the message was not resonating with the
press, and therefore, not the voters. Shuman again urged better staff coordination at getting out the message about Ford's vision:

The basic problem with the Ford Administration, the reason I think
the President has such a weak base of support, is that people do not
perceive him as having a sense of purpose, a vision for the future of
the United States. Although we frequently have the pieces right, there
is no sense of an overall whole, no umbrella under which those pieces
fit, no "New Deal," "New Frontier," "Great Society." It is essential
that we have such a philosophy. It need not be the overblown rhetoric
of a "Great Society," but it ought to be clear and easily understood. It
should take note of where the United States is now, in 1976. Too often
we use the rhetoric of the 1930s, but the United States has changed,
greatly. To cite the most recent change, the 1960s, stripped of their
violent rhetoric, romanticism, and frequently sheer naiveté, represented a major turning point in our history and in the way Americans
view themselves and their relations with the institutions which support and/or service them. No political candidate has yet recognized
this (with the possible exception of Jerry Brown), but Carter, and even
Reagan are reaping the benefits of it, for it expresses itself in part, as
an anti-Washington sentiment. . . . We have done little . . . to articulate
the President's vision of focusing America's third century on the right
of the individual.[28]

In terms of the day-to-day press operation, Ford instituted some
changes in press conferences and also held them much more frequently

than Nixon in an attempt to reopen the White House to the press (each held 39 while in office, but Nixon was in office more than twice as long). Ford's first press conference, held on August 28, 1974, was considered a success, with the new President speaking plainly to reporters and appearing before an open door in the East Room, ridding the event of the ornate blue drapes that Nixon had favored as a backdrop. The press also noticed the change; the headline in *Time* the following week read, "Plain Words Before An Open Door."[29] Ford also permitted follow-up questions at press conferences, which the press had long pleaded for and now finally received. Ford considered press conferences an essential part of governing, and he believed that he personally had a good relationship with the press. As he recalled after leaving office:

> [The press conference] is an institutionalized part of our government, whether it is good or bad. Under no circumstances could a president abandon it. I personally enjoyed the challenge of it. In the first place, I had superb relationships with the members of the White House press corps. I was very fortunate in that regard. I understood their responsibilities and they in turn understood mine. There was no confrontation on a personal basis, so it was an enjoyable experience for me. I used to prepare because I wanted to win! I didn't always win, but at least I thought I was prepared enough to take them on, if that is the right term.[30]

Ford's advisors considered him a solid performer at press conferences and on television in general, especially when dealing with policy specifics. Attention was certainly paid to Ford's image on television, but not to the same extent as previous presidents', such as Johnson, due in part to Ford's insistence on reducing the fanfare associated with the office. Still, minor details were considered by staff members as an essential element to keep Ford looking as presidential as much as possible. Following Ford's sixth press conference on January 21, 1975, Tom DeCair reported to Chief of Staff Dick Cheney on several details about the performance presenting them as areas that needed more polish:

> Apparently the President thought he did poorly. He looked good on t.v. (a little less great in person—but it's t.v. that counts). He should be told he looked good. He should NOT wear the collar pin that looked like it was choking him. He should either wear button-down shirts or shirts with built in collar stays that keep his collar down. He should either completely drop the word judgment (or as he says it, "judge-uh-ment") from his vocabulary or learn how to say it. He used it at least seven times and said it wrong every time. Jerry Warren thinks he makes government a two-syllable word, too, so

you might listen for that sometime. While good on balance, a dry run would have helped him overcome some of the mid-sentence and mid-answer pauses he experienced. If he doesn't want to or doesn't seem to have time for a dry-run, someone should have the balls to tell him that he absolutely MUST. On balance a good performance-although all really depends on the news shows tonight and the papers tomorrow.[31]

The Ford White House continued to rely on the Office of Communications, created during the Nixon administration, as an important public relations tool. However, Ford wanted to distance himself from the heavy-handed public relations tactics that had been developed during the Nixon years in the Office of Communications. He viewed the coordination of White House contacts with members of the press outside of Washington essential, but he wanted to limit use of the Office of Communications as a means to coordinate and control public statements throughout the Executive Branch or as a political tool to sell the President's policy agenda.[32] However, that viewpoint was not always shared by his staff which, as early as February 1975 was discussing ways to both control and improve the administration's "line" about major policy initiatives, such as Ford's energy proposals. Donald Rumsfeld, a key presidential aide, suggested to Ford that this type of strategy was necessary to promote major policy initiatives:

It is important that the President, through Administration spokesmen, say things that are helpful in moving the President towards his goal. The only way I know to do this is to develop an approach to the problem [of sending conflicting views to the press]—an overall approach which then enables Ron [Nessen] and all Administration spokesmen to have a broad sense of how all the various specific questions can best be answered. This requires dissemination of broad policy guidance which is carefully thought through, communicated throughout the Administration, and then repeated and repeated by Administration spokesmen.[33]

The Office of Communications underwent some changes during Ford's tenure in the White House, but its main functions remained similar to those under Nixon—managing a direct mail operation, coordinating regional press briefings, setting up local press conferences and interviews with local anchors, engaging in White House briefings with Ford for media groups, and encouraging cooperation in the area of public affairs among departments and agencies of the Executive Branch. It also prepared the daily news summary, distributed to more than 140 members of the White House staff, and supervised the preparation of presidential briefing books. In 1975, while the office was headed by Margita White, Ford also began a series of "Conversations with the President" for small groups of reporters.[34]

As with previous administrations, Ford's press advisors realized the importance of cultivating positive coverage through local news media outlets throughout the country. This was an especially important aspect of Ford's communication strategy in promoting his first major policy initiatives in early 1975—a tax cut and energy plan. Local media breakfasts were held in several cities, and advisors, including Nessen, believed this was an effective venue for Ford that resulted in positive press coverage: "I strongly believe the President should continue the media breakfasts during his travels. I've never seen him more effective than he is at these breakfasts."[35] The use of local television was also considered crucial during the 1976 campaign, including interviews with local anchors and regional press conferences:

> While traveling, the President should take advantage of local television. Interview requests from local stations and newspapers flood the White House during a campaign period. There are several states which are hooked up by one network of local stations. These should be utilized. . . . In major cities like New York, Chicago, Los Angeles, and in areas where there is a local network of stations, it would be wise and innovative for the President to hold 30-minute news conferences on a three-on-one-basis with the top news "anchormen" of the major television stations in the market. . . . There are instances where time will not permit a half-hour interview with local reporters. However, we could allow a newsman with a popular newscast (high viewership) to interview the President in a controlled situation. That is, present to him the "possible" opportunity to interview the President by being stationed in a strategic location. For example, outside a hotel entrance in the area from the door to the limousine. We could advise the newsman to try to get the President upon his exit. The newsman would of course get his two or three minute interview as it would be programmed into the President's activities. This could be shown in its entirety on the popular news program and provide us a base for psychological cooperation from this program in the future because of our own cooperation and availability. In addition, if desired, the short interview could be purchased by the national networks for their news broadcasts. Doing this at selected locations and not in every city would prevent suspicious criticism. It is answering requests from legitimate newsmen and accommodating when possible.[36]

By 1976, the Office of Communications was used extensively during the presidential campaign, coordinating key aspects of both the

Republican National Convention and the presidential debates with Carter. In July of that year, David Gergen, former Nixon speechwriter, became head of the Office of Communications, and he began to reverse Ford's earlier attempts at decentralizing the information flow within the White House. A "Communications Group" was also organized to develop news plans and themes to promote the administration and its policies. The immediate goal of the group was to control the "line" about the administration and its policies:

> To assist in planning of all major news announcements and newsworthy events coming out of the White House; to coordinate more closely the news flow from the departments and agencies which relates to the President; to stimulate more creative and sustained attention for Administrative initiatives in areas such as the economy, crime, foreign affairs, etc. To be successful, the communications effort must draw upon people from across the staff.[37]

Under Gergen, the Office of Communications took a more programmatic approach to developing a communication strategy, and it became "an important tool for coordinating the administration line and for exercising tight control over information policy and public statements by administration officials."[38]

Overall, a consensus seems to exist that the Ford administration never developed a thorough press and/or communication strategy. Initially, just the fact that Ford was not Nixon seemed to be enough to satisfy the press, and most of the public as well, relieved that the day-to-day drama of Watergate had ended. But with virtually no transition into the office once Nixon resigned, Ford and his advisors did not have an opportunity to develop a coherent communication strategy. The only strategy that existed concentrated on the change in leadership and Ford's desire for an "open" presidency.[39] According to Robert Hartmann, a key advisor and speechwriter for Ford, no press strategy existed,

> except to be open and to be more like previous administrations in our dealings with the press, discounting Johnson and Nixon. I would say that the only organized strategy we had was that set by the outset by the President in promising to meet with reporters approximately every two weeks, and also the innovation introduced at terHorst's suggestion to allow the follow-up question [at press conferences] which had not been common before. . . . [Ford] was very good with the press, in terms of not getting angry and trying to answer the questions rather than being evasive.[40]

However, Ford was hampered, especially during the 1976 campaign, by an image created and perpetuated by the press as often seeming unpresidential. Given the time and circumstances, even a well-developed communication strategy may not have helped Ford, who took over the job of president with many disadvantages, most notably a lack of national recognition among the public and the tainted relationship with the press that both Johnson and Nixon had left behind.

Television also presented a problem for Ford, especially with his image. Like Johnson and Nixon, Ford could never quite measure up to the standard set during the Kennedy years of using television to the president's best advantage. By the mid 1970s, due in part to the changes in the political and cultural environment, as well as the ever-increasing watchful eye of television on the White House, being a moral and honest man with a long and respected career in public service was not enough to satisfy the nation's desire for strong leadership. After leaving office, Ford stated that he believed that too much emphasis was being placed on the electronic media, and not enough on print media or local media outlets. "The television camera takes away some of the substance in the exchange between the two. Those meetings between a president and the writing press can develop a little more in-depth discussion of an issue or problem."[41]

Ford's desire for openness and candor with both the public and the press, along with his desire to hold substantive discussions about important policy initiatives, may have come a bit too late as an effective White House communication strategy:

> The problem was not that Ford did not try to have good relations with the press but that he was too much of a politician to try hard enough. He told correspondents he would be open and candid, but in the end he was closed and self-serving, as political realities dictated.[42]

The political reality for Ford, and also for Carter, would be that Watergate had changed the relationship between the president and the press forever. And while Ford only reluctantly seemed to accept the necessity of controlling various aspects of the presidential image and message, many of the same tactics that ran counter to Ford's desire for accessibility would be openly embraced and heralded as a successful strategy just a few years later when the next Republican president would take office.

FORD'S PUBLIC ACTIVITIES

Ford is remembered as more of a talker than an orator, "a good man speaking plainly, if not always well." However, following what have been called the imperial presidencies of Johnson and Nixon, Ford "restored presidential rhetoric to its rightful place in the process of representative government. More than they, Ford assumed public responsibility for his decisions, explained his reasons, and rarely resorted to blaming others."[43] In his public addresses, particularly obvious during the 1976 presidential primaries with competition from Reagan, Ford was "unable to convey his natural personal charm to large audiences, and his stiff speaking style suffered by comparison to the more folksy, comfortable Reagan."[44] Ford was considered by some as unimaginative and not very articulate, in part from press attention, and in part from Chevy Chase's comedic parodies of Ford's misstatements and physical mishaps. Yet Ford's public strategy was to "parry the barbs of the press with unexpected kindness and access." He granted more than 200 interviews with journalists and held 39 press conferences, averaging 1.3 per month while in office.[45]

The Ford speechwriting process took place in the Editorial Office, which employed 30 to 40 people, was one of the largest staffs in the White House, and it had separate departments for not only speechwriting, but presidential messages, presidential correspondence, and research as well. Most of Ford's speeches were written under the direction of Hartmann and about a dozen others, most notably Paul Theis and Robert Orben, who like Hartmann, also served as advisors to Ford. Occasionally, a particular policy statement or speech was assigned to a speechwriter with a specialty in that area. But most speeches were put together by the entire speechwriting staff, under the guidance of Theis and Orben, who would assign a writer to the speech, outline the subject matter, and determine the appropriate length. The speechwriters had access to Ford during the development stages, and they requested his ideas, as well as those of relevant staff members, for a particular policy. Once a final draft had been prepared, edited, and checked for accuracy, it was sent to various White House and departmental aides for approval, and then to Hartmann and to Ford, who would often make his own additions and deletions, for final approval.[46] However, the speechwriting process did not always run smoothly, particularly during 1976 while Ford was busy campaigning. Teamwork seemed often to be lacking in putting together the final speech, with no coordination between departments. By August of that year, the lack of coordination was obvious, and as Gergen pointed out to Cheney, they were losing the opportunity to place Ford in quality public events to garner positive headlines, pictures and stories:

In too many events, the scheduling operation expects to achieve one result from an event; the policy people are looking for another; and the writers are seeking to achieve still some other goal. Many people on the staff are working very hard for the President, but because they're not working as a team, their efforts are not getting enough traction. . . . The speech drafts are usually prepared without close consultation with policy people. The drafts are circulated so late— often the night before the event—that the rest of the staff has precious little time to comment. After [they] comment, they usually never see the speech again until it is actually delivered. Everyone just holds his breath. The results are painfully obvious. We do not have control or coordination over the messages we are communicating to the country. The writers are frustrated because they feel cut off from much of the staff. The rest of the staff is frustrated because they feel cut off from the President's speeches. And most importantly, the public isn't getting the word. The breakdowns in the system are not so obvious when the President is giving only a few speeches, but in the heat of campaigning, it borders on mass chaos.[47]

During his two-and-a-half years in office, Ford never seemed to stop campaigning, either to introduce himself as President to the public or to win election to the office in his own right. Ford's public activities also relied on an aggressive approach to campaigning for key policy issues, particularly the tax cut and energy package he proposed in January 1975. And, while he lacked a clear-cut communication strategy, there was no lack of public activities or other written communications in the Ford White House. During the first year alone, Ford had "either delivered in person or issued on paper close to one million words. . . . If you include correspondence sent out over the President's name, this count jumps to well over 10 million words."[48] Unlike the Nixon years of avoiding the press and public, Ford averaged well over one public activity per day (see Table 4.1), a rate that would not be surpassed until the Clinton administration. He gave many more policy addresses than Nixon, and he made a point of talking regularly with the press. Ford campaigned almost nonstop in 1976 for election, with 152 campaign speeches or other campaign appearances. A large part of his campaign strategy that year included 57 town meetings/question-and-answer sessions with the public and/or members of the press. During his brief tenure in office, Ford participated in a total of 1,241 public activities between August 9, 1974 and January 20, 1977.

Table 4.1. Ford—Public Activities.[49]

	1974	1975	1976-77
National Address	3	6	2
Policy Addresses	11	27	22
Press Conferences	5	19	15
Radio Addresses	0	0	6
Brief Policy/Ceremonial Remarks	84	255	282
Partisan Remarks/Campaign Speeches	34	36	152
Press Conferences with Foreign Dignitaries	1	0	0
Signing Ceremonies	15	18	51
Teleconference Remarks	0	0	2
Roundtable Discussions	0	0	0
Town Meetings/Q&A Sessions	1	13	57
Remarks to/Exchanges with Reporters	3	29	92
Total	157	403	681
Daily Average	1.08	1.13	1.77

THE FORD POLICY AGENDA

Ford never articulated a long-term or clear policy agenda to the American people, due in part to the fact that Ford and his advisors did not have time with such a quick transition to power. However, the agenda that seemed to emerge was "a continuation of the policies that had been followed by the moderate wing of the Republican party since World War II—a conservative approach to economic and social policy and a cautiously internationalist approach to foreign policy."[50] Ford faced great opposition from a hostile, Democratic-controlled Congress while President, due in part to Congress' many attempts at government reform in the aftermath of Watergate. Like Johnson, Ford had been an experienced lawmaker on Capitol Hill prior to occupying the White House. However, unlike Johnson, he faced poor political timing and a divided government, and he lacked a political mandate. As a result, Ford vetoed 66 bills during his nearly 30 months in office, with Congress overriding 12 of those vetoes. While, in general, Ford's domestic policy was not overly extensive or organized, his attempts at energy policy became the "central battleground for confrontation and deadlock."[51]

During his first few months in office in 1974, Ford focused extensively on the need to fight inflation and the energy crisis in his public remarks (see Table 4.2). During those months, the Trade/Economic category ranked higher than any other issue, due

Table 4.2. Ford's Public Agenda (Major Public Addresses).[52]

	1974	1975	1976-77
Domestic			
Education	24 - 2%	37 - 1%	165 - 8 %
Health Care	9 - 1%	1 - <1%	12 - <1%
Welfare/Entitlements	0 - 0%	3 - <1%	92 - 5%
Anticrime	81 - 8%	248 - 8%	359 - 18%
Political Reform	0 - 0%	4 - <1%	23 - 1%
Science/Technology/			
Transportation	75 - 8%	12 - <1%	8 - <1%
Environment/Energy/			
Land Management	52 - 5%	405 - 15%	68 - 3%
Defense	52 - 5%	86 - 3%	107 - 5%
International			
Diplomatic/Military	67 - 7%	892 - 29%	347 - 17%
Trade/Economic	304 - 31%	240 - 8%	200 - 10%
Economic			
Domestic Fiscal/Monetary	248 - 26%	950 - 30%	519 - 26%
Unemployment/Jobs	59 - 6%	250 - 8%	133 - 7%
Total	N = 971	N = 3128	N = 2033

mostly to Ford's frequent discussions about the need to end U.S. reliance on imported oil. The Domestic/Fiscal Monetary category ranked a close second, reflecting Ford's Whip Inflation Now (WIN) campaign, introduced soon after he took office. During 1975, the Domestic/Fiscal Monetary category ranked first, as Ford campaigned hard for a tax cut to fight the recession. The Diplomatic/Military category also ranked a close second, due mostly to discussions about the continuing withdrawal of American forces in Vietnam and ongoing negotiations with the Soviet Union on the SALT II treaty. Ford's proposed energy program also remained high on the President's public agenda. By the campaign year of 1976, economic matters remained at the top of Ford's priority list, as did other popular campaign topics, such as fighting crime.

THE FIRST TIER: THE TAX CUT OF 1975

The Issue and White House Strategy

When Ford first assumed the presidency, the American economy was troubled by rising inflation, increasing federal expenditures causing greater budget deficits, and declining labor productivity. Ford devoted a great deal of time to the ailing economy during his first months in office and began addressing the issues publicly three days after being sworn in during an address to a joint session of Congress on August 12, 1974. Two months later, in a second address to a joint session of Congress on the economy on October 8, 1974, Ford proposed both a tax increase and his WIN program, a voluntary citizens' program recommended by two of his speechwriters. Ford had declared inflation to be "Public Enemy Number One," but the proposals would not be considered a success. Three months later, Ford would reverse his position on a tax increase to fight inflation, and WIN did not help in establishing Ford as a president firmly in control of the economy:

> The tax increase proposal, just as the economy was heading toward
> a severe recession, and the absurdity of the WIN program severely
> hurt Ford at a time when he was trying to recover from the adverse
> effects of the Nixon pardon and to establish his intellectual creden-
> tials as a president who could successfully manage the economy.[53]

Once the decision was made for the reversal in tax policy—that instead of a tax increase to fight inflation Ford would seek a tax cut to fight the recession—decisions were quickly made on how to sell the new economic plan to the nation just months after Ford had announced a much different plan. The State of the Union Address in January 1975 seemed the logical occasion on which to lay out the new plan to the American public. However, plagued by many leaks and the threat of being upstaged on the issue by the Democratic leaders in Congress, Ford's advisors decided to have the President give an informal address to the nation two days prior to the State of the Union message. Sitting not in the Oval Office, but in a more informal room in the White House with a fireplace and several bookshelves, Ford talked directly to the American people about the economic situation:

> This economic program is different in emphasis from the proposals I
> put forward last October. The reason is that the situation has
> changed. You know it, and I know it. What we most urgently need
> today is more spending money in your pockets rather than in the

Treasury in Washington. Let's face it, a tax cut to bolster the economy will mean a bigger Federal deficit temporarily, and I have fought
against deficits all my public life. But unless our economy revives
rapidly, Federal tax revenues will shrink so much that future deficits
will be even larger. But I have not abandoned my lifelong belief in
fiscal restraint. In the long run, there is no other real remedy for our
economic troubles.[54]

The reviews for Ford's performance for the first speech were
good, but his gloomy message delivered during the State of the Union
was not as well received, in part because the opposition—both from
Democrats who thought the proposed tax cut was not enough to end the
recession and conservatives who did not approve of the inevitable
increase to the deficit—had begun to organize and make their cases
known after the earlier address.[55] However, Ford attempted to talk can-
didly again during the State of the Union:

> . . . the state of the Union is not good. Millions of Americans are out
> of work. Recession and inflation are eroding the money of millions
> more. Prices are too high, and sales are too slow. . . . We depend on
> others for essential energy. . . . Now, I want to speak very bluntly.
> I've got bad news, and I don't expect much, if any, applause. The
> American people want action, and it will take both the Congress and
> the President to give them what they want. Progress and solutions
> *can* be achieved, and they *will* be achieved. . . . The moment has
> come to move in a new direction. . . . Let us mobilize the most pow-
> erful and most creative industrial nation that ever existed on this
> Earth to put all our people to work. The emphasis on our economic
> efforts must now shift from inflation to jobs.[56]

Ford relied on his former contacts on Capitol Hill to try to promote his new tax policy throughout the month of January, vigorously
campaigning on behalf of the plan. He attempted to bring members of
Congress into the decision-making process and also "initiated contact
with different factions of the political elite both to explain his new tax
plan and to expound on its virtues."[57] Ford and his advisors also worked
hard to get the message out about the tax plan through presidential
speeches and news media coverage. In February and March, Ford trav-
eled around the nation to talk about his tax cut plan. In February, Nessen
reported to Donald Rumsfeld that regional press conferences and talks
with other members of local press around the country had garnered Ford
much support, with reaction "overwhelmingly favorable. I urge the continuation of these out-of-town selling trips . . . OOPS . . . explanatory
trips."[58] Ford was also receiving high marks for his breakfast meetings
with media executives across the nation as well:

The reaction . . . has been uniformly positive and their follow-up editorials and columns reflect an increased understanding of and support for the President's economic and energy programs. Stories, columns, and letters about the breakfast sessions refer repeatedly to the President's forthrightness, sincerity, candor, informality, in-depth knowledge, concern with the gravity of the problems facing the nation, and determination to solve them. The editorials highlight the fact that the President has a comprehensive and cohesive program and urge Congress to either come up with one of their own or adopt the President's.[59]

In spite of some of the positive reviews Ford was receiving for his public performance, enacting his proposed $16 billion tax cut was far from smooth sailing for the administration. Congressional Democrats embraced the idea of a tax cut to stimulate the economy, but wanted to raise and redistribute the amounts in Ford's proposal. Ford continued to publicly urge Congress to act on the measure, but it became clear to his advisors that either a compromise by the President or a veto would be the only options once the bill was passed. Congress eventually rushed through a $22.8 billion tax cut with individual tax reductions geared at lower income levels than Ford had planned.[60] Once the decision was made for Ford to sign instead of veto the tax bill, advisors sought the best strategy for Ford to still save face publicly over getting the needed tax cut. Nessen urged Ford to sign the bill, and pointed out how they could use the situation to bolster the President's public image:

You should take full credit for initiating and pushing through a foot-dragging Congress a stimulative tax cut to pull the country out of recession. . . . My observations are based on how I believe the public will perceive your action and not on an expert knowledge of economics. The psychological stimulation of a Tax Cut Bill signing can be magnified by the fact that it comes at the Easter season when the weather is turning good and the first glimmer of hopeful economic news is beginning to show up. This would be a welcome Easter present for the recession-plagued country. On the other hand, a veto would have a psychologically discouraging effect, and would be difficult to explain to the average TV viewer. . . . In addition, a veto now could raise doubts about the consistency of your economic policy and could be interpreted as stubbornness on your part. As Bob Hartmann pointed out the other day, in October you requested a 5% tax increase; in January you requested a 12% tax decrease; and with a veto you would be saying in March a tax cut can wait for Congress to try again. The general view is, as I detect it, that a new bill would be no better and possibly worse than the present one. On the other hand, if Congress overrode your veto, you would lose a considerable amount of authority in future veto confrontations. Up to this point you have come across to the public as a forceful leader in the area of the economy, having scored considerable success despite the overwhelming Democratic majority in Congress. To veto this bill, and especially to be overridden, would damage that image. To sign the bill and then launch a new crusade against irresponsible Congressional spending would enhance that image.[61]

Ford would reluctantly sign the bill on March 29, 1975, stating that it was "within reason" and though he did not approve of all of the provisions, especially giving too much tax relief to the lower rather than the middle classes, he told the nation that "our country needs the stimulus and support of a tax cut and needs it now."[62]

Press Coverage

By January 1975, economic concerns were a top priority with both the White House and Congress, and as a result, the news media was focused on the issue as well. As of January 1, stories began appearing in the *New York Times* speculating about Ford's proposed course of action to fight the recession. Between January and March 1975, a total of 161 news items appeared in the *Times* about Ford's proposed tax cut, with an average of nearly two stories per day (see Table 4.3). Most stories were generated by congressional action on the tax cut (49 percent); the White House ranked second by generating 28 percent of the news items, and interest group activity generated 23 percent. Most of the congressional stories focused on alternative proposals to Ford's as stated during his Address to the Nation and State of the Union messages in January.
    The tone of coverage for news items generated by the White House was mostly balanced, discussing the proposals from both Ford and congressional Democrats (see Table 4.4). Ten editorials appeared during the three-month period on Ford and the tax cut; eight were balanced and two were negative. In general, the *Times* was skeptical of the Ford tax cut, but in January, encouraged that the President was willing to take action in response to tough economic times for the nation. A January 15 editorial stated

> there is much to quarrel with in the President's plan . . . and there is need for a more substantial economic boost than his program provides, but it does give the Congress a running start toward action of the kind the country has been awaiting too long.

Table 4.3. Amount and Type of New York Times Coverage of the Tax Cut Proposal (January 1975-March 1975).

	White House	Congress	Interest Group/Other
News Story	23	50	32
News Analysis	6	11	2
Column	6	7	0
Editorial	10	11	3
Total	45 - (28%)	79 - (49%)	37 - (23%)

Table 4.4. Tone of New York Times Coverage of Presidential Activities on the Tax Cut Proposal (January 1975-March 1975).

	Positive	Negative	Balanced/Mixed	Neutral
News Story	0	0	18	5
News Analysis	0	1	5	0
Column	0	1	5	0
Editorial	0	2	8	0
Total	0	4	36	5

The following day, and the morning after Ford's January 15 State of the Union address, the *Times* again praised Ford's action but criticized the specifics of his plan: "Mr. Ford has undergone a remarkable turn-around in the direction of his policy. But its content remains weak in its priorities and sense of social fairness." By January 28, the *Times* began to take an active stance in urging Congress to "produce an acceptable alternative" to Ford's "poorly conceived program." Specifically, on March 8, the *Times* took issue with the distribution plan for a tax break, urging more money for lower-income Americans, and criticizing the overall political process: ". . . with all the talk about tax cutting, nothing has yet happened to provide fiscal stimulus to the economy." Finally, when Ford signed Congress' tax cut bill, the *Times* praised the President for accepting the proposal, but blasted him for his public urgings for Congress to stop any new appropriations, which was considered by the editorial board as necessary for a complete boost to the economy:

But gratifying as was the President's decision to go along in supplying this needed economic lift, there was a disturbing quality of overkill in his accompanying demand that Congress come to a dead stop on all new appropriations to put the jobless back to work or to meet other needs outside the fields of national security and energy development.

Throughout the policymaking process on this issue, the *Times* never supported Ford's insistence to keep the national deficit as low as possible in dealing with the recession.

THE SECOND TIER: ENERGY CORPORATION

The Issue and White House Strategy

The issue of energy remained a top priority for Ford while in office, but Congress was not always enthusiastic about Ford's approaches to reducing American dependence on foreign oil. Ford would later blame politics on the part of congressional Democrats for little substantive action on energy since the Democratic leadership saw the upcoming 1976 presidential election as an opportunity to get a Democrat in the White House and therefore pursue a different course of action on the issue:

> Tip [O'Neill] wanted to elect a Democratic President. In order to do that, he had to make me look bad. Stalling my energy proposals was one way to achieve that goal, especially when there was little public concern. People still didn't believe that the energy crisis was real. In an attempt to break the deadlock, I did everything I could to convince Congress that it had to move. For nearly a year, I'd been giving speeches about the problem; I sent formal messages up to Capitol Hill, and I met with key lawmakers on at least thirty-three separate occasions.[63]

On October 10, 1975, Ford presented his plan for an Energy Corporation to Congress, a $100-billion government corporation to stimulate commercial development of new energy sources. The plan had been developed by Vice President Nelson Rockefeller as "promoting free enterprise rather than government control" to solve the national energy problem, but it was a source of great dissension among the White House staff. Cheney was one of the earliest critics of the plan, as he outlined in a May 1975 memo:

In my opinion, the proposal is seriously deficient. Contrary to the rhetoric with which it is described, it would constitute substantial government interference into the private economy. . . . I am concerned that the entire proposal has not been given the rigorous scrutiny that it deserves. . . . [Rockefeller] has not submitted the proposal through the staffing mechanism so that other agencies and departments and White House staff members could comment and criticize. His natural tendency is to discuss it with an individual, to express his own unbounded enthusiasm, but not to debate the substantive merits of the proposal. . . . It is important that we try to avoid a confrontation between the Vice President and the White House staff. It is important that the President's decision be consistent with the principles of his previously stated policies. It would be harmful for the President to propose a major new spending program as large as this one after we have finally begun to make progress in holding down the size of the deficit. I would hope that this President can avoid the trap that most previous Presidents have fallen into. There are always enormous pressures to let so-called political pressures generate action and to consider action and initiative more important than the substance of a decision. I think Presidents Kennedy, Johnson and Nixon all fell into the trap sooner or later.[64]

Some modifications were eventually made to the proposal, and Ford first introduced the Energy Independence Authority in an address in San Francisco on September 22, 1975:

Frankly, we cannot wait any longer for the Congress to act on my comprehensive energy program. Long-range security, jobs, and energy are inseparable. The time has come for action on energy independence. Accordingly, I will ask very shortly the Congress to erase all doubt about the capacity of America to respond. I will propose an entirely new $100 billion Government corporation to work, with private enterprise and labor, to gain energy independence for the United States in 10 years or less. This new energy independence authority will have the power to take any appropriate financial action—to borrow or to lend—in order to get energy action. It will serve as a catalyst and a stimulant working through, not in place of, American industry.[65]

Immediately after the address, Ford was questioned by the press about the use of federal money to start the Energy Corporation, and asked whether or not it went against his desire to reduce government spending and the creation of new federal programs. He responded that it is

primarily taking the position from completion of research and development to the first use where there is a hesitancy on the part of investors, because of the uncertainty to invest. This is where I think we have to act. We did in the case of the synthetic rubber plant in World War II. We did it in the Manhattan Project with the atomic bomb. We did it in our effort to get to the Moon.[66]

In the proposed bill to Congress, the Energy Corporation was presented as creating a partnership between the federal government and the private sector

> to assure action on vital energy projects for ten years. Money would be directed toward the commercialization of those new technologies which offer the greatest promise to develop new supplies and conserve present energy resources. Funding would go to projects that would not be started without federal assistance. The EIA would invest up to $100 billion during a seven year period and would terminate after ten years.[67]

However, even before the proposal reached Congress, many doubts about its viability were raised from both sides of the aisle. Many Democrats did not like the idea of creating a new entity that would not be accountable to Congress and that would selectively choose to subsidize segments of the economy, and conservatives did not support creating a new sector of the federal bureaucracy with a $100-billion price tag.[68]

Despite Rockefeller's enthusiasm for the proposal, Ford never placed the issue high on his list of legislative priorities. Many advisors within the White House supported the creation of an energy development fund, but the Energy Corporation never received the full backing of the administration, either internally or publicly. As a result, the bill languished on Capitol Hill with a White House staff that viewed the proposal with great indifference.[69] After introducing the Energy Corporation, Ford would only mention the proposal in one other speech during 1975, an address in Boston to the New England Council on November 17. After that, he only spoke publicly about the plan when asked about it by a reporter during a press conference or interview, and even then, nearly all of the questions to which Ford would respond dealt with the alleged White House disagreement about the plan. After Congress failed to act by the end of 1975, Ford would reintroduce the bill in 1976, but again it was virtually ignored. Congress would only approve a small portion of Ford's energy requests that year, and "the end result was that the nation lacked a coordinated energy policy when the 94th Congress adjourned."[70]

Press Coverage

Coverage in the *Times* on the Energy Corporation was not extensive. Between August 1975, when the first story appeared on Rockefeller's proposal, through December 1975, a total of only 19 news items appeared on the Energy Corporation, an average of less than one news item per week (see Table 4.5). Of those, nine (47 percent) were generated by interest groups or experts on the issue, eight (42 percent) from the White House, and two (11 percent) from Congress. The tone of the news items generated by the White House was mixed (see Table 4.6). A news story appearing on September 5 focused on in-fighting within the White House over the Energy Corporation proposal, and Ford's announcement on September 22 in San Francisco was somewhat upstaged by the second presidential assassination attempt within the month, and which occurred on that same day. Nonetheless, the *Times* still carried its editorial opinion about the proposal on September 23, which was resoundingly negative towards the plan:

Table 4.5. Amount and Type of *New York Times* Coverage of the Energy Corporation (August 1975-December 1975).

	White House	Congress	Interest Group/Other
News Story	6	2	8
News Analysis	1	0	1
Column	0	0	0
Editorial	1	0	0
Total	8 - (42%)	2 - (11%)	9 - (47%)

Table 4.6. Tone of *New York Times* Coverage of Presidential Activities on the Energy Corporation (August 1975-December 1975).

	Positive	Negative	Balanced/Mixed	Neutral
News Story	0	0	4	2
News Analysis	0	1	0	0
Column	0	0	0	0
Editorial	0	1	0	0
Total	0	2	4	2

For all the high-flown rhetoric in which the President clothed the idea, it is essentially a bailout device for large corporations; with particular insensitivity the administration seems to be offering big business just the kinds of Federal guarantees that it refuses to consider for the nation's cities and local governments.

Again, as with the tax cut earlier in the year, the *Times* did not give a favorable view of Ford's economic priorities. Virtually no coverage of the Energy Corporation would appear in the *Times* in the early months of 1976, despite Ford's mention of the plan in his State of the Union address that January.

CARTER AND THE PRESS

Following the imperial presidencies of Johnson and Nixon, and the scandal of Watergate, Jimmy Carter was helped tremendously during the 1976 presidential campaign by his image not only as an outsider, but as an honest and simple man. However, Carter's presidency is a classic example of having an image that may work at winning votes during a presidential election, but which quickly loses its luster once viewed from inside the White House. According to journalist James Reston, Carter

hadn't even had time to find his way around the White House before [the press was] criticizing him for wearing a sweater, working in his own Georgia peanut patch, and carrying his own garment bag over his shoulder. This sort of thing worked fine in the primary elections, but didn't suit the public fancy after he moved into the gracious surroundings of the White House.[71]

Carter wanted to "dismantle the symbols of the imperial presidency," which was a goal in contrast to many of his predecessors. But once elected, the Carter style of governing reflected the desire to maintain the image of an outsider, which hurt his relationship with Congress tremendously, and which hurt the clarity of his message to the American people. Carter had many policy ideas, but he could not communicate the bigger picture effectively to the public.[72]

Carter's overall communication strategy reflected his desire to bring the presidency back to the American people. Johnson and Nixon had relied on the persuasiveness of describing the powers and responsibilities of the office to maintain congressional support for policy initiatives, and they were considered monarchical in the way they spoke about their responsibilities as president—the forceful leadership of commander in chief and chief of state. When depicting his responsibilities through public addresses, Carter (and later Clinton) attempted to develop an intimacy with the American people, placing the emphasis on the "people's presidency." Carter had "promised change, requested public sacrifice, and committed himself to reviving the national economy," but as most presidents experience, depictions of the office often promise more than can be delivered.[73]

Throughout his term, Carter made concerted efforts to remain open with the press, and he started off his first year in office with a regular press conference roughly every two weeks. (This practice would steadily decline each year of the Carter presidency, with only six held in 1980.) Other strategies were also employed early in the administration to keep access open and to provide Carter with a chance to talk informally with both the people and the press. In March 1977, Carter held a national "phone-in" to the White House, where callers spoke to both Carter and Walter Cronkite. In June 1977, a plan was designed to hold informal sessions with several members of the national press corps around the White House swimming pool. In a memo to Carter, Press Secretary Jody Powell explained the effectiveness of such a plan.

> To fulfill your wish to meet informally with reporters covering the White House, I suggest we invite them in groups of 10 or so to talk with you around the White House swimming pool. These meetings could be arranged on the day they are to occur, and they could be held in late afternoon. They would be quasi-social, with the conversation totally off the record (although we could expect almost anything you said to come out sooner or later). The pool would provide a relaxed setting away from "official" surroundings, yet convenient to you.[74]

Powell also recalled that the goal of remaining open and accessible went beyond the national press corps to include non-Washington based news media as well: ". . . the Carter Administration [wanted] to demonstrate its openness and that we were available. We wanted to let people question us and we wanted to get the answers to them."[75]

Carter's attempts to maintain an open presidency often hurt his image in the public, especially as it was portrayed over the longer term by the press once the honeymoon period had ended. During the first few months of the administration, Carter's attempts to bring the presidency back to the people initially helped his image with both the public and the press. Speechwriter Jim Fallows praised Carter's early efforts at image building in this area:

You have been extremely effective in the realm of symbol, in deflating the pretensions of the Presidency. When you walked down Pennsylvania Avenue or sat wearing a sweater on TV, that did not change the fact that your office is the most powerful in the world and that you are the most powerful leader. When you walk into a room without "Hail to the Chief," you are not—and are not perceived to be—any less important a figure. What these gestures show is that you are not a monarch but a democratic leader. You are certainly aware how popular this effort has been. I think you might take one more step in the same direction by trying to have people call you "Mr. Carter" or, perhaps, "President Carter," rather than "Mr. President" or "The President." (*The New Yorker* suggested this in an editorial a few weeks ago). The latter two titles, which do not even include your own name, stress once more the institutional power you hold; they are, in their way, like "Ruffles and Flourishes." You are the one person in the world who needs no props at all to remind people of your importance; what is harder to make people remember is your humanity and individuality. I think that the use of "Mr. Carter" would be a small but worthwhile reminder.[76]

But the honeymoon, especially with the press, faded quickly. Carter was often criticized for trying to do too much at once, for not having a clearly focused agenda, for not understanding how to play the political game in Washington, especially with Congress, and ultimately, for not presenting the image of a strong leader. In a February 1977 memo to Carter entitled "Perceptions of the New Administration," Powell raised concerns about a *Washington Post* column by David Broder that portrayed the new administration as inexperienced and adrift with its foreign policy statements:

Our critics are going to give us trouble over the appearance of flailing about. One aspect which you can directly control is your often-commented-upon tendency to speak in superlatives and hyperbole. For example, had you expressed a desire for the most rapid possible progress toward a cessation of nuclear testing instead of calling for "eliminating the testing of all nuclear devices, *instantly and completely*," your statement would have been viewed as much more reasonable. This problem should be of some concern because it spills over into the area of over-promising. Whether you like it or not or intend it or not, statements about "total," "immediate," "complete" are read by the American people as indications that such possibilities are likely. I believe it is almost always better to understate than to overstate. Whatever you say will be hyped three or four levels before it gets to the average American, anyway. Therefore, your natural tendency to speak in absolutes is aggravated by the traditional press reaction to any statement coming from the President or the White House. In line with our mutual desire for you to develop more direct contact with the press, I suggest that you give David a call and discuss the column with him. He would be most impressed, particularly by a tacit admission from you that he had in fact identified an area of at least potential concern for you.[77]

A little more than 15 months into the Carter administration, an S.O.S. call went out to long-time Carter advisor Gerald Rafshoon to join the administration and shore up Carter's sagging image as a leader with the press and the public. Rafshoon, who was an advertising executive and who had also worked on the 1976 presidential campaign, arrived at the White House in May 1978. Rafshoon was to head the Office of Communication, which would be responsible for long-term communication strategies and for relieving some of the workload of Press Secretary Jody Powell, who dealt more with the day-to-day press operation. The notion of image-making in the Carter administration soon became known as "Rafshoonery" in the press. Rafshoon disputed that his job was to remake Carter's image:

> As soon as I came in there were a lot of stories about Jerry Rafshoon the image-maker. I'm not an image-maker. I used to say in the campaign, and I believe this in political advertising, that 90% of the advertising was Jimmy Carter and 10% was technique. It was my job not to screw up the 10%. In the White House I felt that what the President needed more than anything was to follow his own instincts. I could see that he had been pulled in a lot of directions after he went into the White House. And as best I could I tried to get some order to our priorities, to our public statements, trying to get the administration to speak in one voice and to focus on long range communications. . . . I was involved as an interpreter of our policies, communicating the President's goals, trying to set the agenda, perceptions, developing material for the President and other people on the White House staff and the cabinet to use in speeches and in selling our programs.[78]

Carter's image, as well as his relationship with the White House press corps, was greatly predetermined due to the legacy of Watergate. According to Hedley Donovan, a former reporter and senior advisor to Carter, the White House press corps was "burning to be Woodward and Bernstein; all of them wanted to 'break' something." As a result, the Carter White House "saw the press as hopelessly addicted to stories of conflict, confusion, and scandal, and generally bored by anything 'constructive'"[79] Powell also recalled after Carter left office that the cynicism and distrust by the press towards the White House and, in particular, the press office, put Carter at a great disadvantage in successfully articulating his policy initiatives and goals:

> . . . of all the institutions in our society, the press was probably the most traumatized by Watergate and it probably took it longer to scab over than it did anybody else. If you had to refine it more, I think the White House press corps . . . were even more bloody and bruised from it than the press corps at large.[80]

Carter and his advisors may not have clearly recognized and understood the implications of the cynical shift within the press corps and how it viewed the presidency following Vietnam and Watergate, a lack of understanding which ultimately hurt the administration's overall communication strategy. The news media also did not make much of an effort to understand Carter, but the image they did see was a president who "appeared to regard himself as superior to the reporters in intellect and moral goodness." Carter often criticized reporters for their trivialization of issues, and he also did not have any close friends among the White House press corps to champion him or any of his causes:

> Carter, for his part, failed to grasp the opportunity to educate the press, and to the end of his administration he remained an enigma to those who reported the comings and goings at the White House and on the Hill.[81]

Powell worked hard at being attentive to the day-to-day needs of the press and how they reacted to the President. In December 1977, he devised a plan by which Carter could avoid resentment from some members of the White House press corps by failing to call upon them during press conferences:

> I hate to bother you with such mundane matters, however, I have a suggestion which will be marginally helpful in our relationships with the White House Press Corps. It is, of course, traditional to call upon the wire service reporters first in news conferences. As long as the networks are carrying the news conferences live, it is also proper to call upon one correspondent from each of the three networks. On occasion, you call on two correspondents from one network and no one from another network. In addition, there is a certain resentment if the wire services and the networks completely dominate the questioning at the press conference. Therefore, I suggest that we make it a practice to call upon the two wire service correspondents first. Then I suggest that you call upon one correspondent from each of the three networks. I would also suggest that you do not call upon

any other network correspondents after you have run through one representative from each. This will mean that most of the questions in any 30-minute press conference will come from the balance of the press corps, not just the wires and the networks.[82]

In the fall of 1978, Rafshoon also expressed concern about Carter's performance at press conferences, which was an opportune time to show not only the press but the public that he was an effective leader in charge of his administration. Rafshoon suggested that the President needed to be more concise with his answers, and to rely on a more commanding presence:

> I think your answers at press conferences are generally *too long*. Although your command of the facts is impressive, you often lose your audience. Short, punchy answers allow for more questions. The give-and-take becomes more rapid fire. You appear in command, almost combative. Remember, a half-hour after the press conference is over most viewers probably can't remember a single question or answer. They do have an over-all impression though. That impression should be of you, like a baseball batter, hitting whatever is thrown at you—disposing of pitchers. Occasionally, of course, long answers are required, but these should be the exception not the rule.[83]

Like previous administrations, Carter's advisors realized the usefulness of getting their message out to regional and local members of the press, which often provided more positive coverage than the national press. The Office of Media Liaison, as part of the press office, was structured to help promote the administration with non-Washington based news media and to present its views on policy initiatives. This included coordinating Carter's out-of-town trips with local media representatives, arranging briefings, handling the radio actuality service, and providing videotapes of interviews with administration officials other than Carter to local television stations. Early in Carter's term, the importance of utilizing the Office as part of an overall communication strategy was downplayed.[84] However, once Rafshoon came aboard in 1978, an Office of Communications was created that was separate from the press office. Rafshoon's responsibilities included overseeing the speechwriting operation, press advances, and the television office. "Clarifying the administration's agenda, plotting long-range communications plans, and getting the administration to speak more coherently were the primary tasks of the new office."[85]

Like several presidents before him, Carter became convinced that bad press coverage was hurting his popularity and approval ratings. As a result, with each year in office, he began to deny access to the national press corps, looking even more to the interests of regional and local news media. By mid-1979, Carter moved away from using formal press conferences and instead began to talk with local reporters during trips across the country and to hold private meetings with a variety of journalists and news executives.[86] He and his wife Rosalynn also hosted a number of private dinners with influential members of the press corps in an attempt to build professional relationships that would benefit the promotion of his policy agenda. Carter recalled that his lack of contacts with various Washington elites often hurt his administration's image and the implementation of his policy agenda:

> We came to Washington as outsiders and never appreciably changed this status. Nowhere within the press, Congress, or the ranks of the Washington power structure were there any long-established friends and acquaintances who would naturally come to our defense in a public debate on a controversial issue. Even to those who welcomed us, we were still strangers. Jody Powell said to me that, having never served in Washington, we did not have any outriders posted to defend us from flank attacks. "There never was a honeymoon with the press, but just a one-night stand." After a year or so, Rosalynn and I had a long series of small dinner parties at the White House for the leaders among the news media. They were enjoyable and somewhat beneficial, but failed to compensate for our relative isolation on a more continuing basis with the "movers and shakers" among the Washington elite.[87]

In early 1979, the media dinners were considered an effective strategy to cultivate positive press coverage for the Carter agenda. In a memo to Rafshoon, Greg Schneiders, deputy assistant to Carter on communications, suggested the best use of these events was

> to *really woo* the "heavies." Individual dinners—designed to foster genuine friendships—with [Ben] Bradlee, [David] Broder, [Joe] Kraft, [Hugh] Sidey, [James] Reston and a few others of this type would probably pay off more immediately than continuing to look for new names. Particularly in light of the current media mood, we could use a few understanding columns from the "leaders." (We should also bear in mind that the White House correspondents for the newsweekly magazines have little to do with what appears in these magazines. The appropriate people in New York should be invited here soon.)[88]

The Carter administration continued the use of a news summary, developed by the press office, which was viewed as a useful source of information for communication strategy development. Published six times a week, the news summary included roughly 130 newspapers from across the country, as well as stories from the wire services, a breakdown of network news coverage each night, and a sampling of editorials and editorial cartoons. In addition, a weekly summary of magazines that carried commentary on public affairs and current events was produced. According to Claudia Townsend, a member of the Press Office, the intention of the news summary was to supplement the information that Carter was already getting for himself by keeping up with the major dailies:

> In that sense, it's different from the way it [was with Reagan] and the way it was before the Carter Administration. We knew that the President would read for himself the *New York Times* and the *Washington Post* and the Washington media and what we aimed to do with the news summary were two things. One was to give him an idea of what was going on in the rest of the country in terms of trends and news events that might not yet be covered in Washington and in terms of editorial comment from other papers, a variety of voices. The other was to give some idea of how the things that were going on in Washington were being portrayed through the outlets that reached the largest numbers of people.[89]

The list of newspapers also included at least one from every state, as well as several Black, Hispanic, Jewish, Italian, Greek, and other ethnic publications.[90]

Polling was also an important tool for White House advisors. The Carter administration was among the first to begin to rely on public opinion polling in the formation of public strategies. Pollster Pat Caddell was a valuable resource to Carter in letting him know how the nation viewed his policies, but according to Powell, funding was not adequate to utilize Caddell as often as the White House would have liked. Polling, though limited, did have an impact on the specifics of the communication strategy:

> There's always that tendency to look for the numbers, as soon as you look at them, to start arranging themselves in conformity with whatever your fondest hopes or darkest fears look like. For President Carter, the town hall meetings were an attempt to do that. The press conferences with local and regional press that Pat [Caddell's] operation set up on a pretty regular basis were an attempt to do that.[91]

During an interview within days of the inauguration in January 1977, Powell recommended to Carter that he focus on the issues that polling had determined to be at the top of the American public's agenda: jobs and the economy, welfare reform, and tax reform:

> It is an opportunity to score some political points—your determination to live up to your campaign promises and not to become enmeshed in the trappings of the office—you can tick off the issues that Caddell found to be uppermost in peoples' minds as those you plan to move on or have already begun to work on.[92]

By the end of 1978, the administration had also recognized the importance of Carter's image in the press and having him portrayed as a President with an effective working relationship with Congress, which did not often occur during his first two years in office. Frank Moore, head of the Office of Congressional Liaison, received advice from Rafshoon on cultivating his relationship with influential reporters on the Hill to help in the promotion of Carter's agenda:

> There is no general feeling that this year will be a very harmonious one between the President and the Congress. The budget, SALT, real wage insurance, China and the rest will mean plenty of friction and, in the end, a judgment by the media and the public as to whether the President and this Administration have a productive, if not loving, relationship with Congress. I would suggest that you take several steps to establish closer contacts with the media. You will need to identify reporters and columnists who have an interest in both process and results, and sell them on some consistent "themes" which describe your work and the relationship of this President to the Congress.
>
> The leadership can no longer just pull the string on behalf of a Democratic President. . . . A Democratic President can no longer present a Democratic Congress with a laundry list of programs and then hope to wheel, deal and jam them through. Read LBJ's 1964 State of the Union. Jimmy Carter would be laughed out of town if he proposed one-fourth of what Johnson did.[93]

Those themes encouraged by Rafshoon included focusing on how Carter had become a stronger leader while in office and that he had a new approach to dealing with Congress, specifically that he was willing to stand up to the special interests and fight publicly for his agenda. Also, Rafshoon acknowledged the changes that had occurred within the structure of Congress due to the decentralization of power through congressional reforms and that members were now more independent:

According to Rafshoon, Carter never got credit from the press for his many legislative successes while President:

> We had as good a legislative record as anybody. As far as in the per-
> centages. But what you would see happening was that the process in
> getting something passed was so bloody that the press would focus
> so much on the process and not enough on what actually happened.
> Every president from Eisenhower or from Truman would sweep the
> Panama Canal problem under the rug. Carter got the damned thing
> passed. He gets so little credit on that because the right wing was
> very unhappy and the liberals said so what, it's only right. Civil ser-
> vice reform. For better or worse we had the first energy program.
> But so much was always not about what the energy program was all
> about, but the process and the ball scores on it, Carter not being able
> to work with Congress to get the energy program through.[94]

Due to his leadership style and his desire for an open presidency, Carter also often hurt himself with the press due to overexposure.
This was an issue of great discussion among the top advisors. Rafshoon
recalled the negative impact that too much public exposure had for
Carter's image as an effective leader:

> Limiting extraneous presidential activity I thought was important.
> By initiating public activity by administration figures, we tried to
> coordinate but also to really get other people in the administration
> to go out and carry some of the water and not always depend on the
> President to walk out and deliver the good news or the bad news.
> I'm afraid what was happening and what happened a lot was that
> this President did decide to deliver a lot of the bad news and then
> cabinet members would deliver their good news, which is a reverse
> of what [happened with the Reagan administration] where Reagan
> [did] not ever deliver any bad news. Some people have said that if
> James Watt were Jimmy Carter's secretary of the interior they'd have
> impeached Carter and Watt would have testified.[95]

Rafshoon also believed that Carter was much too eager to talk publicly
about every issue—whether large or small—that arose, which hurt his
image as a focused leader. "In some areas the President was overex-
posed, jumping out and making a statement on every issue, which I
thought was just awful. It showed he had no priorities."[96]

This problem also went hand-in-hand with the lack of coordination to have the administration speak in one voice, which became apparent within a few months of Carter's inauguration. In a handwritten note
to "Cabinet and Other Officers," Carter expressed concern about the

administration's inability to speak in one voice on major policy positions:

> Too much confusion exists concerning the *one* spokesman for me on major issues, particularly in dealing with congressional leaders. Conflicting positions have hurt us on occasions. On some matters, responsibility is clear. Broader issues, though should be decided through thorough consultation, then a single spokesman should deal with the committee members on the hill.[97]

Schneiders addressed the issue with Powell in May 1977 and suggested that members of the Cabinet were afraid to "get too far out front" on issues that Carter was still undecided about, which was causing key administration officials to either avoid the press or to speak anonymously:

> Neither approach helps our cause. In the first instance the President is forced to be identified as the "lead person" on too many issues, he floats his own trial balloons and pays the political price when they pop. The latter, with rare exceptions, is not a healthy situation. I suggest that the President instruct the Cabinet to begin to speak out on the issues that concern them. . . . I think the results would be surprising, namely: 1. More genuinely open government. 2. Greater opportunity to air issues publicly before involving the President. 3. Less need for the President to be publicly identified with every tidbit of federal business so that he can husband his resources and concentrate them on only his top priorities.[98]

Powell responded that Schneiders' ideas had some merit although he had not noticed "any reluctance of administration people to talk to the press whenever an opportunity arises."

> First, the President's inclination to discuss ideas and tentative conclusions does cause some problems, but they are based upon his style of operation and cannot be corrected by urging others to do likewise. Second, it is crucial that Cabinet members and others make it explicit that they are not speaking for the administration when they are not. When this is done, they often assume an advocacy role for a point of view that may be opposed by others in the administration. The inevitable result is a publicity contest within the administration which saps time and resources from the main job of presenting, explaining and advocating administration policy. The press will always play an internal fight higher than a well-thought-out, comprehensive proposal.[99]

In early 1978, Powell suggested dealing with the lack of coordination between advisors on the President's agenda by holding regular meetings among the senior staff, as he proposed in a memo to Carter:

> Although some of the criticism of your staff is overdone, one valid criticism is the lack of coordination among key senior staff. This is generally agreed, but no one is in a position to really do anything on it since we are "all equals." At present there is no effective, daily coordination procedure. This is unprecedented in a White House so far as I have been able to tell. I suggest that you *direct* [Presidential Assistant] Hamilton [Jordan] to convene and chair an early morning meeting composed of himself, [National Security Adviser] Zbig [Brzezinski], [Domestic Affairs Adviser] Stu [Eizenstat], [Head of the Office of Congressional Liaison] Frank [Moore], [Vice Presidential Adviser] Dick Moe and myself to deal ostensibly with legislative matters. . . . The main point is that there is a great need for more coordination and that *you* must insist that these meetings be held and be religiously attended.[100]

Carter supported Rafshoon's coordination of appearances by cabinet members on weekend political shows although he was not always optimistic that the plan would unify the administration's message.

> One of the first things I said when I came in was that the cabinet people are just talking too much and with so many different voices and I would really have liked to be able to coordinate them. The President said good luck. . . . We weren't trying to muzzle, we weren't trying to censor, but before that you could have [Treasury Secretary] Mike Blumenthal on *Meet the Press* and [Chairman of the Council of Economic Advisors] Charlie Schultze on *Face the Nation* and saying two different and contradictory things. Not for any malicious reason, but the press sometimes could elicit an answer that the other person hadn't heard about, and the two programs may not be back to back. . . . Our plan worked with a majority of the cabinet. There were some that were irrepressible, you'd have to kill them. You'd have to shoot them to keep them from talking anytime a camera was within a hundred miles of Washington.[101]

As with other administrations, leaks to the press also plagued the Carter White House at times, especially in the area of foreign policy. In March 1977, as Carter and his advisors were preparing to meet with the Soviets on the Strategic Arms Limitation Treaty, administration leaks on Carter's plan to revamp the U.S. approach in this area led to "Freeze on SALT" stories in the press, which effectively prohibited talks between the two countries for more than a year. In July 1978, administrative leaks were still occurring over Carter's negotiations with the Soviets on SALT, which Powell addressed to the President in a memo:

From what I know of this issue, this sort of leak should not be allowed to pass. Clearly, it came from those who oppose the multiple-hole option [a strategy to increase the survivability of the U.S. nuclear deterrent]. It was done to influence policy and narrow your options. I recommend that you do one of two things: 1. Call in the principals who attended the SALT meeting where this option was discussed and chew them out good. Let them know that you expect your displeasure to be conveyed to their subordinates. 2. Call [Paul] Warnke ([Arms Control Disarmament Agency] is the most likely source) and let him know that you are upset and want him and his people to know about it. Only if the bureaucracy begins to feel that there is some penalty for this sort of behavior will we see some restraints on their part. Otherwise, the problem will continue to grow worse. There is no doubt in my mind that this leak came from the same people who leaked the "Freeze on SALT" story to the same two reporters.[102]

While many of Carter's advisors recognized the need for an effective communication strategy, the specific strategies employed did little to minimize the critical and negative reporting about the administration. Both in-house and external strategies were used in an attempt to control the message coming out of the White House, as well as what was being reported about Carter in the press across the country.[103] But by 1979, a crisis mentality began to emerge in the White House about the direction and image of the administration. As a result, the President and his top advisors met at Camp David to reassess their strategies on how better to lead the nation. Carter recalled the criticisms that were raised about public perceptions of the White House:

They thought the relationship between the White House staff and the White House press corps was especially bad and, that in spite of Jody Powell's efforts, it was unlikely to improve. Everyone agreed that the news media were superficial in their treatment of national and international events and tended to trivialize the most serious problems with a cynical approach. However, they reminded me that I could not win a war with the press, and advised me to stop having so many news conferences.[104]

Part of Carter's image problem, especially with the press, came as a result of the political time. The nation was dealing with an ongoing recession, record levels of inflation, the continuing energy crisis, and a lack of American prestige on the world stage. During his infamous "malaise" speech in July 1979, Carter attempted to address the leadership problem and urged Americans to rally together to make the nation strong again: "All the legislation in the world can't fix what's wrong with America. It is a crisis that strikes at the very heart, soul, and spirit of our national will."[105] While many initially praised Carter's honesty, the strategy itself may have been ill-advised. In his memoirs, Reston recalled Carter's impatience with the mood of the nation:

> Unlike Nixon and Johnson, however, he didn't blame the press for his failures and misfortunes. He usually said in public roughly what he was saying in private. He thought the American people were too impatient, and excessively anticommunist, and there was, he added, a malaise in the country. This undoubtedly was true, but the people didn't hire him to tell them they were down in the dumps. He was widely criticized in the press for this unfortunate remark, and he followed it by the uncharacteristic and politically damaging decision to fire some members of his cabinet.[106]

Carter's image as a weak leader would plague his entire administration, aided in part by international events such as the Iranian Hostage Crisis. But even during the 1980 reelection effort, many in the Carter White House were still convinced that Carter could win the election based in part on his honesty and open style of governing. According to Associate Press Secretary Patricia Bario, the Press Office had a distinct public relations function:

> . . . the basic philosophy was that if we did our job very well as a press operation, if we were open and we answered the questions quickly and sincerely and honestly that this would create such a nice impression of the President across the land, that he would be reelected.[107]

Prior to the 1980 presidential campaign, Rafshoon reported to Carter that his image as a leader needed shoring up since it was one of his weaknesses going into the election: "This is the single biggest weakness in the public perception of you. You are seen to be weak, providing no sense of direction, unsure yourself about where you want to lead the country and unable to lead if you do discover where you want to go."[108]

All things considered, Carter's relationship with the press and his administration's communication strategy may have been hindered the most by his failure to meet the expectations for leadership that the press had placed on him. Carter was criticized for ignoring political elites, not limiting his agenda to achievable goals, and not tailoring his public remarks to positive press coverage. In the eyes of the press, Carter never showed strong leadership or command of his position within the government.[109] The timing of Carter's administration, with Watergate still fresh in the minds of Washington reporters, as well as the public, also harmed Carter's efforts at effective communication and, ultimately, policy implementation. Assessments of the Carter presidency have focused more often on what Carter did not represent, as opposed to what he did represent, as president. While the public initially liked Carter's down-to-earth approach to the presidency, the nation quickly tired of the image of a weak leader:

> We may like the boy next door, we certainly entertain nostalgic feelings for him. But, as Gerald Ford discovered, we do not want him to be president. After a time, the public simply tired of the same old symbols. The president who carried his own bags, who refused the perquisites of the office, also seemed to be a president who did not understand the grandeur and majesty of the presidency.[110]

The grandeur of the office, and how it related to the public aspects of leadership, would be much better understood by Carter's successor.

CARTER'S PUBLIC ACTIVITIES

In general, Carter is not remembered as a good communicator, especially when compared to presidents like Kennedy or Reagan. Throughout his term, Carter attempted to present himself as humble to the American public, and to speak plainly to them about important issues facing the nation. He was a

> beneficiary of the demand for a scaling back from the imperial legacy, and his early symbolic actions after taking the office, his walk to the White House after the inauguration, appearing on television in an open shirt and sweater, and attending town meetings, were calculated to demonstrate his non-imperial approach.[111]

His speaking skills, however, lent themselves more to some venues and topics than others, and his analytical approach to solving problems did not always resonate as a persuasive message to the American people:

> Jimmy Carter had a range of style and skill that ran the gamut from the rhetorical to the analytical. When he campaigned he could be a preacher and before a knowledgeable audience he could be a lucid

speaker in exposition of a complex problem. He used both moral
appeals and knowledgeability in persuasion and negotiation and
was capable of hard and dispassionate analysis in addressing problems. But the underlying theme was Carter's search for achievement.
. . . He believed that correct answers to problems could be developed
through study and analysis.[112]

For most of Carter's administration, the speechwriting process
involved a back-and-forth effort between Carter and his key advisors to
create a specific speech. The process would begin with an outline, then
move to a first draft, then more meetings and readings of the draft
among Carter and his key advisors, and then the creation of a final
draft.[113] Carter spent much time as a wordsmith on the preparation of
speeches, but not as much time either discussing the remarks with
appropriate advisors or on preparing to actually give the remarks. This
frustrated many advisors, including Rafshoon:

> I think one of our problems and I told him this, was that he spent
> more time on preparations of the speech and less time in preparing
> his delivery. He'd get into the text too much sometimes. . . . [There]
> was a never-ending fight of keeping other people out of the speech-
> writing area. Everybody wanted a piece of the speech. And we'd try
> to enforce discipline, and after a certain point you could not come to
> the president on that. . . . He liked to tell us what he wanted to say
> and then he'd want a first text. He didn't spend enough time with
> the speechwriters.[114]

Many advisors also continually urged Carter to work with a
speech coach to improve his delivery, but to no avail. According to
speechwriter Jim Fallows, Carter refused to "tamper with his unvar-
nished, natural style of delivering things," and he never took the advice
of his staff to seek professional coaching:

> I don't know of any case in which he has accepted coaching. None of
> us after the first couple of months even bothered to mention it again
> because it was clear that there was no market for it. Rafshoon, I
> think, [did] a very delicate job of trying to introduce a little bit of it,
> but I'm sure it's much milder than Kennedy or Nixon or Ford did.
> Johnson, too, took speech lessons. But Carter [would] just have none
> of that. I think [that was] a mistake, but it's part of his traits.[115]

Rafshoon continued to urge Carter to use some coaching for his speeches as he began to prepare for the 1980 presidential campaign. "Your
speaking style is a serious problem. I know you don't want to talk to a

speech coach about it (although I really wish you'd reconsider). You should, however, practice more."[116]

Carter's public activities closely reflect the themes of his administration (see Table 4.7). He remained accessible to the press throughout his four years in the White House, and he utilized townhall meetings and question and answer sessions, either with the public or with various groups of journalists outside of the White House press corps, more so than any president before him, in an attempt to gain support for his policy agenda. These public venues remained a top priority for his communication strategy; Carter held a total of 163 during his four years in office. Carter's public activity level remained fairly consistent for each year, with an expected increase during his reelection bid in 1980. However, while the use of policy addresses increased each year, the number of formal press conferences decreased each year. Carter held 22 press conferences in 1977, but that number had fallen to just 6 in 1980-1981. Overall, Carter participated in a total of 1,431 public activities between January 20, 1977 and January 20, 1981.

Table 4.7. Carter—Public Activities.[117]

	1977	1978	1979	1980-81
National Addresses	5	5	4	4
Policy Addresses	9	13	15	16
Press Conferences	22	19	12	6
Radio Addresses	0	0	0	2
Brief Statements/Nonpolicy Remarks	146	180	166	174
Partisan Remarks/Campaign Speeches	12	50	19	106
Press Conferences with Foreign Dignitaries	0	0	0	0
Signing Ceremonies	30	29	13	43
Teleconference Remarks	2	0	2	1
Roundtable Discussions	0	1	0	0
Town Meetings/Q&A Sessions	43	42	33	45
Remarks to/Exchanges with Reporters	57	23	21	61
Total	326	362	285	458
Daily Average	0.94	0.99	0.78	1.19

THE CARTER POLICY AGENDA

One of the overriding factors of the Carter policy agenda was his view of himself as the representational "trustee" of the nation—"an official entrusted to represent the public or national interest, downplaying short-term electoral considerations."[118] Taking care of the nation's business in pursuit of the public good seemed to influence much of the Carter agenda, as well as his political actions on that agenda. Carter believed that he had a moral obligation to identify the needs of the nation, and his "conception of presidential leadership as practicing the politics of the public good meant that he would pursue policies regardless of their immediate political benefits."[119] While his advisors had tried to associate Carter with the liberal tradition of Franklin Roosevelt during the 1976 presidential campaign, the Carter agenda represented more of a centrist position. He was also not perceived as a traditional liberal by many congressional Democrats, due in part to his "outsider" status as a southerner, the high expectations during 1977 of returning the party to its glory days under Roosevelt and Johnson, and Carter's tendency to submit leaner and tighter budgets to Congress then many in his party would have liked. Nonetheless, Carter's agenda did include a wide variety of domestic programs, including energy, urban programs, maintaining the solvency of Social Security, welfare reform, environmental protections, consumer protections, government reform, youth employment programs, and job training programs. He also created the departments of Energy and of Education, and he campaigned for passage of the Equal Rights Amendment. Items on the foreign policy agenda included the Panama Canal Treaty, the continued SALT talks with the Soviet Union, the Camp David Accords with Israel and Egypt, and securing international human rights.[120]

Foreign policy concerns dominated Carter's public agenda during each of his four years in office (see Table 4.8). Carter dealt with a variety of issues in this area involving U.S.-Soviet relations, negotiating the Panama Canal Treaty, and attempts to broker peace deals in the Middle East. Also, Carter talked publicly a great deal about Iran after American citizens were taken hostage in Tehran in November 1979. The frequency with which Carter spoke publicly during major addresses about economic issues peaked during campaign years—both the congressional midterm elections in 1978 and his own reelection effort in 1980. In the domestic area, discussions of defense issues increased during 1980, mostly in response to criticisms from Reagan during the presidential campaign. Energy was a clear priority for the Carter public agenda, both in 1977, when he first introduced his national energy plan, and in 1979, when he continued his fight for extensive legislation in this area.

Table 4.8. Carter's Public Agenda (Major Public Addresses).[121]

	1977	1978	1979	1980-81
Domestic				
Education	5 - <1%	6 - <1%	11 - 1%	72 - 3%
Health Care	39 - 2%	34 - 1%	24 - 1%	9 - <1%
Welfare/Entitlements	90 - 5%	18 - 1%	21 - 1%	19 - 1%
Anticrime	2 - <1%	18 - 1%	0 - 0%	0 - 0%
Political Reform	39 - 2%	99 - 4%	105 - 5%	115 - 5%
Science/Technology/				
Transportation	0 - 0%	2 - <1%	94 - 4%	6 - <1%
Environment/Energy/				
Land Management	539 - 28%	55 - 2%	551 - 26%	139 - 6%
Defense	12 - 1%	53 - 2%	35 - 2%	157 - 7%
International				
Diplomatic/Military	798 - 41%	916 - 39%	931 - 43%	995 - 41%
Trade/Economic	166 - 9%	298 - 13%	150 - 7%	212 - 9%
Economic				
Domestic Fiscal/Monetary	165 - 9%	674 - 29%	168 - 8%	394 - 16%
Unemployment/Jobs	79 - 4%	185 - 8%	69 - 3%	295 - 12%
Total	N = 1934	N = 2358	N = 2159	N = 2413

For both years, the Environment/Energy/Land Management category ranked second only to the Diplomatic/Military category. And other than energy, no other domestic issues ever merited much attention during Carter's major public addresses. Most of Carter's discussions of his broad domestic agenda were reserved for formats such as question and answer sessions with the press and/or townhall meetings with citizens, and they were not discussed in major public addresses.

THE FIRST TIER: ENERGY

The Issue and White House Strategy

No other issue on Carter's domestic agenda received as much attention from the White House as the President's national energy plan. As Carter recalled in his memoirs, "Throughout my entire term, Congress and I struggled with energy legislation. Despite my frustration, there was never a moment when I did not consider the creation of a national ener-

gy policy equal in importance to any other goal we had."[122] Many
believe in retrospect that the struggle for passage of the energy program
defined the weaknesses of Carter's presidency, namely his "difficulty in
building political coalitions, his inability to marshal his party, and his
failure to inspire confidence in his ability to lead the nation."[123] Pursuing
comprehensive energy legislation had not been high on Carter's 1976
campaign agenda, but once elected, he turned to advisor James R.
Schlesinger to develop an energy plan within 90 days to present to
Congress. To avoid press leaks and pressure from special interest
groups, the plan was devised in secret. This left out members of
Congress, as well as most of the President's own advisors, from the for-
mulation of the plan, and put the inexperienced President at an early
disadvantage with important political supporters. Carter did, however,
pursue a strategy in the early months of the plan that included informing the public about the need for energy legislation, even if he was not
revealing the details of his plan. Carter may have "failed to do some
early congressional bridge building, [but] he did not neglect his role as
educator."[124]

In addition to his inaugural address, Carter would give four
other national addresses during 1977, and all four would deal with energy. In a report to the American people in early February 1977, Carter
held a "fireside chat" in the White House library. Wearing a cardigan
sweater and surrounded by books and a roaring fireplace, Carter talked
to the nation about important issues on his agenda, particularly about
the need for a comprehensive energy plan. By all accounts, it was an
impressive performance that showed him as confident in his new role as
president, and willing to face the reality of the energy crisis:

> One of our most urgent projects is to develop a national energy poli-
> cy. As I pointed out during the campaign, the United States is the
> only major industrial country without a comprehensive, long-range
> energy policy. . . . Our program will emphasize conservation. . . . We
> must face the fact that the energy shortage is permanent. There is no
> way we can solve it quickly.[125]

When the energy package was ready to present to Congress and the
American people in April, with Schlesinger having met his 90-day deadline to formulate the plan, Carter, in a sense, broke the bad news to the
nation in a televised address from the White House:

> Many of these proposals will be unpopular. Some will cause you to
> put up with inconveniences and to make sacrifices. The most impor-
> tant thing about these proposals is that the alternative may be a
> national catastrophe. Further delay can affect our strength and our

power as a nation. Our decision about energy will test the character of the American people and the ability of the President and the Congress to govern this Nation. This difficult effort will be the "moral equivalent of war," except that we will be uniting our efforts to build and not to destroy.[126]

The program came under immediate criticism by members of Congress from both parties who had not been consulted by the White House or involved in the development of such a large scale energy plan, especially since the program had been developed almost entirely in secret by Schlesinger and his staff. The public, along with most of the Cabinet and White House staff, had also been kept in the dark about the plan.[127]

Two days later, Carter officially presented his plan to Congress in an address to a joint session. The main goal of Carter's "National Energy Plan" was to increase energy efficiency and to decrease the need for oil, especially from foreign sources. The specifics included "an exceedingly complex package of regulatory and tax measures" aimed mostly at the oil industry and businesses to meet the proposed standards of efficiency.[128] During the address, Carter acknowledged the difficulty of the situation:

This cannot be an inspirational speech tonight. I don't expect much applause. It's a sober and a difficult presentation. During the last three months, I have come to realize very clearly why a comprehensive energy policy has not already been evolved. It's been a thankless job, but it is our job. And I believe that we have a fair, well-balanced, and effective plan to present to you. It can lead to an even better life for the people of America.[129]

The plan immediately ran into political resistance, both from Congress and from powerful special interest groups. In response, Carter sent various members of his cabinet across the nation on a public campaign to gain support for the plan. Along the way, the defects of the plan, including technical flaws in its hasty drafting, became obvious. And despite heavy arm-twisting by the Democratic leadership in both the House and the Senate to push the bill through in its entirety, by the end of the first session of the 95th Congress Carter would still have no energy bill to sign. After its passage in the House in August, but before a similar result in the Senate, the nation's attention was refocused away from the energy plan and on to the Bert Lance affair. Lance, a longtime friend and economic advisor to Carter, resigned as a result of discovered improprieties stemming from his pre-Washington banking days.

Afterwards, the all-important momentum for the plan was lost. In October, the White House attempted to regroup and "make an all-out effort over the next four to six weeks to arouse public support for our energy plan as adopted by the House." The strategy included the following advice to Carter from Schlesinger and Eizenstat:

> A major Presidential speech or other public presentation could rekindle the public sense of urgency which was so widely felt after your April 20 speech. Such a speech should focus on the larger picture—why we need an energy program and what its basic elements must be. It could also serve to remind the public that the energy problem is getting worse, not better. Develop a press plan to ensure that the rationale for and the Congressional process on energy legislation stays in the news. Jody is working on this now. This could include having editors of major newspapers around the country in for a Presidential-Schlesinger briefing.[130]

The Senate did pass a version of the bill in late October, and Carter made a public plea for the bill's survival in the conference committee:

> The choices facing the Members of Congress are not easy. For them to pass an effective and fair plan, they will need your support and your understanding—your support to resist pressures from a few for special favors at the expense of the rest of us and your understanding that there can be no effective plan without some sacrifice from all of us.[131]

But Congress would adjourn for the year before final action could be taken.

During 1978, Congress would chip away at Carter's comprehensive plan. Carter continued to talk publicly about the need for an energy plan, but he did not give any more national addresses on the subject. However, his advisors did devise a plan for gaining public support of the energy proposal which, among other things, developed themes and a tone for presidential public activities. Rafshoon presented a detailed plan to several key White House advisors, with many of the specifics developed by Schneiders:

> *The theme we don't want.* The public will probably not be receptive to the argument that we need energy legislation because we are running out of fuel. There is significant disagreement among experts about this point; the public sees no tangible evidence—like gas lines or rationing—to support the position; we tried this approach before to mixed reviews; the public likes to think that technology will bail us out—and it might well; and at the very time we hope to have public concern peak—July and August—there will probably be a

glut of oil on the market (much of it from Alaska). It is not surprising that Pat [Caddell's] figures show "real energy shortages" running a poor third (38%) to "the way oil companies act" (58%) and "high fuel prices" (65%) as a cause of concern about energy. *The theme we do want.* Americans are most concerned about economics—particularly inflation. It is not difficult to tie energy to these concerns. . . . *Presidential Activity.* Between now and passage of the full energy plan the President should mention energy in every major public statement. It should be his dominant theme. His statements should be general and variations on a single theme: "We need an energy plan. Congress has *still* not acted. Inflation, dollar, etc., etc." . . . The President should be *consistent* and should place himself above the battle, imploring Congress to set aside their petty differences and give the country an energy plan. . . . *Media.* We should begin working with influential columnists, editorial writers, and television types to drive home the fact that passage of an energy plan is the President's number one priority because of its economic implications.[132]

Finally, more than 18 months after it had been presented to Congress, Carter signed an energy bill into law in November 1978. Although what Carter signed was a much altered, much watered-down version of his original plan. Most of the proposed taxes were gone, but regulation of natural gas, coal conversion, and utility rates remained. But while parts of the plan had been approved, the overall plan had failed due to its complexity, not only in getting a comprehensive plan passed through Congress but in the difficulty in convincing Americans about the urgency of the problem, and that energy "lacked a built-in constituency. No coalitions of any significance backed the comprehensive energy package. It was too liberal for conservatives and too conservative for liberals."[133] However, Carter's greatest victory on energy policy with Congress would come in late 1979 and 1980, when panic hit the nation due to gas shortages and the Iranian hostage crisis: "Not until the United States experienced the economic dislocations that Carter had predicted could he finally mobilize the public and Congress to pursue significant change in energy policy."[134] Carter kept energy high on his public agenda in 1979 in a renewed effort to expand the plan and solve the nation's energy problem. Unfortunately for him, that effort would not salvage the damage that had been done early on in the administration, and it would not help win a second term in office.

Press Coverage

Carter's expansive national energy proposal, as well as the many political battles with Congress that ensued after its introduction, garnered much attention from the news media. Between April 1977 and November 1978, a total of 288 news items appeared in the *New York Times* about Carter's proposed energy plan, with an average of one story every other day (see Table 4.9). Most stories were generated by congressional action on the energy plan (48 percent); stories on interest group activity ranked second (35 percent); and the White House ranked a distant third (17 percent). Of the news items generated by White House activity, most were balanced or mixed in their presentation of the energy plan (see Table 4.10). Much information was presented on both the positive aspects of the proposal—in terms of meeting the national need for energy conservation, as well as on the weaknesses and criticisms from opponents of the plan.

The *Times* expressed its opinion about Carter and his energy plan in five separate editorials during the time period analyzed. One was coded as positive, and the remaining four were coded as balanced/mixed. In general, the *Times* praised Carter's efforts for proposing much needed legislation, but it criticized him for his political efforts at getting the plan through Congress. Soon after Carter announced the plan, an editorial on April 22, 1977 expressed concern over the President's ability to achieve passage of the complex program: "When the President promised a detailed, comprehensive energy policy, he meant it. . . . Much as the plan is needed and as much as we therefore applaud the President for it, it is too complex for fast or full absorption." Two days later, the *Times* acknowledged that Carter's inexperience with Washington politics might completely derail the energy plan: "However shrewdly the Carter program addresses energy pricing, it is studded with odd omissions and large question marks. . . . Emerging facts, insights—and politics—may extensively alter the specifics of the ultimate program." However, in that same Sunday edition of the *Times*, columnist James Reston praised Carter for his efforts at leadership on the energy issue:

> Washington is not sure yet that it has an energy policy, but it is beginning to get the idea that it has a President. . . . It is with Carter a sense that there is something good at the bottom of the barrel, a purpose in his human rights arguments, in his insistence on cutting down strategic arms and pork-barrel projects, and facing up to the energy problem.

But as the energy proposal continued on its long journey through Congress, the attitude about Carter's leadership capability with this issue became more skeptical. In an October 14, 1977 editorial, which came after Carter had publicly declared the nation's oil companies as

Table 4.9. Amount and Type of *New York Times* Coverage of the National Energy Plan (April 1977-November 1978).

	White House	Congress	Interest Group/Other
News Story	27	111	80
News Analysis	3	14	8
Column	13	2	11
Editorial	5	11	3
Total	48 - (17%)	138 - (48%)	102 - (35%)

Table 4.10. Tone of *New York Times* Coverage of Presidential Activities on the National Energy Plan (April 1977-November 1978).

	Positive	Negative	Balanced/Mixed	Neutral
News Story	1	1	23	2
News Analysis	0	0	3	0
Column	1	4	8	0
Editorial	1	0	4	0
Total	3	5	38	2

"the biggest rip off in history," the *Times* declared Carter's tough stand against interest group pressure as "brave" and "necessary" talk, but it doubted that Carter would be able to push his comprehensive plan through Congress and affect much change in the nation's attitude about the seriousness of the energy crisis.

THE SECOND TIER: CIVIL SERVICE REFORM

The Issue and White House Strategy

While his overall record with Congress may not be his greatest legacy, Carter did achieve legislative success with the Civil Service Reform Act of 1978. Carter believed that the nation needed strong leadership in this policy area, and that "his election was a mandate for better government."[135] The first major reform to the system in nearly a century, the act created a Senior Executive Service to replace the Civil Service Commission. The bill also included a merit pay system for middle-level management, increased flexibility in firing incompetent employees, statutory labor rights for federal employees, and protection for whistle-blowers. The proposal, developed by a commission of 100 civil servants and members of the business and academic communities, represented Carter's desire to seriously pursue government reform in the first few years after Watergate, a theme he spoke of often during the 1976 presidential campaign. Carter signed the bill into law in October 1978, and the only aspect of the plan that was left out was a proposal to scale back preference for hiring veterans to federal positions. When introduced, the bill had raised serious objections from federal employee unions, but most of Carter's original plan remained intact.[136]

Carter first publicly introduced his plan for reform of the federal civil service system during his 1978 State of the Union Address:

> Even the best organized Government will only be as effective as the people who carry out its policies. For this reason, I consider civil service reform to be absolutely vital. Worked out with the civil servants themselves, this reorganization plan will restore the merit principle to a system which has grown into a bureaucratic maze. It will provide greater management flexibility and better rewards for better performance without compromising job security. Then and only then can we have a government that is efficient, open, and truly worthy of our people's understanding and respect. I have promised that we will have such a government, and I intend to keep that promise.[137]

Carter's advisors, including Eizenstat, believed that legislative efforts on such issues as civil service reform in early 1978 would resonate with the mood of the public for reform, especially if portrayed as an issue that Congress was reluctant to consider:

> After conversations with Pat Caddell and a number of other people, I am convinced that your rating in the public opinion polls is increasingly a function of your relations with Congress and their capacity to pass legislation. While that is to some extent inevitable, your Presidency risks being measured just by legislative accomplishments. I believe that is dangerous because Congress, in my estimation, has become increasingly unwilling to tackle the tough, substantive issues we have presented and will continue to present through-

out your Administration. I think that it is therefore critical that we attempt to define as much as possible your success as President in non-legislative terms while, of course, continuing to pursue our legislative program with all our resources.

Eizenstat suggested executive actions in the area of government reform, ones which would not require congressional approval and

> would thereby fit nicely with your concentration on that subject and with the country's anti-government mood. . . . [W]e could provide you with regular opportunities to make brief statements on administrative actions being taken to improve government efficiency and eliminate unneeded government regulation. Through such regular statements you can become much more identified with government reform than you presently are. Given the country's mood, that identification should rebound in the polls. More importantly, the sense of Presidential action, control and leadership can be regularly demonstrated.[138]

In March, Carter sent his proposal for Civil Service Reform to Congress, in which he stated:

> My proposals are intended to increase the government's efficiency by placing new emphasis on the quality of performance of Federal workers. At the same time, my recommendations will ensure that employees and the public are protected against political abuse of the system.[139]

As the political debate on Capitol Hill began on the President's proposal, and as interest groups began to weigh in on the subject, Carter stood firm publicly for the need for strong government reform. He addressed the proposal during the opening statement of a press conference on April 25:

> Nearly everyone in our country will benefit from the civil service reform proposals. . . . When criticism and debate in the Congress lead to a stronger plan, then I'll support those changes. But I will object very strenuously to weakening our proposal. And I do object also very strenuously to false accusations, specifically one that's been raised recently that this will intrude into the privacy of public servants and injects politics and possible abuse into the system to damage those who serve the Government. In fact, to the creation of a merit protection board and an office of special counsel, political abuse is specifically removed.[140]

He also spoke about his proposal during another press conference in May, this one in Portland, Oregon, attempting to highlight the importance of federal government reform to even those who lived outside of Washington:

> Since so many critical decisions are made in Washington, and Washington is physically remote from the West, responsiveness of our Government depends upon the ability to learn your needs and to give them a full and a fair consideration. A government whose capital is a whole continent away has to be that much more alert and responsive and competent.[141]

In a memo from Rafshoon to Carter in July 1978 on the President's 90-day public activity plan, civil service reform was listed the third highest legislative priority behind the economy and energy, respectively:

> *Civil Service Reform*: This is the heart of government reform. It looked like it was going to pass without a big fight. This is no longer so. We must pull out all stops to get it passed and to show your total commitment to reorganization. As with energy, prior to passage we should identify you with the bill whenever possible and post passage we should be sure to get credit. It is important that we begin now to revise the criteria, established during the campaign, on reorganization. We are going to eliminate 1,600 agencies so we should begin to claim major success for the reorganization effort on the basis of civil service reform.[142]

On August 3, Carter participated in a roundtable discussion on civil service reform with various civil service employees; it was held in Fairfax, Virginia and broadcast live on local radio and television. Carter also made civil service reform a campaign issue during the midterm elections. Civil service reform is seen as one of Carter's greatest legislative accomplishments, in part because of the administration's acknowledgment that "support for reform is typically broad and thin, while opposition is typically narrow and deep." The strategy of including career civil servants in the drafting of the policy and coordinating it with key members of Congress allowed for swift passage of the bill before strong opposition, especially from organized labor, could be pursued.[143]

Press Coverage

Unlike higher profile policies like energy, Carter's civil service reform proposal did not receive much coverage by the news media. The *Times* included only 38 news items between March and October 1978, an average of one news item every six days. Of those, only 21 percent were generated by the White House, while 47 percent were generated by Congress and 32 percent were generated by interest group activity (see Table 4.11). Of the eight White House news items, the tone was evenly balanced in all four categories (see Table 4.12). The two columns included in this time frame addressed criticism about proposal specifics, such as the changes to hiring preferences for veterans. Only one editorial on March 8, 1978 appeared in the *Times* on this policy, which was positive in its support for Carter's plan, calling his civil service reform proposal "a tough, comprehensive set of reforms," and praising his efforts in this area of policy-making: "The President's proposals to make the bureaucracies that serve the nation efficient and responsive are long overdue."

Table 4.11. Amount and Type of *New York Times* Coverage of Civil Service Reform (March 1978-October 1978).

	White House	Congress	Interest Group/Other
News Story	4	15	10
News Analysis	0	0	0
Column	3	0	0
Editorial	1	3	2
Total	8 - (21%)	18 - (47%	12 - (32%)

Table 4.12. Tone of *New York Times* Coverage of Presidential Activities on Civil Service Reform (March 1978-October 1978)

	Positive	Negative	Balanced/Mixed	Neutral
News Story	1	0	1	2
News Analysis	0	0	0	0
Column	0	2	1	0
Editorial	1	0	0	0
Total	2	2	2	2

CONCLUSION

Limited leadership potential existed during the Ford and Carter years as both the public and the press had high expectations for cleaning up Washington after Watergate. Both men were somewhat successful, but they mostly fell short in many areas. Ford's most enduring legacy, despite the pardon of Nixon, has been his reputation as an honest and ethical man, and his efforts to restore the office of the presidency to a respected and dignified political position.[144] Ford also brought a humility back to the White House that it had lacked for many years. Certainly, the same could be said of Carter. The public aspects of presidential leadership became more important during the decade of the 1970s, and during this time, "the nation's institutions, including the news media, would undergo a wholesale reappraisal of basic values."[145] While the theme of reform was evident in both administrations, the news media began to shift its attention during this time toward a trivialization of news, especially about the president.

In spite of many efforts at having an open and accessible White House that did not rely on heavy-handed public relations to sell the presidency, Ford and his advisors relied on many of the same tactics as his predecessors, finding that they could not function without the aid of the Office of Communications and controlling the image as much as possible. Carter had much the same experience, and his tendency to share too many details with the public about mundane policy matters turned off some Americans. Also, both presidents worked overtime at convincing the American public that a crisis existed in its energy policy, but the results of those efforts would not be realized until the Reagan years. Reagan would also be the beneficiary of the mood for reform, as his public discussions about reducing the size of the federal government would become a core principle of both his presidential campaign in 1980 and his administration, especially in the news media. And while both Ford and Carter relied on innovative public techniques to bring the presidency back to the people, especially the use of townhall meetings and informal question and answer sessions with both the public and the press, neither would enjoy an overly successful communication strategy. Many of the problems with constructing a positive public image and a strong vision for a legislative agenda would be solved during the 1980s by the Reagan administration, which pursued one of the most successful communication strategies on record.

ENDNOTES

1. John Robert Greene, *The Presidency of Gerald R. Ford* (Lawrence, KS: University Press of Kansas, 1995), 192.
2. Michael Emery and Edwin Emery, *The Press and America: An Interpretive History of the Mass Media*, 8th ed. (Boston: Allyn and Bacon, 1996), 460.
3. Ibid., 458-9.
4. Greene, *The Presidency of Gerald R. Ford*, 31-4.
5. Richard Reeves, *A Ford, not a Lincoln* (New York: Harcourt Brace Jovanovich, 1975), 68.
6. Gerald R. Ford, *A Time to Heal: The Autobiography of Gerald R. Ford* (New York: Harper & Row, 1979), 126-7.
7. Letter from John Chancellor to Jerry terHorst, 8/20/74, Jerald terHorst Files, Box 3, Gerald R. Ford Library.
8. Memo from Pat Buchanan to Jerry terHorst, 8/17/74, Ron Nessen Papers, Box 24, Gerald R. Ford Library.
9. Ibid.
10. Mark J. Rozell, *The Press and the Ford Presidency* (Ann Arbor: University of Michigan Press, 1992), 54.
11. Ron Nessen, *It Sure Looks Different from the Inside* (Chicago: Playboy Press, 1978), 29.
12. Greene, *The Presidency of Gerald R. Ford*, 63-4.
13. John Tebbel and Sarah Miles Watts, *The Press and the Presidency: From George Washington to Ronald Reagan* (New York: Oxford University Press, 1985), 518-20
14. Ibid., 520.
15. Nessen, 50-3.
16. Letter from John Osborne to Ron Nessen, 11/27/74, Ron Nessen Papers, Box 5, Gerald R. Ford Library.
17. Memo from Jack Hushen to Ron Nessen, 6/26/75, Ron Nessen Papers, Box 23, Gerald R. Ford Library.
18. Addendum to memo from Jack Hushen to Ron Nessen, 6/26/75, Ron Nessen Papers, Box 23, Gerald R. Ford Library.
19. Rozell, 2-4.
20. John Robert Greene, "'A Nice Person Who Worked at the Job': The Dilemma of the Ford Image," in *Gerald R. Ford and the Politics of Post-Watergate America*, Vol. 2, Eds. Bernard J. Firestone and Alexej Ugrinsky (Westport, CT: Greenwood Press, 1993), 636-7.
21. Interview with John G. Carlson by Mark J. Rozell, 5/2/90, Mark J. Rozell Files, Gerald R. Ford Library.
22. Memo from Jim Shuman to Ron Nessen, 10/15/75, Ron Nessen Papers, Box 133, Gerald R. Ford Library.
23. Memo from Dorrance Smith to Doug Blaser, 7/26/76, Ron Nessen Papers, Box 24, Gerald R. Ford Library.
24. Ibid.
25. Ibid.

26. Memo on Press Office Staff Meeting, 6/27/75, Ron Nessen Papers, Box 23, Gerald R. Ford Library.
27. Memo from Jim Shuman to Ron Nessen, 8/6/75, Margita E. White Files, Box 1, Gerald R. Ford Library.
28. Memo from Jim Shuman to David Gergen, 5/18/76, Ron Nessen Papers, Box 135, Gerald R. Ford Library.
29. Reeves, 83.
30. Gerald R. Ford, "The President and Political Leadership," in *Twenty Years of Papers on the Presidency*, Ed. Kenneth W. Thompson (Lanham, MD: University Press of America, 1995), 14-5.
31. Memo from Tom DeCair to Dick Cheney, 1/21/75, Ron Nessen Papers, Box 132, Gerald R. Ford Library.
32. John Anthony Maltese, *Spin Control: The White House Office of Communications and the Management of Presidential News*, 2nd rev. ed. (Chapel Hill: University of North Carolina Press, 1994), 118.
33. Memo from Donald Rumsfeld to Gerald Ford, 2/21/75, Ron Nessen Papers, Box 132, Gerald R. Ford Library.
34. Maltese, 124-8.
35. Memo from Ron Nessen to Jim Connor, 3/12/75, Ron Nessen papers, Box 24, Gerald R. Ford Library.
36. Memo from Bob Mead to Don Rumsfeld, Dick Cheney, Ron Nessen, Jerry Jones, Howard Callaway, and Terry O'Donnell, 7/2/75, Helen M. Collins Files, Box 3, Gerald R. Ford Library.
37. Memo from Jim Cavanaugh, Mike Duval, and David Gergen to Dick Cheney, 4/23/76, Jerry Jones Files, Box 19, Gerald R. Ford Library.
38. Maltese, 135-48.
39. Rozell, 162-4.
40. Interview with Robert Hartmann by Mark J. Rozell, 12/15/89, Mark J. Rozell Files, Gerald R. Ford Library.
41. Ford, "The President and Political Leadership," 14-5.
42. Tebbel and Watts, 520.
43. Craig Allen Smith, "Gerald R. Ford," in *U.S. Presidents as Orators: A Bio-Critical Sourcebook*, Ed. Halford Ryan (Westport, CT: Greenwood Press, 1995), 295-6.
44. Greene, *The Presidency of Gerald R. Ford*, 176.
45. Ibid., 62-3.
46. Finding Aid for Paul Theis and Robert Orben, Editorial Office, Gerald R. Ford Library.
47. Memo from David Gergen to Dick Cheney, 8/10/76, David Hoopes Files, Box 10, Gerald R. Ford Library.
48. Memo from Paul Theis to Robert Hartmann, 8/8/75, Ron Nessen Papers, Box 132, Gerald R. Ford Library.
49. Compiled from *The Public Papers of the Presidents of the United States: Gerald R. Ford, 1974-77* (Washington, DC: Government Printing Office, 1975-79).

50. Greene, *The Presidency of Gerald R. Ford*, 191-2.
51. Berman, 295-6.
52. Compiled from *The Public Papers of the Presidents of the United States: Gerald R. Ford, 1974-77* (Washington, DC: Government Printing Office, 1975-79).
53. John W. Sloan, "Groping Toward a Macrotheme: Economic Policymaking in the Ford Presidency," in *Gerald R. Ford and the Politics of Post-Watergate America*, Vol. I, Eds. Bernard J. Firestone and Alexej Ugrinsky (Westport, CT: Greenwood Press, 1993), 279.
54. Address to the Nation on Energy and Economic Programs, 1/13/75, *Public Papers of the Presidents: Gerald R. Ford, 1975* (Washington, DC: Government Printing Office, 1977).
55. Barbara Kellerman, *The Political Presidency: Practice of Leadership From Kennedy Through Reagan* (New York: Oxford University Press, 1984), 166-7.
56. Address Before a Joint Session of the Congress Reporting on the State of the Union, 1/15/75, *Public Papers of the Presidents: Gerald R. Ford, 1975* (Washington, DC: Government Printing Office, 1977).
57. Kellerman, 167.
58. Memo from Ron Nessen to Don Rumsfeld, 2/15/75, Ron Nessen Papers, Box 132, Gerald R. Ford Library.
59. Memo from Margita E. White to Ron Nessen, 3/3/75, Ron Nessen Papers, Box 131, Gerald R. Ford Library.
60. *Congressional Quarterly Almanac, 1975*, Vol. XXXI (Washington, DC: Congressional Quarterly Service, 1976), 95-6.
61. Memo from Ron Nessen to Gerald Ford, 3/28/75, Ron Nessen Papers, Box 131, Gerald R. Ford Library.
62. *Public Papers of the Presidents: Gerald R. Ford, 1975* (Washington, DC: Government Printing Office, 1977).
63. Ford, *A Time to Heal*, 340.
64. Memo from Dick Cheney to Donald Rumsfeld, 5/24/75, Richard Cheney Files, Box 5, Gerald R. Ford Library.
65. Remarks in San Francisco at the Annual Convention of the AFL-CIO Building and Construction Trades Department, 9/22/75, *Public Papers of the Presidents: Gerald R. Ford, 1975* (Washington, DC: Government Printing Office, 1977).
66. Interview With Television Reporters in San Francisco, 9/22/75, *Public Papers of the Presidents: Gerald R. Ford, 1975* (Washington, DC: Government Printing Office, 1977).
67. Letter to the Speaker of the House and the President of the Senate Transmitting Proposed Legislation To Establish an Energy Independence Authority, 10/10/75, *Public Papers of the Presidents: Gerald R. Ford, 1975* (Washington, DC: Government Printing Office, 1977).
68. *Congressional Quarterly Almanac, 1975*, Vol. XXXI (Washington, DC: Congressional Quarterly Service, 1976), 268.

69. Paul C. Light, *The President's Agenda: Domestic Policy Choice from Kennedy to Reagan*, rev. ed. (Baltimore, Johns Hopkins University Press, 1991), 154.
70. *Congressional Quarterly Almanac, 1976,* Vol. XXXII (Washington, DC: Congressional Quarterly Service, 1977), 92.
71. James Reston, *Deadline: A Memoir* (New York: Random House, 1991), 423.
72. Berman, 310-7.
73. Paul Haskell Zernicke, *Pitching the Presidency: How Presidents Depict the Office* (Westport, CT: Praeger, 1994), 2-3, 145.
74. Memo from Powell to Carter, 6/1/77, Jody Powell Papers, Box 39, Jimmy Carter Library. In an attachment to this memo, Powell provides Carter with photos of reporters invited to upcoming pool sessions and brief descriptions about how each has been covering the President and his policies, which is reminiscent of how the Nixon administration categorized members of the press based on their support or opposition to Nixon and his policies. For example, Hugh Sidey of *Time* magazine is described as having "warned that there may be hazards in the President's approaching the Presidency with a missionary-like attitude, comparing the President to Woodrow Wilson." On Helen Thomas of UPI:

> She has lately been much warmer towards you, after initial suspicion of you and your staff's newness and Southerness. She is of Syrian descent, is quite proud of that heritage, and is particularly pleased about your human rights stand—there has apparently been some trouble in that area among her ancestors—also pleased by more "even-handed" approach to the Mideast.

75. Interview with Jody Powell, Patricia Bario, Al Friendly, Rex Granum, Ray Jenkins, Dale Leibach, and Claudia Townsend, Miller Center Interviews, Carter Presidency Project, December 17-18, 1981, p. 34, Jimmy Carter Library.
76. Memo from Fallows to Carter, 2/11/77, Jody Powell Papers, Box 42, Jimmy Carter Library.
77. Memo from Powell to Carter, 2/2/77, Jody Powell Papers, Box 39, Jimmy Carter Library.
78. Interview with Gerald Rafshoon, Miller Center Interviews, Carter Presidency Project, April 8, 1983, p. 4, Jimmy Carter Library.
79. Hedley Donovan, *Roosevelt to Reagan: A Reporter's Encounters with Nine Presidents* (New York: Harper & Row, 1985), 222.
80. Interview with Jody Powell, Patricia Bario, Al Friendly, Rex Granum, Ray Jenkins, Dale Leibach, and Claudia Townsend, Miller Center Interviews, Carter Presidency Project, December 17-18, 1981, p. 17, Jimmy Carter Library.

81. Garland A. Haas, *Jimmy Carter and the Politics of Frustration* (Jefferson, NC: McFarland and Company, 1992), 60-1.

82. Memo from Powell to Carter, 12/1/77, Jody Powell Papers, Box 39, Jimmy Carter Library.

83. Memo from Rafshoon to Carter, 9/26/78, Gerald Rafshoon Papers, Box 28, Jimmy Carter Library.

84. Maltese, 150-9.

85. Ibid., 161-2.

86. Haas, 60.

87. Jimmy Carter, *Keeping Faith: Memoirs of a President* (New York: Bantam Books, 1982), 127.

88. Memo from Schneiders to Rafshoon, 2/26/79, Jody Powell Papers, Box 65, Jimmy Carter Library.

89. Interview with Jody Powell, Patricia Bario, Al Friendly, Rex Granum, Ray Jenkins, Dale Leibach, and Claudia Townsend, Miller Center Interviews, Carter Presidency Project, December 17-18, 1981, p. 68, Jimmy Carter Library.

90. Memo from Pat Bauer to Rafshoon, 6/14/78, Gerald Rafshoon Papers, Box 4, Jimmy Carter Library.

91. Interview with Jody Powell, Patricia Bario, Al Friendly, Rex Granum, Ray Jenkins, Dale Leibach, and Claudia Townsend, Miller Center Interviews, Carter Presidency Project, December 17-18, 1981, pp. 24-5, Jimmy Carter Library.

92. Memo from Powell to Carter, 1/22/77, Jody Powell Papers, Box 39, Jimmy Carter Library.

93. Memo from Rafshoon to Moore, 12/21/78, Gerald Rafshoon Papers, Box 28, Jimmy Carter Library.

94. Interview with Gerald Rafshoon, Miller Center Interviews, Carter Presidency Project, April 8, 1983, p. 12, Jimmy Carter Library.

95. Interview with Gerald Rafshoon, Miller Center Interviews, Carter Presidency Project, April 8, 1983, p. 9, Jimmy Carter Library.

96. Interview with Gerald Rafshoon, Miller Center Interviews, Carter Presidency Project, April 8, 1983, p. 14, Jimmy Carter Library.

97. Handwritten memo from Carter to Cabinet and Other Officers, 4/27/77, Jody Powell Papers, Box 39, Jimmy Carter Library.

98. Memo from Schneiders to Powell, 5/18/77, Gerald Rafshoon Papers, Box 28, Jimmy Carter Library.

99. Memo from Powell to Schneiders, 6/1/77, Gerald Rafshoon Papers, Box 28, Jimmy Carter Library.

100. Memo from Powell to Carter, 1/16/78, Jody Powell Papers, Box 39, Jimmy Carter Library.

101. Interview with Gerald Rafshoon, Miller Center Interviews, Carter Presidency Project, April 8, 1983, p. 8, Jimmy Carter Library.

102. Memo from Powell to Carter, 7/10/78, Jody Powell Papers, Box 40, Jimmy Carter Library.
103. Robert S. Littlefield, "Carter and the Media: An Analysis of Selected Strategies Used to Manage the Public Communication of the Administration," in *The Presidency and Domestic Policies of Jimmy Carter*, Eds. Herbert D. Rosenbaum and Alexej Ugrinsky (Westport, CT: Greenwood Press, 1994), 425-6.
104. Carter, 117.
105. *Public Papers of the Presidents: Jimmy Carter, 1979* (Washington, DC: Government Printing Office, 1980).
106. Reston, 426.
107. Interview with Jody Powell, Patricia Bario, Al Friendly, Rex Granum, Ray Jenkins, Dale Leibach, and Claudia Townsend, Miller Center Interviews, Carter Presidency Project, December 17-18, 1981, p. 7, Jimmy Carter Library.
108. Undated memo from Rafshoon to Carter on 1980 campaign themes, Gerald Rafshoon Papers, Box 24, Jimmy Carter Library.
109. Mark Rozell, *The Press and the Carter Presidency* (Boulder, CO: Westview Press, 1989), 219-29.
110. Mary E. Stuckey, *The President as Interpreter-in-Chief* (Chatham, NJ: Chatham House Publishers, 1991), 102.
111. Dan F. Hahn and Halford Ryan, "Jimmy Carter," in *U.S. Presidents as Orators: A Bio-Critical Sourcebook*, Ed. Halford Ryan (Westport, CT: Greenwood Press, 1995), 300.
112. Erwin C. Hargrove, *Jimmy Carter as President: Leadership and the Politics of the Public Good* (Baton Rouge: Louisiana State University Press, 1988), 170-1.
113. Memo from Fallows to Carter, 11/28/77, Jody Powell Papers, Box 42, Jimmy Carter Library.
114. Interview with Gerald Rafshoon, Miller Center Interviews, Carter Presidency Project, April 8, 1983, p. 20, Jimmy Carter Library.
115. Exit Interview with Jim Fallows, p. 24, Jimmy Carter Library.
116. Undated memo from Rafshoon to Carter on 1980 campaign themes, Gerald Rafshoon Papers, Box 24, Jimmy Carter Library.
117. Compiled from *The Public Papers of the Presidents of the United States: Jimmy Carter, 1977-81* (Washington, DC: Government Printing Office, 1977-82).
118. Charles O. Jones, *The Trusteeship Presidency: Jimmy Carter and the United States Congress* (Baton Rouge, LA: Louisiana State University Press, 1988), 2.
119. John C. Barrow, "An Age of Limits: Jimmy Carter and the Quest for a National Energy Policy," in *The Carter Presidency: Policy Choices in the Post-New Deal Era*, Eds. Gary M. Fink and Hugh Davis Graham (Lawrence, KS: University of Kansas Press, 1998), 173.
120. William E. Leuchtenburg, "Jimmy Carter and the Post-New Deal Presidency," in *The Carter Presidency: Policy Choices in the Post-

New Deal Era, Eds. Gary M. Fink and Hugh Davis Graham (Lawrence, KS: University of Kansas Press, 1998), 8-13.

121. Compiled from *The Public Papers of the Presidents of the United States: Jimmy Carter, 1977-81* (Washington, DC: Government Printing Office, 1977-82).
122. Carter, 91.
123. Barrow, 158-9.
124. Kellerman, 188.
125. Report to the American People, 2/2/77, *The Public Papers of the Presidents: Jimmy Carter, 1977* (Washington, DC: Government Printing Office, 1977).
126. Address to the Nation on the Energy Problem, 4/18/77, *The Public Papers of the Presidents: Jimmy Carter, 1977* (Washington, DC: Government Printing Office, 1977).
127. Haas, 69.
128. *Congressional Quarterly Almanac*, 1977, Vol. XXXIII (Washington, DC: Congressional Quarterly Service, 1978), 708.
129. Address Delivered Before a Joint Session of the Congress, 4/20/77, *The Public Papers of the Presidents: Jimmy Carter, 1977* (Washington, DC: Government Printing Office, 1977).
130. Memo from Schlesinger and Eizenstat to Carter, 12/12/77, Jody Powell Papers, Box 57, Jimmy Carter Library.
131. Address to the Nation on the National Energy Plan, 11/8/77, *The Public Papers of the Presidents: Jimmy Carter, 1977* (Washington, DC: Government Printing Office, 1978).
132. Memo from Rafshoon to White House advisors, 6/1/78, with an undated attached memo from Schneiders to Rafshoon, Jody Powell Papers, Box 46, Jimmy Carter Library.
133. Kellerman, 210.
134. Barrow, 176.
135. Patricia W. Ingraham and James L. Perry, "The Three Faces of Civil Service Reform," in *The Presidency and Domestic Policies of Jimmy Carter*, Eds. Herbert D. Rosenbaum and Alexej Ugrinsky (Westport, CT: Greenwood Press, 1994), 684.
136. *Congressional Quarterly Almanac*, 1977, Vol. XXXIII (Washington, DC: Congressional Quarterly Service, 1978), 818-24.
137. State of the Union Address, 1/19/78, *The Public Papers of the Presidents: Jimmy Carter, 1978* (Washington, DC: Government Printing Office, 1979).
138. Memo from Eizenstat to Carter, 2/21/78, Jody Powell Papers, Box 39, Jimmy Carter Library.
139. Message to the Congress on Federal Civil Service Reform, 3/2/78, *The Public Papers of the Presidents: Jimmy Carter, 1978* (Washington, DC: Government Printing Office, 1979).
140. The President's News Conference, opening statement, 4/25/78, *The Public Papers of the Presidents: Jimmy Carter, 1978* (Washington, DC: Government Printing Office, 1979).

141. The President's News Conference in Portland, Oregon, opening statement, 5/4/78, *The Public Papers of the Presidents: Jimmy Carter, 1978* (Washington, DC: Government Printing Office, 1979).
142. Memo from Rafshoon to Carter, 7/19/78, Jody Powell Papers, Box 46, Jimmy Carter Library.
143. Ingraham and Perry, 683-4.
144 Larry Berman, *The New American Presidency* (Boston: Little, Brown and Company, 1987), 297.
145. Emery and Emery, 459.

5

Reagan and Bush: Stagecraft and its Legacy

If image were truly everything during the 1980s, then Ronald Reagan was the right man in the White House at just the right time. Imagery and symbolism played a vital role in the communication strategy during the Reagan years, which coincided with the burgeoning of the cable television market. In addition to the major networks, radio, and the traditional print press, Reagan would find even more media outlets, aided by expanding technology, from which to speak to the American public than his predecessors had had in the White House. Reagan would enjoy one of the longest honeymoon periods with the press of any president upon entering office, helped in part by the failed assassination attempt in March 1981. However, the communication style of the Reagan presidency was tightly scripted and controlled, and while most of his aides would argue otherwise, he was considered by most accounts one of the least accessible presidents to the national press in the modern era. Nonetheless, Reagan often enjoyed favorable press coverage, and he left office with high approval ratings despite the Iran-Contra scandal during his second term. As Reagan's successor, George Bush and his one-term presidency represent an irony of presidential politics in terms of a communication strategy. Bush may have been the heir apparent to the Reagan system of governing, but he wanted to distance himself from the stagecraft style of communicating and the news management used so

179

successfully by his former boss. Despite providing much greater access to his administration and courting the national press with both formal and informal questioning opportunities, as well as attempting to provide a high level of substantive discussions on policy issues, Bush was not viewed as an effective communicator, and he would never enjoy the same kind of success in the realm of public relations. The imagery and vision provided to the public during the Reagan years would truly be a tough act for future presidents to follow.

REAGAN AND THE PRESS

In the era of modern presidents, Ronald Reagan was perhaps the most successful at controlling his image through the mass media, earning for himself the nickname the "Great Communicator," and for his administration the "Teflon" presidency. Despite his conservative policy views, Reagan also enjoyed fairly high public opinion ratings while in the White House, as his personal popularity with Americans often overshadowed their differing opinions with the President on both domestic and foreign policy issues. A former two-term governor of California, Reagan offered voters an appealing alternative during the 1980 presidential election. He differed from the embattled incumbent, Jimmy Carter, and he offered the hope of restoring credibility to the White House beyond the lingering Watergate scandal of the early 1970s. Having the amiable personality of a grandfather figure and the ability to speak directly to the American people through television seemed to boost Reagan's popularity and appeal. By 1980, American voters were longing "for a tall-in-the-saddle American," and candidate Reagan seemed made to order, perceived as a patriotic and "inspiring leader, someone who would establish broad, basic policies and philosophies to reverse trends they didn't like at home and restore American prestige abroad."[1]

Following his inauguration in 1981, Reagan and his advisors quickly began working to bring the "great presidential propaganda machine up to date, oiling its gears the better to manipulate the media." As a former actor, Reagan seemed a perfect match for the White House at just the right time, in control of a public relations apparatus that had been built up steadily since the Kennedy administration. The Reagan press team was quick to make the necessary changes in dealings with the press so as to portray the President in the most favorable light. As a result, the pressroom was remodeled with permanent seats, and seating assignments were handed out to reporters, with television correspondents earning the coveted seats in the front row. As an attempt to keep the press even more controlled, reporters were instructed to stay in their seats and raise their hands to ask questions. Reagan's advisors claimed that this tactic was to simply bring order to the event, but it also enabled Reagan to selectively call on the reporters of his choice. As if leaving no doubt as to the importance of the President's public image, the Reagan administration included more than 600 employees as part of the press and public relations offices—more than any other president had ever employed—whose job it was to maintain a positive image of Reagan in both the press and the public eye.[2]

One of the greatest successes of the Reagan administration was its ability to control the political agenda, as well as to set the terms of public debate. Seven basic news management principles were applied to news generated from the White House: plan ahead; stay on the offensive; control the flow of information; limit reporters' access to Reagan; talk about the issues the White House wants to talk about; speak in one voice; and repeat the same message many times. The ultimate goal was to always stay in control of a news story so as to avoid being in damage-control mode. This was often managed by delivering the "line of the day" to the press, which was developed each morning during a meeting and then passed throughout the administration. At each morning's press briefing, reporters were pointed in the right direction for a particular story, usually complete with great pictures.[3] Reagan's aides had realized that their greatest asset was the President himself, and they began using two basic tactics to get their message to the American people: public appearances would be carefully staged and controlled in order to emphasize his personality to television viewers, and he would be promoted as a can-do leader rather than by placing any emphasis on a political philosophy.[4]

The Reagan administration has been acknowledged for its "stunningly successful news management." According to *Washington Post* journalist David Broder, Reagan was one of the most difficult presidents to interview since he communicated mostly through anecdotes and sections of his prepared speeches: ". . . the President never thinks of himself as being offstage, at least when reporters are around." Broder also attributes Reagan's inaccessibility to the press, at least compared to other presidents, to the steady stream of inaccuracies he provided the press when talking about policies. But while Reagan's mistakes only seemed to enhance his charm to the public, the gaffes also made his communications staff even more protective. The policies and priorities of the Reagan press team included limiting direct access to the President, making news management a major priority for trusted White House aides and cabinet secretaries, and shutting down the flow of information from lower levels of the administration.[5]

The control of leaks to the press was also a top priority in the Reagan administration. By 1982, following some leaks from within the White House, Reagan issued an order forbidding anyone within the administration to speak to reporters on background information except for his closest advisors, who later talked him into a compromise on the order. But the damage had already been done, at least where the press was concerned, since lower staff members were intimidated about talking to the press, which cut off key news sources for Washington correspondents. Perhaps the most memorable administration news source of all, and the one which angered top White House officials the most, was Budget Director David Stockman, whose revelations about the 1981 economic plan appeared in the *Atlantic.* Stockman claimed that he had played with the budget numbers to make sure that they did not look like the "voodoo economics" that then-candidate George Bush had called the Reagan economic plan during the 1980 Republican presidential primaries. Other actions were taken to limit reporters' access to information, which included attempts to control information coming out of the Justice Department, the Pentagon, and the Central Intelligence Agency. Certain federal employees were also required to sign secrecy contracts upon employment.[6] The Reagan administration as a whole often showed contempt for the role of a free press in Washington, which was summed up by a sign that sat on Deputy Press Secretary Larry Speakes' desk that read: "You don't tell us how to stage the news, and we don't tell you how to cover it."[7]

Despite a less-than-friendly relationship with the press, the Reagan administration was still receiving fairly positive coverage, especially through the use of television. Reagan had established the "heroic presidency" in American culture through myths and values, while image control through carefully planned presentations and appearances allowed him to appear presidential. Through media control, Reagan conformed to the essential needs of television, making it "the instrument of governing."[8] For Reagan, the medium became the message; he would join Americans in their living rooms to discuss the state of the union, providing a strong sense of tradition through very simple talk. He also effectively governed through the daily news by granting the press many photo opportunities, thus allowing the White House to control images presented to the public. Most photo opportunities were granted with no chance for reporters to ask questions, and press briefings were held late in the day, giving networks little time to edit their stories before going on the air. During the first term, Reagan gave numerous interviews and special White House briefings from outside Washington, which would often result in the location distracting the audience and taking precedence in the story over what Reagan was actually saying. Reagan had the perfect television personality, which allowed him to govern through the medium; his simplified, idealistic view of the world played well on television, allowing him to directly relate to his audience, the American public.[9]

Radio provided an additional medium that allowed Reagan to talk directly to the American people about his policy agenda without any distortion by the national news media. Reagan had begun his entertainment career as a radio broadcaster during the 1930s and was a great admirer of Franklin Roosevelt, who had mastered the use of radio with his Fireside Chats. During the television age, presidents had only sporadically used radio addresses to present their policy agendas to the American public. But in April 1982, Reagan began what would become his weekly radio addresses to the nation. The five-minute broadcasts every Saturday would most often be used to reiterate policy issues that had been discussed in other public venues by both the President and his advisors during the week prior. Like his television appearances, Reagan would provide a simplified and straightforward version of Washington politics to his listeners, often appealing to his fellow Americans to aid him in his fight against the evils of the political world. Domestically, that evil was the corruption of big government in Washington that was usually perpetrated by the liberal big spenders in Congress, and internationally, it was the spread of communism around the globe. Reminding his listeners that they had sent him to Washington to fix the problems with the federal government, Reagan's position on policies during his radio addresses was always presented as the reasonable alternative to which the average American living outside the Beltway could relate.

In addition to the importance of television and radio to the Reagan communication strategy, cultivating positive coverage within the print press was also a priority, due to the influence within Washington of national dailies such as the *New York Times* and *Washington Post*. In early 1982, when the administration felt it was receiving unfair coverage from the *Post* on Reagan's New Federalism plan, a White House strategy was devised to educate the editors and reporters at the newspaper with a luncheon for *Post* executives, including Ben Bradlee and David Broder; a luncheon with *Post* key editorial staff, hosted by Stockman and Treasury Secretary Don Regan; and a two-hour briefing session with all *Post* reporters who would be covering any angle of the New Federalism plan. Speakes explained the plan to Chief of Staff James Baker:

> The *Washington Post* continues to cut to ribbons the Administration's "New Federalism" program. . . . With its impact on Congress and the Washington media, these daily curve balls are having a major

impact on our efforts to educate the editors and reporters. We *must*
begin a full-scale effort to educate. . . . This may sound like overkill,
but the influence of *The Post* is so great on decision makers in
Washington, it will be well worth the effort.[10]

Cultivating positive coverage in the local press across the nation
was also an important part of the Reagan communication strategy, which
allowed "out-of-town journalists an opportunity to communicate directly
with the President, as opposed to being forced to rely on the Washington
press corps for all their information."[11] The administration decided early in
1981 to continue the practice of holding White House luncheons for out-of-
town editors and publishers, a practice begun under Kennedy and also
used successfully by the Carter administration. Many newspaper executives encouraged Reagan's advisors to continue the practice, which they
found informative and helpful. The White House had recognized early on
the importance of "making an attempt to meet the needs of the non-
Washington media and not just doing things for the Washington press."[12]
Various departments within the White House Office of Communications
headed up the efforts to cater to the needs of the local news media, which
included granting telephone interviews with the President and other key
administration officials for local television and radio stations, holding news
briefings for out-of-town press representatives, and mailing fact sheets
about Reagan's policy initiatives to local news editors and publishers. The
use of a radio actuality service, similar to the ones used by the Nixon and
Carter administrations, was also continued. Local radio stations around the
country could call in to the White House on a toll-free number and receive
a ready-to-use news clip from the "White House Broadcasting Service," as
it was called during the Reagan years.[13] By June 1981, use of the actuality
service had increased so much, with up to 400 calls daily, that a request
was made for new equipment to meet the demand "to keep this valuable
information outlet in operation."[14] The service had been inaugurated on
March 17, 1981, and by June 12, 1981, it had received a total of 15,042 calls
from local radio stations; Speakes supported the request for new equipment for the actuality service, which he considered "a key part of our communications effort on behalf of the President."[15] Throughout Reagan's
eight years in office, the strategy to gain coverage for administration policies in the local press would become much more aggressive than with previous administrations. Realizing the impact and influence that the White
House would have on small news operations across the country, efforts
were made to contact radio stations directly to promote the actuality service, and to contact local newspapers with White House statements for
inclusion in their stories. Certain states would also be targeted if news out
of Washington was of particular interest to citizens in the area in order to
increase the coverage on the President's policies.[16]

Another holdover from the Nixon, Ford, and Carter administrations which was utilized by the Reagan White House was the use of a daily news summary. Prepared daily by the press office for top advisors such as Baker, Attorney General Ed Meese, and Deputy Chief of Staff Michael Deaver for their reading on the morning drive into the White House, the content, while much less extensive than during the Nixon years, included the major story of the day to "show the play given" in major news outlets such as the *Washington Post*, the *New York Times*, AP, UPI, and Reuters. As Speakes explained to Baker in a June 1981 memo, the news summary was "designed not only to give you the gist of the news, but to give you the twist that various news organizations put on it."[17] Information on press coverage of the administration was also included as part of the weekly update for the President that was developed in November 1981, which included a "Weekly Update" briefing book "to be delivered to the President *each Friday evening*, for his weekend reading" and a "Weekly Update" meeting each Monday "to discuss issues raised by review of the briefing book, along with a weekly selection of other issues that may merit special Presidential attention." A weekly press update from the Office of Communications was included in the briefing book, along with the President's weekly schedule, and summary status reports from the Office of Cabinet Administration and Office of Policy Development, the National Security Council staff, and the Office of Legislative Affairs.[18]

Reagan's advisors also worked hard to develop and maintain the coordination of press contacts, which was handled by the press office. Baker submitted guidelines to the entire White House staff in January 1983 to ensure that all press activities be coordinated and cleared through the press office in order to minimize any inaccuracies or competing viewpoints from administration officials. According to the guidelines, the press office

should remain the first stop for White House reporters seeking information about the President's policies and views. In order to maintain an open Presidency, it is essential that members of the senior staff also be willing to meet with reporters on a frequent basis. As the need arises, the communications department will designate key members of the staff who will be available to the press to answer questions on a specific subject. These "designated hitters" will be expected to take either telephone calls or be personally available to members of the press. . . . The communications department will seek to ensure key members of the staff are sufficiently available to the press, especially on major news stories, to provide an open and full flow of information to the press. . . . On-the-record interviews should be recognized as the best way to conduct most interviews with the press. . . . In keeping with the traditions of this Presidency, these guidelines should be carried out in a way that maintains an atmosphere of openness, professionalism and civility in relations with the White House press corps.[19]

Coordination of press contacts was also considered a vital aspect of the 1984 reelection campaign, with special attention provided to coordination between the White House and the Republican National Committee. Since both would be articulating administration policies and Reagan's views on various issues, Baker reminded senior staff in a May 1983 memo that "for obvious reasons, it is important that the administration be perceived as 'speaking with one voice.'"[20]

Several advisors have been credited with the successful news management techniques employed by the Reagan administration. Controlling the access to the President, as well as the flow of news coming out of the White House, was always a top priority. Speakes (who took charge following the assassination attempt in March 1981 that left Press Secretary James Brady seriously wounded), Deaver, and David Gergen, an assistant to the President in the Office of Communications, among others, made an art form of turning news management into a way of governing, creating coverage that was "extraordinarily positive."[21] Their ability to package the presidency allowed for the successful manipulation of the media, and enabled Reagan "to go over the heads of the media, directly to the American people."[22] Deaver, a top behind-the-scenes strategist, utilized Reagan's on-stage skills to provide nightly footage on the evening news broadcasts to show the President in a positive light, even though public opinion polls routinely showed that many Americans disagreed with him on policies. Showing Reagan against favorable backdrops on television sets gave the President the "ability to step through the television tubes and join Americans in their living rooms; and together they would watch these policies of Washington's and shake their heads—and occasionally their fists—at Washington's policymakers."[23]

Donald Regan, who served as Treasury Secretary during the first term and Chief of Staff during most of the second (before resigning), recalls the great emphasis placed on news control during the Reagan years, and he credits Deaver with successfully maintaining Reagan's public image. It was Deaver who scripted every line, scheduled every moment in public, and even provided Reagan with toe marks so as to stand in exactly the best light or at the best angle for the camera; he considered every public activity as "a one-minute or two-minute spot on the evening network news, or a picture on page one of the *Washington Post* or the *New York Times*, and conceived every Presidential appearance in terms of camera angles." Speakes was also involved in extensive preparation, like cautioning Reagan about certain reporters who were at a press conference and preparing for him the questions they might ask. The scripted part was always flawless, but walking back to the White House with reporters, Reagan often broke from character and answered questions that he should have ignored. Deaver and Speakes would then hurry off to control the damage of the day. Ultimately, Regan recalls, the administration knew that journalists did not agree with Reagan's policies, and they did not love him like many in the public did, so they "decided to control what they could not prevent," making the press dependent on them for stories: "[i]t was raised to the level of an art form under Baker, Meese, and Deaver . . . this organized feeding of the media produced predictable results . . . the creature grew bigger; and the bigger it grew, the hungrier it became."[24]

Early on, Deaver recognized the influential role that the press plays in presidential politics, yet he recalls that he never really felt comfortable in his role of being in charge of crafting Reagan's public persona, always waiting for the other shoe to drop: "Sooner or later, no matter how open you think you have been, or how friendly the relationship, the press will do a job on you." According to Deaver, there were two crucial things for someone in his position to survive in Washington: believing that what you are doing is more important than your personal needs, and not confusing the image with the reality. His job was to inspire support for the President personally, which was necessary to get support for Reagan's policies. And creating Reagan's public image through visuals was the most important aspect of Deaver's job: "You get only forty to eighty seconds on any given night on the network news, and unless you can find a visual that explains your message you can't make it stick."[25]

Speakes also recalls the importance of image building during his years in the Reagan White House. Everything he and other members of the press team did was geared towards television, forcing them to think and plan like television producers. One example of how the President made news was providing the networks with a photo opportunity of Reagan visiting a local school, then holding an education forum with Reagan making a newsworthy statement. Regardless of what Reagan said, the pictures would show him as a President who cared about children and their education. According to Speakes, the rule was, if there were no pictures for television at an event, then there was no coverage, no matter how important the news: "There was no need to have cameras in there and reporters trying to ask questions that would embarrass the President unless we could get our story on TV." Speakes also held great control over which cabinet members or White House advisors would appear on news talk shows. All decisions were based on audience size—

any top-rated shows, like *Good Morning America* on ABC or the *CBS Evening News with Dan Rather*, would get top White House officials, like Secretary of State George Shultz or Secretary of Defense Casper Weinberger, while *MacNeil-Lehrer* on PBS, while well-respected and watched by Washington insiders, was low on the list and got lower-tiered staffers due to its small audience size.[26]

For major policy initiatives, Speakes would develop a communications plan, which would include television appearances and other press contacts for various administration officials. On June 4, 1981, a communications plan was "designed to carry the momentum of the President's announcement on his tax program through the weekend," and it included proposed Friday morning appearances by Regan on NBC's *Today Show*, Baker on ABC's *Good Morning America*, and Meese on CBS's *Morning News*. Later that afternoon, Regan was to meet with 20 top economic reporters "to discuss details of the tax program and its impact," while Baker would meet with 20 political reporters, bureau chiefs, and columnists "to discuss the political and legislative aspects of the President's tax program." Finally, top administration officials were to appear on the Sunday morning news shows, including a proposed appearance by Baker on CBS's *Face the Nation*.[27] A similar communications plan was developed for Reagan's tax bill in August 1982. A week of activities included a marathon interview schedule for Lyn Nofziger, head of the Political Affairs Office, with eight major print outlets (including the *New York Times, Washington Post, Los Angeles Times, Baltimore Sun, Wall Street Journal, New York Daily News, Gannett,* and *Business Week*), television interviews with CBS, NBC, ABC, CNN, ITNA, and INN, and radio interviews with Mutual, AP Radio, UPI Audio, RKO General Broadcasting, and Voice of America. Other aspects of the plan included Sunday news shows, the development of "talking points for all spokesmen, including press office, reciting solid facts," and a "strong insert [on the tax bill in Reagan's midweek] Billings, Montana political speech. . . . The trip is a certain TV story, and a tax bill appeal is a certain lead."[28] As Speakes wrote in a memo to Baker about the major press events on the 1982 tax bill:

> I think scheduling and timing are critical to indicate buildup of momentum. I recommend the following: Wednesday—President devotes major portion of his political speech in Billings to the tax bill. Thursday—*Washington Times* interview. (This should be done Thursday rather than Friday because the *Times* has no weekend editions and publication would be held up until the following Monday). Friday—Press Q&A availability. (I recommend Friday because if done on the same day as the *Washington Times* interview, the points would be duplicated and would be a "wash"). Sunday—

Television speech (if we decide to go ahead). We will need after we
return here on Thursday to begin producing "converts." If we do not
have some crossovers by that time, the story will be old and momentum will be lost.[29]

Another key element of Speakes' job was preparing Reagan for
press conferences, which would always begin 10 to 14 days in advance
of the actual event. Speakes would get questions and answers from
departments and agencies about anticipated topics that would be coming from reporters. Reagan would spend the entire weekend before the
press conference rehearsing at Camp David. Speakes justified the large
amount of preparation time, saying that press conferences were "one of
the primary ways in which a President communicates directly with the
American people, and there's nothing wrong with trying to make sure
you're properly prepared for one." But not everything at each press conference could be anticipated. Thanks to the prepared seating chart that
was used for the press, Reagan once confidently called on a reporter
who was not in attendance that day. Speakes and his staff also routinely
identified reporters who would ask "softball" questions, and put them
on the right side of the room so Reagan could go there if he was being
battered by other reporters. But often the set-up became obvious.
Speakes even orchestrated the altering of the pressroom so that Reagan
could exit from doors right behind the podium, allowing him to avoid
the press afterwards and minimizing any of his famous off-the-cuff
gaffes.[30] Despite holding infrequent formal press conferences, much
coordination and planning by Speakes and other members of the White
House staff went into the events in an attempt to control both the atmosphere and outcome, as Speakes reported to Deaver in April 1983:

We have implemented a policy of having reporters raise their hands
and wait to be recognized. This has eliminated much of the raucous
atmosphere of past Presidential press conferences and has allowed
reporters to concentrate on the President's answers, rather than trying to outshout their colleagues. Also, this has eliminated confusion
over who the President has recognized. Additionally, we have made
certain that every reporter who is recognized is able to ask a follow-
up question. This allows for a more thorough treatment of the issue
they have raised. And we have rotated reporters in the front row of
chairs, so as to allow as many "regulars" as possible an opportunity
to be called upon.[31]

The administration also showed concern for "misconceptions"
about Reagan's policies that often appeared in the press. Following a
press conference in January 1982, Speakes suggested a plan to deal with

errors that were "creeping into newspaper columns, television news-casts, and weekend interview shows" since, if left unchallenged, they would "become fact in the public mind." He suggested a "research oper-ation to ferret out and promptly challenge each and every error," which would include sending a letter filled with facts to correct the error to the guilty reporter.[32] Misstatements by Reagan and the play they received in the press were, according to Gergen, a "sensitive issue" between the President and the press. Gergen wrote in a 1982 memo to Reagan that "the press is watching like hawks for any misstatements of facts. RR's good humor has helped a great deal on this front."[33] There were also efforts by the White House to prevent bad press coverage before it occurred. One example involved the dedication of the Vietnam Veterans Memorial in November 1982. Speakes told Baker in a memo that the

> press is rumbling a bit about the White House participation in the Vietnam Veterans Memorial dedication. Our participation—or lack of it—may end up as a story by the end of the week. I would suggest we send somebody such as Secretary Weinberger to the Saturday dedication. The highest ranking Administration official going now is the Acting Administrator of the VA.[34]

By mid-1982, Speakes was also concerned that Reagan's schedule did not permit enough time for the President to be thoroughly briefed about current issues for press conferences and other media events. Speakes urged Baker to reinstate a daily meeting time for the press team with Reagan, to keep the President abreast of key questions, thus "preparing him for unexpected questions." Speakes lamented:

> In three instances, my public statements—based on guidance—have not reflected the President's view and/or facts. . . . Five minutes a day in the Oval Office would save us a lot of headache and heartache—not to mention pain elsewhere.[35]

One of the most quoted examples of how the Reagan adminis-tration used the media to its advantage is from 1984, when CBS White House Correspondent Leslie Stahl attempted to show the American peo-ple what was behind the "Great Communicator" image of Ronald Reagan. In a tough, critical story that lasted nearly 5 minutes, an eternity for a 22-minute evening news broadcast, Stahl's biting commentary painted an accurate picture of how the White House was manipulating the press to get its message out, and how the networks were broadcast-ing a picture that did not match up with Reagan's policies:

How does Ronald Reagan use television? Brilliantly. He's been criticized as the rich man's president, but the TV pictures say it isn't so.
At seventy-three, Mr. Reagan could have an age problem. But the
TV pictures say it isn't so. Americans want to feel proud of their
country again, and of their president. And the TV pictures say you
can. The orchestration of television coverage absorbs the White
House. Their goal? To emphasize the President's greatest asset,
which, his aides say, is his personality. They provide pictures of his
looking like a leader. Confident, with his Marlboro Man walk. A
good family man. They also aim to erase the negatives. Mr. Reagan
tries to counter the memory of an unpopular issue with a carefully
chosen backdrop that actually contradicts the President's policy.
Look at the handicapped Olympics, or the opening ceremony of an
old-age home. No hint that he tried to cut the budgets for the dis-
abled and for federally subsidized housing for the elderly. . . .
Another technique for distancing the president from bad news—
have him disappear, as he did the day he pulled the Marines out of
Lebanon. . . . There are few visual reminders linking the President to
the tragic bombing of the Marine headquarters in Beirut. But two
days later, the invasion of Grenada succeeded, and the White House
offered television a variety of scenes associating the President with
the joy and triumph.

While Stahl was afraid of the negative reaction that the story might get
from the White House, especially the possibility that key administration
sources would suddenly dry up, just the opposite occurred. The White
House loved the piece, claiming that all the wonderful pictures used in
the story provided better public relations than money could buy, since
not many people heard Stahl's commentary about staging the news over
the patriotic backdrops and visuals provided by the many Reagan
clips.[36]
     Most scholars agree that the Reagan administration deserves
much credit for its successful use of the mass media as a governing tool,
but like many other presidents, Reagan did not cultivate a warm and
friendly relationship with many in the White House press corps. His
limited access to reporters, including few press conferences and many
staged events where questions were not allowed, frustrated members of
the press. They may have admired his courtesy and good humor, but
they found out quickly in 1981 that access would not be a high priority
for the Reagan administration.[37] The President and his advisors had discovered that, unlike earlier administrations that had closely monitored
the day-to-day stories in the press, the mass media would best serve
them as a public relations outlet. They also had at their disposal sophis-
ticated new polling techniques, funded by the Republican National
Committee, to keep track of the public's priorities, which helped

Reagan's advisors to prioritize the White House policy agenda.[38] Ultimately, Reagan proved a different kind of challenge than that with which Washington reporters had dealt in the past:

> The press found itself almost completely unable to deal with Reagan in the usual way. His mock humility, his seemingly total amiability, and his appearance as the big, rich, smiling daddy for whom the voters had yearned so long obliterated the fact that he meant to take the country back to the nineteenth century, if possible, and to impose on the most diverse nation in the world a uniformity of thought and belief that belonged to a nostalgic past where it had never actually existed.[39]

The cultivation of the image and the strategic use of the mass media had set a new standard for presidential communications that would challenge both of Reagan's immediate successors in the White House.

REAGAN'S PUBLIC ACTIVITIES

The Reagan oratory style, as well as the content of his speeches, has been well documented by both presidency and communication scholars. With his previous career experience as a radio announcer and actor, Reagan possessed the skills necessary to master the rhetorical presidency. He preferred delivering a speech that included "clarity, directness, and simplicity" in its message, and he "judged writing by how it would sound to the ear, not how it would appear to the eye in print." Reagan relied on public events to promote his core political ideology of conservatism, smaller government, deregulation, and free enterprise. Reagan was perhaps at his best when delivering a speech on foreign policy, which would include hard-line rhetoric against the Soviet Union; his anticommunist theme would continue in his public addresses even as U.S.-Soviet relations improved during the late 1980s.[40]

Also well noted as part of the Reagan style was his reliance on humor and anecdotes when delivering a speech. Humor helped to soften his conservative rhetoric, "promoting the image of a concerned citizen of goodwill, rather than an ideologue of the far right." The anecdotes and stories, which were rarely lacking in any speech, were Reagan's attempt to present himself as an average citizen who could relate to the everyday concerns of Americans.[41] However, while stories may have pleased his audiences, they often annoyed the press. By early 1982, the press began complaining about Reagan's continued use of stories from California, as Speakes was informed by a press relations staffer:

The press is getting tired of hearing the President refer to his days as Governor of California. He has been President for over a year now and has a record and experience in office. The California memories might have been valid early on, but their validity seems to be wearing off with the press. Plus, his recollections seem to contribute to the errors in stories.[42]

But even more famous than his penchant for storytelling was Reagan's use of political symbolism. He often discussed his conservative viewpoints on issues such as abortion, school prayer, and welfare reform in his public addresses, yet these often proved more symbolic than substantive since Congress, with a Democratically controlled House of Representatives, stood in the way of great change in these areas.[43] However, Reagan showed great skill at portraying right from wrong by relying on contemporary folklore to paint a picture of the American dream:

The symbols, stories, and heroes that Reagan uses to connect so deeply with us reveal our wish to be, as he has said, "a giant on the scene." The people of America in the first half of the 1980s gazed approvingly at his depiction of us as a pious, strong, aggressively competitive, winning society basking in the grace of a beneficent God. Reagan's speeches resemble the paintings of Norman Rockwell in their portrayal of simple, cleanly drawn, and unconfused men and women.[44]

Reagan's public addresses also relied on two types of metaphors to provide a connection to his audience. The first, path metaphors, represented a clear choice between policy alternatives as well as action by the President. Examples include: "I will not stand by and watch this great country destroy itself under mediocre leadership that drifts from one crisis to the next" and "the question is, are we simply going to go down the same path we've gone down before." The second, health metaphors, were some of Reagan's favorites: "Our federal government is overgrown and overweight. Indeed, it is time for our government to go on a diet," and "the 1981 budget hemorrhaged badly." Health metaphors represented positive images to which a public interested in health and fitness could relate. Americans seemed more than willing to follow Reagan on his rhetorical journeys since "he spoke our language, thereby gaining our acquiescence for the journey even though we were suspicious of some of his chosen vehicles."[45]

Like his recent predecessors in the White House, Reagan relied on the speechwriting department, which included six full-time writers, to prepare his public remarks. But unlike other presidents such as

Kennedy and Nixon, Reagan did not have much involvement in the initial speechwriting process. Also, high turnover occurred in the speechwriting department during the Reagan years. Speechwriters were never afforded great access to the President, but they were grateful for editorial remarks that Reagan would sometimes provide on rough drafts. In perfecting the final draft, Reagan was "passionately involved" in making sure the right message, stories and all, was conveyed.[46] In order to facilitate the White House staff of speechwriters, upon arrival in 1981, Reagan provided a packet of old speeches from his days as Governor of California so that his past style could be imitated.[47] But no matter how much preparation the staff put into Reagan's speeches, they could not prevent the President from committing one of his infamous gaffes, also known as "Reaganisms," like his contention that trees and other plants were responsible for most of the nation's air pollution. While he enjoyed reading, like many other presidents before him, Reagan would trust too much of what he read in sources such as *Reader's Digest* or local newspapers, and he would make statements based loosely on random facts that he retained.[48]

In addition to the six main speechwriters, dozens of researchers and secretaries within the Speechwriting Department aided in the development of Reagan's public remarks. A simple routine existed for the writing and editing of speeches, which would begin with head speechwriter Bently Elliott assigning a particular event to either himself or one of the other writers. (Policy did not dictate the assignment since none of the six writers specialized in a particular policy area as part of their job.) A first draft would be returned to Elliott for editing and then circulated within the White House and other relevant agencies for comments. The speech would then go back to the author, and a second draft would be produced and submitted to Reagan for his comments and approval. Ultimately, Reagan would have the final say on the content of each of his speeches. Since Reagan's speeches represented the "force of policy within the executive branch," the drafts, once circulated, often caused much contention between members of the administration, who wanted their particular objectives and programs highlighted. However, the speechwriters maintained control of the content of the speech, with Reagan's approval, and they would often serve the role as mediators between warring factions within the administration. Reagan enjoyed a good relationship with his speechwriters, whom he recognized as playing an important role in developing the voice of his administration.[49]

The amount of Reagan's public activities (see Table 5.1) shows an overall increase when compared to his television-age predecessors. Also, Reagan increased his public activities with each year of the first term, with the 1984 total reflecting his reelection campaign schedule.[50]

Table 5.1. Reagan—Public Activities.[51]

	1981	1982	1983	1984	1985	1986	1987	1988-89
National Addresses	7	7	5	4	6	12	6	3
Policy Addresses	16	23	29	26	18	13	25	18
Press Conferences	6	8	7	5	6	7	3	4
Radio Addresses	0	30	54	43	49	52	52	55
Brief Statements/Nonpolicy Remarks	149	185	198	202	170	144	198	192
Partisan Remarks/Campaign Speeches	18	34	19	85	21	45	7	47
Press Conferences with Foreign Dignitaries	0	0	0	0	1	0	0	0
Signing Ceremonies	14	26	16	20	10	14	16	25
Teleconference Remarks	0	1	3	0	1	1	1	0
Roundtable Discussions	0	0	1	2	0	0	1	0
Town Meetings/Q&A Sessions	4	23	29	12	11	8	9	10
Remarks to/Exchanges with Reporters	38	41	44	42	24	21	48	40
Total	252	378	405	441	317	317	366	394
Daily Average	0.73	1.04	1.11	1.21	0.87	0.87	1	1.02

The total number of yearly public activities would drop slightly during the second term, but overall, Reagan's public schedule remained fairly consistent throughout his eight years in office. While much of Reagan's public strategy focused on the use of television and radio, formal press conferences were not a top priority, as Reagan averaged only 0.5 per month during both terms, one of the lowest totals during the twentieth century. A change in public strategy did occur in 1982, as Reagan began his weekly radio addresses, a five-minute address each Saturday morning on selected topics. Also, in April 1982, Reagan began holding question and answer sessions with various groups across the nation, as well as "mini press availabilities" with the press for additional questioning sessions outside of regular press conferences and scheduled interviews.[52] By the end of 1983, Gergen reported to Speakes, Deaver, and Baker that he was convinced that regular and controlled opportunities for Reagan to meet with and answer questions from the press were an essential part of the President's press routine and a good strategic move: "[Reagan] did that in California with great success, and he has repeatedly demonstrated his effectiveness in these "mini" press availabilities and other forums while here."[53] In total, Reagan participated in 2,870 public activities during his eight years in office.

THE REAGAN POLICY AGENDA

From the time of his inauguration in January 1981, Reagan made economic policies a centerpiece of the presidential agenda. During the 1980 campaign, he had promised voters an economic recovery, as well as a tougher approach to U.S.-Soviet and other foreign relations. Reagan had also campaigned on a conservative social agenda, which included support for tough anticrime legislation and a school prayer amendment, and opposition to abortion and school busing for desegregation. But the social agenda would wait, as Reagan's first year in office was spent pushing through Congress his economic package that included $700 billion in budget cuts, $50 billion in tax cuts, and a 27 percent increase in the defense budget. While his early legislative success was "linked to his early strategic control of the agenda," other proposals later on would meet with much more resistance in Congress.[54] By 1982, Reagan was still discussing economic policies quite extensively and had begun to focus on his plans for a "New Federalism," where states would begin to take more responsibility for many social and other spending programs paid for by the federal government. However, Reagan would not experience a legislative victory in this policy area as he had with the economic package in 1981.[55] The Reagan agenda during the first term represents a compromise on the part of the administration. They made the decision to spend much of their political capital on the budget and tax cuts during the first year, which meant postponing other social issues like the school prayer amendment, a legislative ban on abortion, a line-item veto, a balanced budget amendment, and tuition tax credits for private schools. These issues did not become a priority until 1983, after Reagan had lost his initial opportunity for a honeymoon with Congress, and as the Republican majority in the Senate—won in 1980—began to shrink.[56] By the second term, foreign policy dominated more of the administration's attention as it focused on U.S.-Soviet relations, on stopping the spread of communism in Central America—most notably in Nicaragua—and on international trade issues. Domestic economic issues, however, still remained high on the Reagan policy agenda, including the President's public campaigns for tax reform, deficit reduction, and a reform of the budget process, including his pleas for a constitutional amendment for both a balanced budget and a line-item veto.

When looking at the Reagan policy agenda presented in his major public addresses (see Table 5.2), foreign policy and economic issues clearly appear to have been the top priority. Domestic Fiscal and Monetary policies dominated Reagan's speeches during 1981, as he aggressively pursued the various aspects of his economic recovery package. By 1982, while the economy was still a top concern of the administration, a shift began to occur with public discussions of Diplomatic/Military policies increasing greatly from the previous year. Then, in 1983 and 1984, the Diplomatic/Military policy category ranked first, as Reagan addressed the issues of U.S.-Soviet relations, including arms reduction talks and the Strategic Defense Initiative, as well as other foreign policy concerns in the Middle East and the U.S. military invasion of Grenada. The Diplomatic/Military category would also rank first in each of the four remaining years, as Mikhail Gorbachev came to power in the Soviet Union and summit talks between the two nations increased. Reagan also used many of his public appearances to discuss the need for U.S. support of the "Freedom Fighters" in Nicaragua who were attempting to overthrow a communist-backed regime. Economic issues remained a close second in priority for Reagan's addresses in 1985, as he pushed for continued economic growth and tax reform, and in 1987, with many public discussions on deficit reduction and budget reform. Even though several domestic issues, such as reforming Social Security and welfare, garnered much attention from the administration on Capitol Hill, these issues did not take center stage in Reagan's public addresses. Beyond statements in his State of the Union addresses or an occasional radio address on a given domestic issue, most major public addresses during the first term dealt with foreign or economic issues.

Table 5.2. Reagan's Public Agenda (Major Public Addresses).[57]

	1981	1982	1983	1984	1985	1986	1987	1988-89
Domestic								
Education	22 - 1%	76 - 2%	478 - 10%	151 - 5%	109 - 4%	24 - <1%	88 - 2%	47 - 1%
Health Care	6 - <1%	7 - <1%	189 - 4%	13 - <1%	6 - <1%	1 - <1%	101 - 3%	10 - <1%
Welfare/Entitlements	115 - 7%	46 - 1%	58 - 1%	22 - <1%	26 - <1%	53 - 2%	130 - 3%	56 - 2%
Anticrime	122 - 7%	75 - 2%	132 - 3%	269 - 9%	53 - 2%	110 - 3%	52 - 1%	304 - 9%
Political Reform	21 - 1%	172 - 5%	72 - 1%	171 - 6%	45 - 2%	48 - 1%	116 - 3%	25 - 1%
Science/Technology/ Transportation	14 - <1%	48 - 1%	38 - <1%	133 - 5%	31 - 1%	8 - <1%	50 - 1%	43 - 1%
Environment/Energy/ Land Management	13 - <1%	5 - <1%	121 - 2%	34 - 1%	3 - <1%	48 - 1%	0 - 0%	0 - 0%
Defense	49 - 3%	92 - 3%	281 - 6%	107 - 4%	197 - 7%	312 - 9%	98 - 3%	111 - 3%
International								
Diplomatic/Military	196 - 11%	1040 - 31%	1907 - 38%	832 - 29%	1105 - 38%	1664 - 48%	1370 - 35%	1902 - 55%
Trade/Economic	215 - 13%	265 - 8%	297 - 6%	218 - 7%	176 - 6%	447 - 13%	627 - 16%	488 - 14%
Economic								
Domestic Fiscal/ Monetary	790 - 46%	1301 - 38%	764 - 15%	512 - 18%	1068 - 36%	667 - 19%	1040 - 27%	388 - 11%
Unemployment/Jobs	143 - 8%	270 - 8%	635 - 13%	455 - 16%	124 - 4%	65 - 2%	195 - 5%	80 - 2%
Total	N = 1706	N = 3397	N = 4972	N = 2917	N = 2943	N = 3447	N = 3867	N = 3454

THE FIRST TIER:
SOCIAL SECURITY REFORM OF 1982-1983

The Issue and White House Strategy

From early on in his political career, social security had been a touchy political issue for Reagan, described as being "more tar baby than Teflon." Reagan had spoken publicly as early as 1964 about the possibility of social security becoming a voluntary system, and he made the suggestion again during his bid for the Republican presidential nomination in 1976. While conservatives had long supported the idea, Gerald Ford's campaign staff used the issue against Reagan during the primaries, scaring many elderly voters about Reagan's desire to cut their benefits. During the 1980 campaign, Reagan was routinely advised to offer support for continuing social security programs, but to otherwise avoid the politically explosive issue.[58] After his election, the Reagan transition team drafted a proposal to deal with social security and its impending financial crisis. But Reagan was not particularly interested in the policy, and advisors decided not to make the issue a high priority in the administration during the early months of 1981, choosing instead to focus on budget and tax cuts.[59]

However, confident from the congressional success over the budget plan, the administration announced in May 1981 its support for cuts in social security so as to save the program. As a result, the administration suffered one of its worst defeats, with the Senate rejecting any cuts in a 96-0 vote. In an attempt to save political face, the administration then began to talk with members of both parties about the "healthy diversity" in alternatives for saving social security.[60] On the issue of social security, Reagan also faced intense political pressure from senior citizens' groups who supported many of Reagan's policies in other areas but fought hard against any cuts to their benefits.[61] Yet, as partisan bickering on the issue continued throughout 1981, Reagan appointed a National Commission on Social Security Reform at the end of the year in an attempt to take the issue off the political agenda.[62] As a result, not only was Congress able to mostly skirt the issue in 1982, the issue of entitlements in general was barely mentioned by Reagan for the entire year (see Table 5.2). Despite the magnitude of the issue—especially given its portion in the national budget—Reagan did not give a single address on social security in 1982, and when he did mention the issue, it was only to reassure the public that he did not intend to support cuts in funding.

Finally, by early 1983, the Commission had agreed on recommendations, and Congress then swiftly acted to save social security from insolvency. The bipartisan agreement that included increasing payroll taxes and taxing the benefits of high-income recipients ended the nearly two-year battle that had begun in 1981 when Congressional Democrats accused the Reagan administration of "trying to balance the budget at the expense of the elderly."[63] Reagan signed the bill at a large White House ceremony on April 20, 1983, and despite the earlier defeat in the Senate over proposed cuts, the Reagan press team promoted the event as the culmination of the President's campaign to preserve the social security system. The "Social Security Media Plan" outlined six groups to which the administration would target its message: the general public, Republican and administration supporters, out-of-town press and editors, columnists, aging groups, and business groups. The social security "line of the day" emphasized how the bill was

> . . . a balanced package based on reforms, not exorbitant tax increases or benefit cuts; demonstrates Presidential leadership and the ability of the President to work with Congress in a bipartisan way on a major issue; and, [was] fair to workers, employers, and beneficiaries.[64]

Following the bipartisan agreement, Reagan never seriously returned to the issue, insisting that social security not be a part of any future discussions on balancing the budget. Throughout his remaining years in the White House, Reagan would remain opposed to any cuts in social security, instead sitting by and watching the cost of the program continue to grow.[65]

Press Coverage

Despite Reagan's reluctance to talk about social security, the *New York Times* provided fairly extensive coverage of the issue between January 1982 and April 1983, with a news item appearing, on average, every two out of five days. Not surprisingly, the White House generated the least amount of stories with only 13 percent of the coverage; Congress generated the most with 50 percent, followed by interest groups with 37 percent (see Table 5.3). Of the news items generated by presidential activity, the tone was mixed, with the numbers fairly distributed over the four categories (see Table 5.4). Most news stories were positive, giving extensive coverage to Reagan's views when he did express them. Only one editorial appeared on Reagan's plans for social security, which was negative. Overall, the *Times* coverage of the issue seemed to reflect the fact that the key political participants, namely the President and Congress, chose to rely on a bipartisan commission for a solution. Therefore, the

Table 5.3. Amount and Type of *New York Times* Coverage of Social
Security Reform (January 1982-April 1983).

	White House	Congress	Interest Group/Other
News Story	17	89	52
News Analysis	6	1	4
Column	1	3	12
Editorial	1	5	4
Total	25 - (13%)	98 - (50%)	72 - (37%)

Table 5.4. Tone of *New York Times* Coverage of Presidential
Activities on Social Security Reform (January 1982-April 1983).

	Positive	Negative	Balanced/Mixed	Neutral
News Story	7	1	4	5
News Analysis	0	2	3	1
Column	0	0	1	0
Editorial	0	1	0	0
Total	7	4	8	6

usual back-and-forth between the White House and Capitol Hill was not
occurring, disrupting the usual pattern for covering political news in
Washington.

THE SECOND TIER: STUDENT AID CUTS IN 1982

The Issue and White House Strategy

More than likely, Reagan will not be remembered as the most pro-edu-
cation president ever to occupy the White House. Reagan had promised
to abolish the Department of Education during the 1980 campaign,
which had only just been established under the Carter administration.
However, the department would remain intact, despite Reagan's

promise and his desire to remove education from his list of agenda priorities. After several national reports emerged during the early 1980s about the decline in quality of American education, Reagan realized that taking a hard-line stance on federal budget cuts for education programs would send the wrong message to the public.[66] In 1983, with polls showing a two-to-one disapproval of Reagan's proposed cuts to federal student aid programs, the White House began a "communication offensive" designed to promote American excellence in education, merit pay for teachers, and classroom discipline. Reagan would make approximately 25 appearances to discuss education during the year, most of them Deaver-style photo opportunities, where he often repeated the same message to those in attendance. Despite some unfavorable coverage from the White House press corps, according to Deaver, the focus of the public relations blitz was the local network newscasts, which gave favorable coverage on education. As a result, by the end of 1983, the public opinion polls had reversed to a two-to-one favorable rating for the President.[67]

However, it was Reagan's proposal to cut federal aid to students, including student loans, which had prompted the negative polling numbers. In 1981, Congress had approved the Reagan administration's proposals to trim federal spending for college student assistance as part of the budget package. But by 1982, the administration wanted further cuts, which prompted an ongoing battle with Congress, since many members were not willing to cut the politically popular programs. Under the Reagan proposal in 1982, all graduate and professional students would lose eligibility for Guaranteed Student Loans, the income requirement for family eligibility would be raised, and Pell grants for low-income students would be drastically cut. Initially, Reagan vetoed legislation that included much more funding than he had wanted, calling the appropriations bill a "budget buster." Congress, however, overrode the veto to finally reject the President's proposed cuts, approving funding for the 1983-1984 school year in September without cutting the student aid budget and restoring eligibility for many veterans that had been cut in 1981. Throughout 1982, Congress had been deluged with lobbying efforts—especially from colleges, students and parents—to save student loans.[68] And despite Reagan's insistence on lowering the federal budget for student aid, he rarely spoke publicly about his proposal, with the exception of one radio address in April in which he devoted a little more than half the speech (only about three minutes) to the proposed cuts—an attempt to reassure listeners that the cuts would not be drastic and that they were necessary to streamline the program.[69]

Press Coverage

Reagan's proposed cuts to student aid in 1982 were not a top priority on the President's public agenda, and as a result, they did not receive much coverage in the *New York Times*. Between January and October 1982, a total of 57 news items appeared on the issue, an average of roughly one story every five days. Most stories did not appear until Congress began debating the issue during the summer and early fall. However, interest group activities and other political participants generated the most coverage with 54 percent, compared to 30 percent for Congress and 16 percent for presidential activities (see Table 5.5). Many stories in the *Times* focused on profiles of middle-class families with college-aged children who would be adversely affected by the cuts in the Reagan proposal. While only nine news items appeared in the *Times* that were generated by the White House, none was positive and most were negative (see Table 5.6), including two harshly-worded editorials taking the Reagan administration to task for its short-sighted education policies.

Bush and the Press

The successful communication strategy of the Reagan years would be a tough act to follow for future presidents, especially for George Bush. The heir apparent to the Reagan system of governing, Bush instead sought to distance himself from the staged photo opportunities and "line of the day" news management style that the Reagan administration had raised to an art form. Bush, the ultimate Washington insider, courted the press as members of the political elite. He afforded the press great access to not only himself, but to his advisors as well, and he held many informal discussions with reporters. The Bush administration did not want the reputation of being a "symbolic presidency" that relied on the "stagecraft" developed during the Reagan years. Bush maintained a high level of public discussion of issues, but he relied on an overall lower public profile.[70] For example, he increased the number of press conferences immediately upon taking office, but since his advisors believed that he did not perform well on television, they became informal and often impromptu early morning events with little news value. This meant that many news organizations did not provide coverage, yet the press could not complain about Bush being inaccessible.[71]

Bush had wanted to develop a better relationship with the press, especially in providing more real interaction between himself and the White House press corps. He courted members of the press, seeking a "mutually beneficial relationship" with several journalists.

Table 5.5. Amount and Type of *New York Times* Coverage of Proposed Student Aid Cuts (January 1982-October 1982).

	White House	Congress	Interest Group/Other
News Story	3	16	27
News Analysis	1	1	1
Column	3	0	3
Editorial	2	0	0
Total	9 - (16%)	17 - (30%)	31 - (54%)

Table 5.6. Tone of *New York Times* Coverage of Presidential Activities on Proposed Student Aid Cuts (January 1982-October 1982).

	Positive	Negative	Balanced/Mixed	Neutral
News Story	0	2	0	1
News Analysis	0	1	0	0
Column	0	1	2	0
Editorial	0	1	1	0
Total	0	5	3	1

> It is evident that by making himself accessible, drawing journalists into his network of personal relationships and speaking frankly to them, Bush hoped in the early days of his presidency to neutralize potential media hostility and to enhance thereby his governing capability.[72]

Bush did not enter the White House with the intention of continuing the image making that had occurred during the Reagan years. While a primary goal of the Reagan administration was to get their president on the evening news, Bush emphasized "continuity, conciliation and compromise," which did not make for exciting pictures on television. "There was to be no equivalent of Michael Deaver to take charge of Bush's image; there would not be a theme of the week and presidential trips would not be tailored to meet the requirements of nightly television news broadcasts."[73] However, while Bush held many more press conferences than Reagan did, and met with reporters regularly on an informal basis, he did not use these events as a means to advance his own policy agenda to the American public. Instead, he simply allowed reporters to ask him questions: "Bush made little connection between his public relations and his policy initiatives. . . . He talked *to* the press, not *over* it."[74]

Much of Bush's communication strategy focused on his use of press conferences. Most were aimed at meeting the needs of newspapers—and not the network news—unlike during the Reagan years. Bush relied on numerous informal, last-minute press sessions in an attempt to create an open and friendly presidency. This strategy reflected what Bush considered to be his greatest asset, which was "face-to-face, personal contact" with reporters. What the strategy lacked, however, was an overall message to the American public about the Bush policy agenda.[75] The Bush administration continued to rely on the Office of Communications in relating information to members of the press from around the country in the form of press releases, background information, radio actualities, and satellite feeds. The news media had come to rely on this information over the years in helping them do their job, and the "mutually beneficial aspects of the office helped to ensure the office's institutionalization."[76] Bush also continued to rely on the coverage provided by non-Washington members of the press as a means to communicate, a tradition that had begun during the Kennedy years and a strategy upon which every president since (including Clinton) has relied to get his message out to the American public.[77]

In spite of Bush's attempts at an open and friendly relationship with the press, news coverage during the Gulf War in 1991 was closely monitored and tightly controlled by the government. Only Pentagon-approved pool reporters were allowed to report on action, and stories were subject to military censorship. Most coverage consisted merely of official military briefings and technological light shows that highlighted night bombings. Unlike the experience during Vietnam, when the American press brought the fighting into the living rooms of Americans on a nightly basis via the network news, the press, especially television, maintained the visual image of American military strength until Iraq surrendered. "Persian Gulf coverage was a classic example of government and the media collaborating to manipulate popular passions and shape our nation's political discourse."[78] This also helped Bush achieve high public approval ratings during the conflict, some as high as 90 percent in February 1991 for approval of job performance. However, that number would plummet to about 40 percent over the next 12 months as an economic recession took hold.[79]

The recession, while not the worst or the longest that Americans had ever endured, would nonetheless hurt Bush's presidency in a vari-

ety of ways. First, the news media covered the recession extensively during the 1992 presidential campaign, often showing the current administration and its domestic policies, or lack thereof, as a big part of the
problem. Second, a tighter economic climate for the news media as an
industry made for tougher competition, which resulted in more critical
coverage of the Bush administration. Third, the news media, particularly
the White House press corps, was still recovering from the "PR
machine" and its manipulations during the Reagan era.[80] As a result,
Bush was the unfortunate recipient of negative coverage, especially during his reelection bid, and he often showed his impatience and testiness
with the press: "[Bush devoured] everything printed and broadcast
about him and [seemed] to take criticism personally."[81] Critical stories
about members of his family, like stories about his son Neal's involvement in the Savings and Loan banking scandal, upset Bush more than
any other coverage. According to C. Boyden Gray, counsel to Bush:

> . . . I think he was increasingly disenchanted with the hammering he
> and his family were getting. He knew that public scrutiny and pub-
> lic criticism came with the territory and didn't complain about it
> publicly, but he would complain to me privately. His bitterness
> about the press may have taken some of the fun out of the job for
> him.[82]

Bush's public image also posed challenges for developing an
effective communication strategy. He had two images to live down once
he became president. The first, which emerged during his victory over
Massachusetts Governor Michael Dukakis during the 1988 campaign,
was that of a "mud-slinging, whining, nasty man who had used negative advertising to downgrade his opponent." Bush had to deal with the
"wimp" image that had manifested itself in the press, and he countered
with a tough, aggressive campaign style. The second was to convince the
American public that while he had been the "invisible man" of the
Reagan administration, a loyal vice president who had escaped public
scrutiny over Iran-Contra, he was up to the task of providing strong
American leadership for what was being called "the new world order."[83]

In 1988, Bush had campaigned on a theme of maintaining continuity with the Reagan years, but he did move away from some of the
Reagan themes by talking about such issues as improving education and
the environment. He also made his infamous "read my lips, no new
taxes" promise during the campaign, which he would break when he
signed the tax compromise bill in 1990. While president, Bush's image
was hurt by his lack of a clear vision for the country, something that
Reagan had possessed. Instead, Bush presented the image of "steward-

ship of competence without a compass," which left him unable to relate to the strong values of many of his conservative backers. Bush was often criticized in the press for "either lacking such a vision, failing to articulate one effectively, or both."[84] But his trouble with "the vision thing" and his failure to articulate a clear message and vision to the American people "raised the art of empty rhetoric to new heights." By 1992, Bush was viewed as out of touch with average Americans, especially those affected by the 1991 recession, which hurt him in his reelection bid. The image of a strong, competent leader (which is what emerged during the Gulf War) never seemed to consistently appear during the Bush years.[85] And this made for repeated criticisms by the press, as noted by James Reston:

> I had thought I knew George Bush fairly well, but I didn't recognize his warrior pose. I longed for years that some gentleman president would come along and set an example of calm thinking and honest talking, and I felt that George Bush was precisely that sort of man. . . . But something happened to him on his way to the White House. He campaigned like Richard Nixon and talked like Lyndon Johnson, saying publicly that Saddam Hussein was worse than Hitler, and vowing publicly to "kick him in the ass." And when it was said that maybe he was a bit of a wimp, he disproved it by plunging into two wars in his first two years in office.[86]

Ultimately, the Bush administration viewed the press differently than Reagan had, and this affected the relationship. While the news media was a vehicle through which Reagan excelled at communicating, Bush's advisors considered the press more of a hindrance. This view is evident in Press Secretary Marlin Fitzwater's description of the press in his memoirs:

> The press corps is an unwanted appendage, like a cocklebur that attaches to your pants leg. For the White House staff, it's a problem to be managed, a block of people to be moved around like a checker—brought into the Oval Office at the top of each meeting, ushered into the Rose Garden to witness a bill signing, and wedged into a maze of hallways that can't be freely entered.[87]

Other members of the administration have also stated their opinions about how unfairly Bush was treated by the press. According to former Agriculture Secretary and Republican National Committee Chairman Clayton Yeutter, Bush may never receive the recognition he deserves for his accomplishments while in the White House:

. . . the Bush administration accomplished much more than most people realize, but the media never focused on anything positive related to the President. The media biases in recent years were the worst I have ever seen, as some of the polls indicate. History, too, may well overlook the positive accomplishment and focus on President Bush's mistakes.[88]

In an interview after he left office, Bush stated that the thing that he missed least about Washington was dealing with the press:

By that I mean the Washington, inside-the-Beltway press. I don't say that bitterly, just as a matter of fact. They do their thing, now I'm free to do mine. I have no desire to get back into the media game, to interact with the press. And I don't miss the political infighting, either. Not one bit.

He also discussed his biggest disappointments as president, which related in part to his style of communicating:

There were several, foreign and domestic. But I think my biggest was that I wasn't articulate enough to overcome the politically-driven, press-driven perception that the economy in 1992 was in a deep recession. In the third quarter of '92, and indeed the beginning of the fourth quarter, during the campaign, things were going better. But when I tried to point that out, the perception was that I was totally out of touch. I just wasn't a good enough communicator. If [Reagan] had been in my place, he'd have cut through the opposition fog that everything was going to hell. He'd say, "Wait a minute, here are the facts, the reality." And the reality was that the recession had bottomed out in 1991, and the economy had grown not just by the 2.7 percent I claimed for the third quarter, but by 3.4 percent. And in the fourth quarter, it grew at a very robust 5.8 percent—not exactly a recession . . . but I failed as a communicator.[89]

Overall, Bush's communication strategy was not effective, and it contributed, at least in part, to his loss of the presidency to Clinton in 1992. And like Ford and Carter, Bush's attempts at an open administration and good relationships with the press did not guarantee positive, or even fair, coverage. This, according to Fitzwater, frustrated Bush tremendously:

. . . to the last day of his administration, [Bush] could not understand how the press could be so bad to him when he had been so good to them. He held 280 press conferences, at least twenty minutes long and open to questions on any subject, and had been generally more accessible than any president in modern history. He had them over to the White House for drinks, to his Kennebunkport home for hot dogs, and to the Oval Office for chats.[90]

The prevailing irony of the Bush years seems to suggest that, while Reagan's successor received the backlash from the image manipulation by the "Great Communicator," reversing course in communication strategy did not please the press either. Perhaps the timing and style of the Bush presidency presented a no-win situation for successful White House communications, no matter what the strategy.

BUSH'S PUBLIC ACTIVITIES

While more accessible to the press and public than Reagan, Bush was reluctant to speak directly to the American public as often as Reagan did, and this hurt his ability to lead. Bush also had the ability to see the complexity of many issues, particularly in the domestic arena, while Reagan viewed things in black and white, as right or wrong, which made for a clearer, more concise message to Americans. Also, while Reagan had seen himself as an "agent of change," Bush represented a "guardianship" president: "Bush's reluctance to mount the bully pulpit was a matter of aptitude and inclination. Even the sturdiest of Bush loyalists readily concede that he lacked the exceptional talent for communication possessed by his predecessor."[91] While the comparisons to Reagan in the area of public speaking were inevitable, Bush was never able to live up to that standard, no matter how good his public performances. Even his closest advisors, like Gray, admitted this: "President Bush could be a very good speaker, but he was no Ronald Reagan. Very few people are, will be, or have been as effective as Reagan."[92]

The speechwriting process in the Bush White House included five full-time writers, a dozen researchers, and several outside consultants. Tony Snow, a writer for the *Washington Times*, became one of Bush's favorite writers. (Speeches by others had rarely impressed Bush, and turnover was high in the speech office before Snow arrived.) While Bush usually provided substantive speeches, the style was often lacking, due in part to the President's reluctance to practice his delivery. Off-the-cuff remarks by Bush were also not his strong suit since "Bush had little training in public speaking . . . [and] when he spoke extemporaneously, he often mangles syntax and used incredibly cryptic phrases obviously assuming the audience could read his mind or that they possessed the same special knowledge he did."[93]

While Bush participated in a lot of public activities, he was "more comfortable building consensus one-on-one, behind closed doors."[94] Nonetheless, his public activities show a slight increase from the totals of the Reagan years (see Table 5.7). Bush relied extensively on press conferences, and by 1991, he also began to hold formal press conferences with foreign dignitaries. Bush also gave more policy addresses than Reagan, with a dramatic increase in these appearances during his reelection campaign in 1992. A slight increase in the total number of public activities occurred in 1991, especially in national addresses, due mostly to U.S. military involvement in the Persian Gulf. And like most incumbent presidents, Bush also campaigned extensively for reelection. During 1992, one of the newer strategies that he relied on was townhall meetings and roundtable discussions. He also gave 13 radio addresses in 1992, after only giving a total of five in the three years prior to 1992. Overall, Bush participated in a total of 1,992 public activities during the four years between January 20, 1989 and January 20, 1993.

THE BUSH POLICY AGENDA

During the 1988 campaign, Bush had promised an extensive domestic agenda, including initiatives and programs for education, the environment, crime control, and banking reform. But the situation of a

Table 5.7. Bush-Public Activities.[95]

	1989	1990	1991	1992-93
National Addresses	6	4	12	5
Policy Addresses	22	20	17	20
Press Conferences	28	28	27	13
Radio Addresses	0	0	5	13
Brief Statements/Nonpolicy Remarks	254	223	256	256
Partisan Remarks/Campaign Speeches	21	76	15	149
Press Conferences with Foreign Dignitaries	3	8	20	15
Signing Ceremonies	28	27	23	17
Teleconference Remarks	0	0	12	5
Roundtable Discussions	0	0	0	6
Town Meetings/Q&A Sessions	13	13	5	27
Remarks to Exchanges with Reporters	52	82	109	57
Total	427	481	501	583
Daily Average	1.23	1.32	1.37	1.51

Democratic Congress, as well as his promise for no new taxes—which meant limited spending opportunities given the size of the national budget deficit—left little opportunity to achieve substantial policy changes. The Bush administration believed that major changes to policies were not necessary, but simply intended to focus on certain areas. The public, however, viewed this as a lack of momentum on behalf of the president's agenda. Nothing dominated the political agenda during the Bush years since the President sought only incremental changes to policies that had already been changed during the Reagan years. "The administration's policy agenda in its first year seemed to be reactive rather than strategic. It reflected the president's style, which was to be a problem solver rather than a visionary, a doer rather than a dreamer."[96]

Like many other presidents before him, Bush's public agenda focused more often on international issues than any other type (see Table 5.8). During each of his four years in office, the Diplomatic/Military category greatly outpaced all other categories during his major public addresses. Given Bush's experience in the international arena prior to winning the presidency, as well as the major international events while Bush was president (pro-democracy events in Tiananmen Square in China, the fall of the Berlin Wall, the U.S. invasion of Panama, the collapse of the Soviet Union, and the Gulf War), these figures are not surprising. During each year except 1989, the International Trade/Economic category ranked second, since Bush often talked about NAFTA, GATT, and international economic development around the globe. Economic issues were not high on Bush's public priority list until his 1992 campaign for reelection. (Bush often responded to claims made by other candidates about economic issues.) Bush also occasionally focused on domestic issues during his public addresses. For example, the Anticrime category ranked second in 1989, as Bush promoted his proposals to reduce crime and fight drug abuse. Education was also a consistent domestic issue that Bush discussed, but in comparison to the percentages for the Diplomatic/Military category—particularly during 1990 and 1991—the numbers for domestic issues are relatively low. During the campaign year of 1992, the Diplomatic/Military category was at its lowest for Bush, and more economic and domestic issues received attention in his major public addresses, which represents the most evenly distributed year for policies across all categories.

Table 5.8. Bush's Public Agenda (Major Public Addresses).[97]

	1989	1990	1991	1992-93
Domestic				
Education	214 - 7%	61 - 2%	266 - 11%	116 - 4%
Health Care	20 - 1%	5 - <1%	10 - <1%	112 - 4%
Welfare/Entitlements	90 - 3%	47 - 2%	22 - 1%	78 - 3%
Anticrime	582 - 19%	58 - 2%	120 - 5%	133 - 5%
Political Reform	82 - 3%	7 - <1%	102 - 4%	252 - 9%
Science/Technology/ Transportation	9 - <1%	72 - 3%	37 - 1%	13 - <1%
Environment/Energy/ Land Management	82 - 3%	42 - 1%	9 - <1%	17 - 1%
Defense	99 - 3%	29 - 1%	102 - 4%	110 - 4%
International				
Diplomatic/Military	1122 - 37%	1690 - 59%	1339 - 53%	789 - 29%
Trade/Economic	337 - 11%	501 - 18%	299 - 12%	504 - 19%
Economic				
Domestic Fiscal/Monetary	233 - 8%	282 - 10%	144 - 6%	423 - 16%
Unemployment/Jobs	189 - 6%	58 - 2%	58 - 2%	147 - 5%
Total	N = 3059	N = 2852	N = 2508	N = 2694

THE FIRST TIER: THE EDUCATION EXCELLENCE ACT

The Issue and White House Strategy

While Bush may have campaigned on the promise of becoming "the education president," many doubted any president's ability to have much impact, beyond that of the bully pulpit, on a policy that is so dominated by state and local decisions. Nonetheless, Bush began addressing educational issues immediately after becoming president. During an address to Congress just weeks after taking office, Bush seemed to place the issue high on his legislative priority list:

> When some of our students actually have trouble locating America on a map of the world, it is time for us to map a new approach to education. We must reward excellence and cut through bureaucracy. We must help schools that need help the most. We must give choice to parents, students, teachers, and principals; and we must hold all concerned accountable. In education, we cannot tolerate mediocrity.

I want to cut that dropout rate and make America a more literate
nation, because what it really comes down to is this: The longer our
graduation lines are today, the shorter our unemployment lines will
be tomorrow.[98]

He continued with a similar theme during a public address in March
1989, stating that America needed to maintain its competitive edge in
the global marketplace with a superior educational system:

All of you have heard me say that I intend to be the "Education
President." And let me say now, I can't think of any issue that is
larger or more far-ranging in its impact than the education of our
young people. Think about the great issues of the day. Do we want
to talk about America's place in the world? Then we'd better think
about education. Do we want to talk about competitiveness and how
we can improve it? Again, we'd better think about education. . . .
Education is long-range planning at its best. It's a solution for the
next century, for problems we haven't even begun to recognize.[99]

In April 1989, Bush sent a proposed Educational Excellence Act
to Congress, which requested $423 million for cash awards to be given
to excellent schools and teachers, math and science scholarships, and
alternative methods for certifying teachers. The bill also dealt with litera-
cy programs and teacher recruitment methods. As Bush stated in his
message to Congress:

The Educational Excellence Act of 1989 [is] a bill to provide incentives to attain a better-educated America. I believe that greater educational achievement promotes sustained economic growth,
enhances the Nation's competitive position in world markets,
increases productivity, and leads to higher incomes for everyone.
The Nation must invest in its young people, giving them the knowledge, skills, and values to live productive lives.[100]

Bush also convened a two-day education summit in September 1989
with the nation's governors, where national performance goals were set
for education. Among the goals included school readiness, student
achievement in math and science, a reduction in the national dropout
rate, recruitment and retention of qualified teachers, and providing safe
and drug-free schools.[101]

    While the summit and creating national goals with the help of
the nation's governors may have been unprecedented, most of Bush's
actions on education during 1989 were merely media events to maximize news coverage. These included visits to the White House by stu-

dents and teachers, speaking engagements at various schools, and participation in a few education forums.[102] He only introduced his small package of spending initiatives, which advanced solely in the Senate that year and not in the House. Bush may have publicly addressed "the widespread anxiety about the declining performance of American education," but he argued that spending more federal dollars on education would not solve the problem. Instead, the current levels of funding needed to be better spent.[103] This strategy left little room for major policy initiatives to be developed with the Democratic Congress.

During 1990, Bush continued to push for his education bill to progress through Congress, even though the bill did not really address the goals that he and the governors had set for improving national education standards. Bush included a statement in the 1990 State of the Union address, where he outlined his administration's educational goals, including school readiness, improving the graduation rate, and improving student assessment:

> Education is the one investment that means more for our future because it means the most for our children. Real improvement in our schools is not simply a matter of spending more: It's a matter of asking more—expecting more—of our schools, our teachers, of our kids, of our parents, and ourselves. . . . Every school must offer the kind of disciplined environment that makes it possible for our kids to learn.[104]

But education seemed to drop from Bush's public priority list during 1990. Even his advisors recognized that only limited changes could come at the federal level when dealing with education. As a result, most of Bush's education proposal died at the end of the congressional session of 1990. The only part of the bill that Bush signed into law was that which dealt with the creation of new math and science scholarships. While Bush had attempted to use the bully pulpit—at least during his first year in office—as a means to address education in America, a sound public strategy does not guarantee congressional action. According to Gray, the Bush administration did achieve limited success in bringing the issue to the forefront of the national agenda:

> Nine out of every ten dollars of public money spent on education is spent at the state level, not the federal level. The federal government can't really do much to force people to act differently. It is a bully pulpit more than a budgetary or regulatory matter. The President, with the help of Mrs. Bush's efforts at improving literacy, set the stage for the revolution now occurring at the state level of education.[105]

However, Bush's legacy in the area of education is less than what he had originally promised, and while he is remembered for at least talking about education, substantive policy changes did not occur during his four years in the White House.

Press Coverage

Aside from specific public events, Bush's educational initiatives received little coverage and analysis from the press. Between April 1989, when Bush first proposed his Education Excellence Act to Congress, and October 1990, when Congress adjourned without acting on most of the proposal, a total of only 30 news items appeared in the *Times* on this issue, which equaled one news item, on average, every 19 days (see Table 5.9). Bush's public activities did garner a majority of the coverage (60 percent), compared to Congress (10 percent) and interest group (30 percent) activity. However, 19 of the 30 news items appearing during this time period were news stories about the education summit with the nation's governors and other public events where Bush mentioned education. Only a handful of editorials, columns, or news analysis stories appeared on education. Also, most of Bush's coverage on this issue was categorized as balanced or mixed, due to the *Times'* skepticism about the President's ability to impact the state of America's public school system (see Table 5.10).

In keeping with the low amount of news coverage on Bush's education initiative, the *Times* weighed in only twice with their opinion about Bush's action on this issue. Following the education summit, a September 24, 1989 editorial claimed that Bush had a long way to go before the American educational system would be improved:

> It's one thing to call a summit meeting on education. It's quite another to follow through with ideas, support and, yes, dollars. Only if this meeting proves to be a gathering of national resolve and not simply a political showcase will Mr. Bush earn the right to be called the education President.

In a March 3, 1990 editorial, the Times remained skeptical and critical of Bush's plan to improve education without spending any additional federal funds: "It will take more than money to solve America's education deficit. But without money, national educational goals are meaningless. Mr. Bush and the governors have only done the easy part." And while the *Times* may have covered the education summit and other news events on this issue, the lack of substantive congressional activity left little in terms of real political action to generate press coverage.

Table 5.9. Amount and Type of *New York Times* Coverage of the Education Excellence Act (April 1989-October 1990).

	White House	Congress	Interest Group/Other
News Story	10	3	6
News Analysis	1	0	1
Column	4	0	1
Editorial	3	0	1
Total	18 - (60%)	3 - (10%)	9 - (30%)

Table 5.10. Tone of *New York Times* Coverage of Presidential Activities on the Education Excellence Act (April 1989-October 1990).

	Positive	Negative	Balanced/Mixed	Neutral
News Story	0	0	8	2
News Analysis	0	0	1	0
Column	0	0	4	0
Editorial	0	0	3	0
Total	0	0	16	2

THE SECOND TIER: THE CLEAN AIR ACT OF 1990

The Issue and White House Strategy

During the 1988 presidential campaign, Bush had promised new leadership in the area of environmental policy, and once he took office, he gave high priority to amending the Clean Air Act. The Bush administration actively sought out the advice of members of Congress, industry spokespeople, and environmental interest groups in developing a proposal. The bill presented to Congress in June 1989, which "sought to strengthen environmental protection without imposing excessive costs on industry," also got the attention of the Democratic Congress and showed Bush's intention to get a bill passed.[106] Despite the resistance to toughen environmental protections during the Reagan presidency, Bush responded to the increased public awareness about environmental issues, including reports of global warming and a hole in the ozone layer, with his proposal to overhaul the existing Clean Air Act of 1970. He included this issue in his first address to Congress in February 1989:

> If we're to protect our future, we need a new attitude about the environment. We must protect the air we breathe. I will send to you shortly legislation for a new, more effective Clean Air Act. It will include a plan to reduce by date certain emissions which cause acid rain, because the time for study alone has passed, and the time for action is now.[107]

Bush's proposal to Congress in June, the first put forward by the White House since 1977, focused on acid rain, urban air pollution, and toxic air emissions. Bush stated that his plan was

> a fresh approach to the Clean Air Act [to] help meet the Nation's environmental needs without compromising our record of unprecedented economic growth. . . . Draconian limits on economic growth and on the use of the automobile should not be necessary in order to give Americans clean air at levels they are willing to pay for, but it will require significant Federal, State, and local leadership and innovative approaches from government and industry.[108]

Bush's public strategy in this area differed from that of his education initiatives since the President talked mostly about the Clean Air Act in press conference or question and answer sessions with reporters. However, the bill was able to move through both houses of Congress with some compromises, but it was cleared for Bush's approval in late October 1990 as a sweeping piece of legislation that would impose stricter federal standards on urban smog, automobile exhaust, toxic air pollution and acid rain.[109] Bush signed the bill into law on November 15, 1990, taking credit for his role in a major legislative accomplishment: "This legislation isn't just the centerpiece of our environmental agenda. It is simply the most significant air pollution legislation in our nation's history, and it restores America's place as the global leader in environmental protection."[110]

Press Coverage

While Bush may have talked publicly about environmental issues less often than education, this issue received slightly more news coverage.

Between June 1989—when Bush first proposed his amendments to the Clean Air Act to Congress, and November 1990—when he signed the bill into law—a total of 65 news items appeared in the *Times*, which equaled one news item, on average, every eight days. However, congressional action on the issue received a majority of the coverage (58 percent), followed by interest group activity (23 percent) and White House activity (18 percent) (see Table 5.11). This is consistent with a low-profile public strategy on the part of the White House. Again, as with education, little analysis in the form of editorials, columns, or news analysis stories appeared in the *Times* on this issue. And most of Bush's coverage was categorized as balanced/mixed since, again, the *Times* remained skeptical of a Republican president pursuing sweeping changes to a traditionally Democratic issue such as environmental protection (see Table 5.12).

Table 5.11. Amount and Type of *New York Times* Coverage of the Clean Air Act of 1990 (June 1989-November 1990).

	White House	Congress	Interest Group/Other
News Story	8	28	12
News Analysis	0	4	2
Column	1	0	1
Editorial	3	6	0
Total	12 - (18%)	38 - (58%)	15 - (23%)

Table 5.12. Tone of *New York Times* Coverage of Presidential Activities on the Clean Air Act of 1990 (June 1989-November 1990)/

	Positive	Negative	Balanced/Mixed	Neutral
News Story	0	0	6	2
News Analysis	0	0	0	0
Column	1	0	0	0
Editorial	0	0	3	0
Total	1	0	9	2

Only two editorials appeared in the *Times* about Bush's action on amending the Clean Air Act. When Bush first proposed his plan to Congress, the *Times* was cautiously optimistic that the White House was finally recognizing the need for action on the environment. The June 14, 1989 editorial states:

> For years, the fight against dirty air has missed a crucial element: a President who thinks the nation deserves clean air. George Bush's proposals to overhaul the antiquated Clean Air Act of 1970 aren't perfect. But they represent a major departure from years of official indifference.

However, in less than two months, the *Times* had become more critical; in its July 25, 1989 editorial of Bush's proposal, as the details of the plan began to emerge. The *Times* noted,

> Now Mr. Bush has unveiled the fine print. The applause has turned to skepticism, even anger. . . . Cleaning the nation's air will be an expensive, contentious business. But as poll after poll shows, Americans are prepared to pay for cleaner air. Mr. Bush is sailing slowly, but at least the wind is up.

No other editorials generated by Bush's leadership on the issue would appear in the *Times*, despite the proposal becoming law in November 1990.

CONCLUSION

Overall, the two case studies for Reagan and Bush provided in this chapter show that, at least for these policy issues, neither president spent a great deal of time selling his domestic proposals to the public through major addresses. Like many other presidents, both Reagan and Bush preferred to discuss foreign and economic policies during major addresses. But for Reagan, even discussions of economic policies dropped off after his early budget victory in 1981. His overall public agenda shows that domestic policies never received high priority. The Reagan administration preferred to rely on staged media events to get out many of their domestic policy messages, especially using photo opportunities with no chance for reporters to quiz the President on his proposals. The inception of weekly radio addresses also provided the perfect outlet for brief discussions on domestic policies, leaving no room for rebuttal from reporters. While it is not surprising that the President did not attempt to aggressively sell his proposed cuts to student aid since it was not a politically popular avenue for budget cutting, Reagan also stayed relatively quiet on social security, an issue that could have seriously affected millions of Americans had the fund gone bankrupt. Reagan does represent, however, a president who effectively used the "hit the ground running" strategy to pass a sweeping budget deal during his first year in office, and who utilized a hands-off media strategy when dealing with several policy issues which were not overwhelmingly popular with the public.

While the jury may still be out regarding many aspects of the Reagan presidency, no administration had ever had such success at managing the news so as to portray the president in such a favorable light. That is not to say that Reagan escaped his eight years in office completely unscathed by the press. Certainly, his second term in office was marred by the unfolding of the Iran-Contra scandal, as well as other minor scandals involving administration officials. Yet, while the White House press corps may have figured out some of the behind-the-scenes secrets as to how the administration was orchestrating the news, with little access on their own, they mainly failed to find ways to circumvent the public relations apparatus so effectively installed by such advisors as Speakes, Deaver, and Gergen. While administration officials believed that they provided great access to the press, most members of the White House press corps did not share in that opinion. In 1983, Speakes reported to Deaver on the many ways in which they had improved access for the press, including several informal press availabilities, various interviews, and press activities both at and away from the White House:

> Despite the traditional complaints from the resident White House press corps, the President has been accessible and we have done many new things to improve the way in which the President communicates with the press. . . . To a reporter, there is no such thing as "enough" access. But . . . we can tell our side of the story, which I think is pretty good.[111]

No president had ever fit into the role of national leader during the television age of politics quite so easily, nor used the medium of television to his advantage quite so well. If image truly is everything, then at least from the standpoint of communication strategies, the Reagan presidency was an unqualified success.

The Bush presidency, on the other hand, would suffer as a result of Reagan's successes. While Bush promised to be both the "education" and "environmental" president, presenting a "kinder and gentler" conservative agenda that highlighted public service and his selftitled "thousand points of light," Bush is remembered best for his international leadership, particularly in the Gulf War. He never clearly articulated a domestic agenda to the public, and he never proposed sweeping changes to domestic issues, mainly preferring to "stay the course" that had been developed during the Reagan era. As Bush's legacy continues to develop, perhaps historians and political pundits will be kinder than were the voters during 1992, ousting the current president for a promised change in the area of economic and domestic policies. Continuity, coupled with only mediocre communication skills, as Bush discovered, does not make for a strong public image as an effective and active leader in the White House.

ENDNOTES

1. David Shaw, "Did the Press Apply the Teflon to Reagan's Presidency?" *Los Angeles Times*, 27 October 1992, A-20.
2. John Tebbel and Sarah Miles Watts, *The Press and the Presidency: From George Washington to Ronald Reagan* (New York: Oxford University Press, 1985), 535-7.
3. Mark Hertsgaard, *On Bended Knee: The Press and the Reagan Presidency* (New York: Farrar Straus Giroux, 1988), 33-7.
4. Ibid., 105-6.
5. David S. Broder, *Behind the Front Page: A Candid Look at How the News is Made* (New York: Simon & Schuster, 1987), 176-99.
6. Tebbel and Watts, 540.
7. For a discussion of the animosity between the Reagan administration and the press, see Mary E. Stuckey, *Playing the Game: The Presidential Rhetoric of Ronald Reagan* (New York: Praeger Publishers, 1990), 15-22.
8. Robert E. Denton, Jr., *The Primetime Presidency of Ronald Reagan: The Era of the Television Presidency* (New York: Praeger Publishers, 1988), 10-1.
9. Ibid., 63-77.
10. Memo from Larry Speakes to James Baker, 2/1/82, Larry Speakes Files, Box 13880, Ronald Reagan Library.
11. Memo from Larry Speakes to Michael Deaver, 4/18/83, Larry Speakes Files, Box 13880, Ronald Reagan Library.
12. Memo from Lou Gerig to Jim Brady, Max Friedersdorf, Karna Small and Larry Speakes, 3/9/81, Document #017365, WHORM: Public Relations, Box 1, Ronald Reagan Library.
13. John Anthony Maltese, *Spin Control: The White House Office of Communications and the Management of Presidential News*, 2nd rev. ed. (Chapel Hill: The University of North Carolina Press, 1994), 183-94.
14. Memo from Bill Hart to Larry Speakes, 6/10/81, Larry Speakes Files, Box 13880, Ronald Reagan Library.
15. Memo from Larry Speakes to John Rogers, 6/12/81, Larry Speakes Files, Box 13880, Ronald Reagan Library.

16. Maltese, 203-4.
17. Memos from Larry Speakes to James Baker, 5/21/81 and 6/12/81, Larry Speakes Files, Box 13880, Ronald Reagan Library.
18. Memo from Richard Darman and Craig Fuller to Martin Anderson, Joseph Canzeri, Max Friedersdorf, David Gergen, and James Nance, 11/30/81, Michael Deaver Files, Box 7621, Ronald Reagan Library.
19. Memo from James Baker to White House Staff, 1/10/83, Larry Speakes Files, Box 13880, Ronald Reagan Library.
20. Memo from James Baker to Senior White House Staff, 5/11/83, Larry Speakes Files, Box 13880, Ronald Reagan Library.
21. Hertsgaard, 3-6.
22. David Shaw, 27 October 1992.
23. Martin Schram, *The Great American Video Game: Presidential Politics in the Television Age* (New York: William Morrow and Company, 1987), 26-32.
24. Donald T. Regan, *For the Record: From Wall Street to Washington* (New York: Harcourt Brace, 1988), 247-254.
25. Michael K. Deaver, *Behind the Scenes* (New York: William Morrow, 1987), 139-41.
26. Larry Speakes, *Speaking Out: The Reagan Presidency from Inside the White House* (New York: Charles Scribner's Sons, 1988), 220-1.
27. Memo from Larry Speakes to James Baker, 6/4/81, Larry Speakes Files, Box 13880, Ronald Reagan Library.
28. Memo from Larry Speakes to James Baker, 8/9/82, Larry Speakes Files, Box 13880, Ronald Reagan Library.
29. Memo from Larry Speakes to James Baker and Lyn Nofziger, 8/10/82, Larry Speakes Files, Box 13880, Ronald Reagan Library. Reagan did give an address to the nation on the tax bill on August 16, 1982.
30. Speakes, 236-8.
31. Memo from Larry Speakes to Michael Deaver, 4/18/83, Larry Speakes Files, Box 13880, Ronald Reagan Library.
32. Memo from Larry Speakes to David Gergen, 1/25/82, Larry Speakes Files, Box 13880, Ronald Reagan Library.
33. Memo from David Gergen to Ronald Reagan, 3/19/82, David Gergen Files, Box 10530, Ronald Reagan Library.
34. Memo from Larry Speakes to James Baker, 11/8/82, Larry Speakes Files, Box 13880, Ronald Reagan Library
35. Memo from Larry Speakes to James Baker, 7/28/82, Larry Speakes Files, Box 13880, Ronald Reagan Library. In a handwritten note on the bottom of the memo, Baker responded: "As I told you the other day, just flag me or Senior Staff—the time has always been (and still is being) held for this on RR's schedule."
36. As discussed and quoted in Schram, 23-6.
37. *Ten Presidents and the Press*, Ed. Kenneth W. Thompson (Washington, DC: University Press of America, 1983).
38. Tebbel and Watts, 541.

39. Ibid., 536.
40. Kurt Ritter, "Ronald Reagan," in *U.S. Presidents as Orators: A Bio-Critical Sourcebook*, Ed. Halford Ryan (Westport, CT: Greenwood Press, 1995), 316-31.
41. Ibid., 325-32.
42. Memo from Mark Weinberg to Larry Speakes, 2/10/82, Larry Speakes Files, Box 13880, Ronald Reagan Library.
43. Robert Dallek, *Ronald Reagan: The Politics of Symbolism* (Cambridge, MA: Harvard University Press, 1999), viii.
44. Paul D. Erickson, *Reagan Speaks: The Making of an American Myth* (New York: New York University Press, 1985), 116-7. For a discussion of Reagan's use of symbolism, see also Dallek, *Ronald Reagan: The Politics of Symbolism*; and Lou Cannon, *President Reagan: The Role of a Lifetime* (New York: Simon & Schuster, 1991).
45. Robert E. Denton, Jr. and Dan F. Hahn, "Reagan's Persuasiveness: An Exploratory Interpretation," in *Presidential Communication, Description and Analysis*, Eds. Robert E. Denton, Jr. and Dan F. Hahn (New York: Praeger Publishers, 1986), 66-72.
46. Ritter, 334-5.
47. Erickson, 8.
48. See Cannon, 128-32. Cannon, who penned the term "Reaganism," would routinely end his weekly column in the *Washington Post* with a "Reaganism of the Week."
49. William Ker Muir, Jr., *The Bully Pulpit: The Presidential Leadership of Ronald Reagan* (San Francisco: ICS Press, 1992), 23-35. For a discussion of the speechwriting process in the Reagan White House, see also Peggy Noonan, *What I Saw at the Revolution: A Political Life in the Reagan Era* (New York: Random House, 1990).
50. The total number for 1981 is lower than other years due in part to the assassination attempt in March; several of Reagan's scheduled speeches in April were delivered instead by Vice President George Bush, and were not included in this total.
51. Compiled from *The Public Papers of the Presidents of the United States: Ronald Reagan, 1981-89* (Washington, DC: Government Printing Office, 1982-91).
52. Notice to the Press from the Office of the Press Secretary, 4/5/82, Box 13885, Marlin Fitzwater Files, Ronald Reagan Library.
53. Memo from David Gergen to James Baker, Michael Deaver, and Larry Speakes, 12/1/83, James Baker III Files, Box 10513, Ronald Reagan Library.
54. Larry Berman, *The New American Presidency* (Boston: Little, Brown and Company, 1987), 324-5.
55. Jeff Fishel, *Presidents & Promises* (Washington, DC: CQ Press, 1985), 163-6.
56. Paul Light, *The President's Agenda: Domestic Policy Choice from Kennedy to Clinton* (Baltimore: Johns Hopkins University Press, 1991), 242-3.

57. Compiled from *The Public Papers of the Presidents of the United States: Ronald Reagan, 1981-89* (Washington, DC: Government Printing Office, 1982-91).

58. Cannon, 243.

59. Paul Light, *Artful Work: The Politics of Social Security Reform* (New York: Random House, 1985), 118. Light provides an extensive review of the policymaking process on social security in this book.

60. Richard P. Nathan, "The Reagan Presidency in Domestic Affairs," in *The Reagan Presidency: An Early Assessment*, Ed. Fred I. Greenstein (Baltimore: Johns Hopkins University Press, 1983), 56.

61. W. Lance Bennett, *The Governing Crisis: Media, Money, and Marketing in American Elections*, 2nd ed. (New York: St. Martin's Press, 1996), 100.

62. Light, *Artful Work*, 4.

63. *Congressional Quarterly Almanac, 1983*, Vol. XXXIX (Washington, DC: Congressional Quarterly Service, 1984), 219.

64. Memo from Mike Baroody to David Gergen, undated, Mike Baroody Files, Box 11219, Ronald Reagan Library.

65. Paul E. Peterson and Mark Rom, "Lower Taxes, More Spending, and Budget Deficits," in *The Reagan Legacy: Promise and Performance*, Ed. Charles O. Jones (Chatham, NJ: Chatham House Publishers, 1988), 225.

66. Norman C. Thomas, Joseph A. Pika, and Richard A. Watson, *The Politics of the Presidency*, 3rd rev. ed. (Washington, DC: CQ Press, 1994), 328.

67. Hertsgaard, 48-50.

68. *Congressional Quarterly Almanac, 1982*, Vol. XXXVIII (Washington, DC: Congressional Quarterly Service, 1983), 483-5.

69. Ronald Reagan, "Radio Address to the Nation on the Caribbean Basin Initiative and Student Loans," 4/10/82, *The Public Papers of the Presidents of the United States, 1982* (Washington, DC: Government Printing Office, 1983).

70. John Anthony Maltese, "Spin Control in the White House," in *Understanding the Presidency*, Eds. James P. Pfiffner and Roger H. Davidson (New York: Longman, 1997), 112-3.

71. Samuel Kernell, *Going Public: New Strategies of Presidential Leadership*, 3rd ed. (Washington, DC: CQ Press, 1997), 93.

72. David Mervin, *George Bush and the Guardianship Presidency* (New York: St. Martin's Press, 1996), 50-1.

73. Ibid., 52.

74. George C. Edwards, III and Stephen J. Wayne, *Presidential Leadership: Politics and Policy Making*, 5th ed. (New York: St. Martin's Press, 1999), 152.

75. George C. Edwards, III, "George Bush and the Public Presidency: The Politics of Inclusion," in *The Bush Presidency: First Appraisals*, Eds. Colin Campbell and Bert A. Rockman (Chatham, NJ: Chatham House Publishers, 1991), 148-9.

76. Maltese, 216.
77. Kernell, 91.
78. Maltese, 220-1.
79. Lyn Ragsdale, *Vital Statistics on the Presidency: Washington to Clinton* (Washington, DC: CQ Press, 1996), 184.
80. For a discussion of the news media environment during the early 1990s, see David Shaw, "Not Even Getting a First Chance, *Los Angeles Times*, 9/15/93.
81. Edwards, *The Bush Presidency: First Appraisals*, 149.
82. C. Boyden Gray, "The President as Leader," Presented in a Forum at the Miller Center of Public Affairs on 2/17/94, in *The Bush Presidency: Ten Intimate Perspectives of George Bush*, Ed. Kenneth W. Thompson, (Lanham, MD: University Press of America, 1997), 6-7.
83. Michael Emery and Edwin Emery, *The Press and America: An Interpretive History of the Mass Media*, 8th ed. (Boston: Allyn and Bacon, 1996), 474.
84. Edwards, *The Bush Presidency: First Appraisals*, 145.
85. For a discussion of Bush's many images, see Richard W. Waterman, Robert Wright, and Gilbert St. Clair, *The Image-Is-Everything Presidency: Dilemmas in American Leadership* (Boulder, CO: Westview Press, 1999), 57-62.
86. James Reston, *Deadline: A Memoir* (New York: Random House, 1991), 447.
87. Marlin Fitzwater, *Call the Briefing! Bush and Reagan, Sam and Helen: A Decade with Presidents and the Press* (New York: Random House, 1995), 81.
88. Clayton Yeutter, "Accomplishments and Setbacks," Presented in a Forum at the Miller Center of Public Affairs on 4/30/93, in *The Bush Presidency: Ten Intimate Perspectives of George Bush*, Ed. Kenneth W. Thompson, (Lanham, MD: University Press of America, 1997), 50-1.
89. Victor Gold, "George Bush Speaks Out," *Washingtonian*, February 1994.
90. Fitzwater, 11-2.
91. Mervin, 47-9.
92. Gray, 10.
93. Craig R. Smith, "George Herbert Walker Bush," in *U.S. Presidents as Orators: A Bio-Critical Sourcebook*, Ed. Halford Ryan (Westport, CT: Greenwood Press, 1995), 349.
94. Edwards, *The Bush Presidency: First Appraisals*, 145.
95. Compiled from *The Public Papers of the Presidents of the United States: George Bush, 1989-1993* (Washington, DC: Government Printing Office, 1990-93).
96. James P. Pfiffner, *The Strategic Presidency: Hitting the Ground Running*, 2nd rev. ed. (Lawrence, KS: University of Kansas Press, 1996), 141-3.

97.   Compiled from *The Public Papers of the Presidents of the United States: George Bush, 1989-1993* (Washington, DC: Government Printing Office, 1990-93).

98.   Address on Administration Goals Before a Joint Session of Congress, 2/9/89, *The Public Papers of the Presidents of the United States: George Bush, 1989* (Washington, DC: Government Printing Office, 1990).

99.   Remarks at the Junior Achievement National Business Hall of Fame Dinner in Colorado Springs, Colorado, 3/16/89, *The Public Papers of the Presidents of the United States: George Bush, 1989* (Washington, DC: Government Printing Office, 1990).

100.   Message to the Congress Transmitting Proposed Legislation on Educational Excellence, 4/5/89, *The Public Papers of the Presidents of the United States: George Bush, 1989* (Washington, DC: Government Printing Office, 1990).

101.   *Congressional Quarterly Almanac, 1989*, Vol. XLV (Washington, DC: Congressional Quarterly Service, 1990), 191-2.

102.   Ibid.

103.   Paul J. Quirk, "Domestic Policy: Divided Government and Cooperative Presidential Leadership," in *The Bush Presidency: First Appraisals*, Eds. Colin Campbell and Bert A. Rockman (Chatham, NJ: Chatham House Publishers, 1991), 82.

104.   Address Before a Joint Session of the Congress on the State of the Union, 1/31/90, *The Public Papers of the Presidents of the United States: George Bush, 1990* (Washington, DC: Government Printing Office, 1991).

105.   Gray, 18.

106.   Quirk, 86.

107.   Address on Administration Goals Before a Joint Session of Congress, 2/9/89, *The Public Papers of the Presidents of the United States: George Bush, 1989* (Washington, DC: Government Printing Office, 1990).

108.   Message to the Congress Transmitting the Report of the Council on Environmental Quality, 6/23/89, *The Public Papers of the Presidents of the United States: George Bush, 1989* (Washington, DC: Government Printing Office, 1990).

109.   *Congressional Quarterly Almanac, 1990*, Vol. XLVI (Washington, DC: Congressional Quarterly Service, 1991), 229.

110.   Remarks on Signing the Bill Amending the Clear Air Act, 11/15/90, *The Public Papers of the Presidents of the United States: George Bush, 1990* (Washington, DC: Government Printing Office, 1991).

111.   Memo from Larry Speakes to Michael Deaver, 4/18/83, Larry Speakes Files, Box 13880, Ronald Reagan Library.

6

Clinton:
Years of Scandal and Spin

Bill Clinton's relationship with the news media, like that of many of his predecessors in the White House, was nothing if not complex. As early as the 1992 presidential primaries, Clinton's media advisors worked overtime to keep a positive spin on stories about their candidate. The barrage of the negative press coverage began in January of that year, even before the New Hampshire primary, and continued through the November election. When the mainstream press picked up on Gennifer Flowers' story of a 12-year relationship with Clinton, published in the tabloid newspaper *The Star*, and for which she had been paid $50,000, a new precedent had been set for acceptable sources and news content in political reporting. Some of the more memorable and prominent headlines from Clinton's press coverage throughout the campaign included continuing stories of marital infidelity and draft dodging, and debates over whether or not he had inhaled while experimenting with marijuana. In an earlier time, such stories might have knocked many presidential candidates right out of the water. Clinton, however, relied on his polished communication skills and proved he deserved the early campaign nickname of the "Comeback Kid." He overcame the negative press coverage and appealed to many voters by keeping his message focused primarily on the need to improve the nation's slumping economy. His campaign also utilized an approach to press strategies that included townhall meetings and appearances on radio and television talk shows, going over the heads of the national press and directly interacting with the voters. Clinton sold himself to the American public as a "New Democrat," not the tax-and-spend liberal of years past, but a fiscally responsible moderate who promised to reduce the deficit while stimulating the economy, provide national health care, and get the country back on track.

Not much changed for Clinton after his scandal-ridden campaign in 1992. His leadership style was mostly defined by the ability of his advisors to perpetually spin their president out of trouble with both the press and the public. As the first president born after World War II to occupy the White House, Clinton represented the baby boom generation that had been raised during the television age. As a high school student, he had shaken hands with his political hero John F. Kennedy on the lawn of the White House in 1963 while attending a leadership conference. Less than 30 years later, he would return to Washington as the second youngest president ever elected; he was 22 years younger than his most recent predecessor, George Bush. Along with the many policy hopes pinned to the Clinton administration was the assumption that the media-savvy Clinton, who had performed well for the television cameras and had survived the media onslaught of negative coverage during the presidential election, would rival Ronald Reagan's skill at controlling the public agenda and managing news coming out of the White House. But his relationship with the press was rocky, and at times, filled with animosity. Yet, with many political odds against him, including a less-than-friendly press and a less-than-sweeping mandate to govern, Clinton was, at times, able to achieve a fairly impressive legislative record. And despite the many times his presidency was declared dead by political commentators, Clinton still managed to be reelected for a second term in 1996, and he survived a presidential impeachment following the Monica Lewinsky scandal in 1998. In terms of a communication strategy, this chapter only considers Clinton's first term in office. However, the political spectacle of 1998 perhaps exemplifies Clinton's greatest accomplishment, and in which his communication strategy played an integral part—his political survival.

CLINTON AND THE PRESS

With a Democratic Congress and a newly unified government, the Clinton team sat poised to ambitiously begin work on creating the many changes in the federal government that had been promised during the 1992 presidential campaign. As Clinton stated in his inaugural address:

"And so today we pledge an end to the era of deadlock and drift, and a new season of American renewal has begun."[1] However, there was one major problem for the new administration—no one told the news media. Clinton is perceived as having had one of the shortest honeymoons on record with the Washington press corps; some would argue that he had no honeymoon at all. Press relations got off to a bad start immediately after the election when the slowness of the transition team in making any announcements on staffing irritated the press. The shutdown of information did not allow for any "feeding of the beast," a ritual in which previous administrations had participated. The Clinton team also was forced to begin in damage-control mode. Within days of the inauguration, following Zoe Baird's withdrawal of her nomination for attorney general and the flap over ending the ban on gays in the military, the Clinton presidency was declared dead on arrival. Political pundits had a field day focusing on the early miscues of the administration. One of the biggest, at least in the eyes of the press, was the closing of the press room door in the White House by Communications Director George Stephanopoulos, which took away a major access route for reporters to get the information they needed. Four months into the presidency, press relations hit rock bottom with a flood of stories about Clinton's $200 Hollywood haircut and the firing, and subsequent re-hiring, of the White House travel staff. White House blunders, not policies, were making headlines and leading the nightly newscasts. According to David Shaw of the *Los Angeles Times:* "Clinton received no free shave from the nation's news media; he was nicked, cut, sliced and slashed by the barbers of the Fourth Estate—and instead of a honeymoon, he got an autopsy."[2]

For the Clinton administration, control over defining both the national agenda and the President's image in the press was elusive during the first months in Washington. As a candidate, change was Clinton's favorite topic of discussion. But as President, bringing about that change to the American political system was easier said than done, as Clinton and his advisers learned early on. Though Clinton promised to focus "like a laser beam" on the economy immediately following his inauguration, the administration's lack of experience at the national level led to other issues taking center stage. Poor execution on the part of the White House forced Clinton to spend important time on damage control, which raised questions about who was in control of the political agenda. Clinton's leadership style also hurt the clarity of his message; his insistence on consensus and compromise, along with needing to be a part of every decision made, were perceived as weak and inefficient.[3]

During the 1992 presidential campaign, the Clinton team forged a new path in how to deal with the news media, often sidestepping the traditional outlets so as to speak more directly to the American people—

through talk shows like *Larry King Live* and *Phil Donahue*, appearances on MTV, and various forms of electronic townhall meetings. But that skill of dodging the mainstream press and their constant attacks did not automatically follow Clinton to Washington. The negative coverage of the new administration during the first few months can be attributed, in part, to an ineffective press strategy. However, the situation greatly improved with the hiring of David Gergen to head the communications team in May 1993. A former communications adviser to Presidents Nixon, Ford, and Reagan, Gergen, rather than the younger Clinton staffers, better understood how to play the press game in Washington, including providing the White House press corps with a more courteous attitude and better access to information. With Gergen on board and a reshuffling of staff within the Communications Office, including the reassignment of Stephanopoulos to the post of senior advisor, the tone of Clinton's coverage began to improve. But aside from press strategy, the timeliness, or untimeliness, of outside events seemed to affect Clinton's portrayal in the press as well. The summer and fall of 1993 found Clinton rebounding in the eyes of the public with a solid choice for the Supreme Court, the passage of his budget, and a series of effective discussions on his health care policy. But by the end of the year, stories about Whitewater and Paula Jones' allegations of sexual harassment began to appear, reinvigorating Clinton's critics in the press.[4]

Communication strategies are often considered the "hallmark of a presidency." Three key elements help to shape this crucial relationship, including the President's personality and style, the goals of the administration, and the party in control of the White House. (Republicans opt for a more centralized, planned approach controlled by senior advisers, while Democrats favor a loose organization of advisers that deal with the day-to-day issues of the press.) Clinton and his advisors maintained an attitude from the campaign that they did not need the mainstream press, and unlike Kennedy, Clinton had no close friends among the media elite. Despite his disastrous start with the press, Clinton did learn from his mistakes by recognizing the need to sell his programs to the public through the established Washington press corps. By the end of his first year in office, the constant negative stories which had come from every angle had subsided, and he saw a boost in public opinion, with a 60 percent approval rating in December 1993.[5]

Clinton's campaign style of governing, which greatly involved press coverage of administration policies, was evident in how Clinton attempted to pass key economic legislation in his first 18 months in office. In this case, a strategy to deal with the press developed within days of the inauguration, as leaks about the President's proposed economic program began shaping the debate in the press before Clinton himself was able to discuss the issue. Consultants from the campaign, including James Carville, Paul Begala, and Mandy Grunwald, were immediately put to work to sell the program to the American people. The goal was to "recreate the urgency of the campaign" by reminding Americans how bad the economy really was. The media plan did not include discussing specifics of the economic plan, but instead dispatched the White House line on the issue in broad-based terms. The purpose of the media blitz was to sell Americans on why Clinton was capable of turning the economy around.[6]

Another factor that affected Clinton's press coverage was that he had two alternating yet distinct leadership styles. One was a "no-holds-barred" style that ignored the political environment in an attempt to meet all the goals of his legislative agenda at once, while the other was his capability of focusing on specific issues and working hard to sell them to the public. Clinton set a new standard for the presidency in terms of interest in both politics and policy; this was aided greatly by his ability to debate the specifics of key policy issues while maintaining his personal charm. Unfortunately, this also hurt his ability to communicate directly with the American public since he had difficulty presenting the "big picture" to citizens, often getting bogged down in the specifics of proposals.[7] Clinton lacked a "rhetorical definition" of his agenda during his first two years in office. He also had "an undisciplined personal style, tremendous energy, a desire to please many sides, a mind stuffed with policy ideas, and a party of interest groups clamoring for policy."[8] As a result, he had trouble keeping his message focused and was viewed as disorganized and ineffective, which hurt his working relationship with Congress and muddled his message to the American people.

Unlike presidents such as Ford, Carter, and Bush, who all attempted to provide an open presidency with the press, Clinton's initial press strategy centered on avoiding the mainstream press whenever possible by relying on informal media formats. This allowed the Clinton White House to target specific audiences through events such as talk show appearances, reaching audiences that may not read newspapers or watch the traditional evening newscasts. Also, the viewers would see a more personalized version of their president. Similarly, townhall meetings also provided Clinton with an outlet for policy discussions with everyday American citizens, a format that definitely accentuated his abilities to retain facts and to connect with the public.[9] The Office of Communications continued its role as a public relations outlet for the White House, and under Clinton, devised several new techniques to keep in touch with both the press and the public in the new computer age. These included an increased access to information through a White House web page, which provided information available to computer users such as Clinton's public remarks, his daily schedule, transcripts of press briefings, and photos. A White House e-mail address was also set up to respond to questions from citizens about Clinton's policies: "This electronic channel bypassed the filter of reporters who used to be the only source for transmitting such material."[10] However, despite the strategy to steer clear of the traditional political press, Clinton was criticized as being too accessible and too informal with the press. Some argued that his attempts to avoid the Washington news media through talkshows and townhall meetings threatened to diminish the prestige and the myth surrounding the presidency, which are often considered important aspects of the office for a president to respect and use to his advantage in leading the nation.[11]

Regardless of any White House communication strategy, coverage of Clinton was resoundingly negative during his first year in office. Clinton received no honeymoon, usually afforded to new presidents while they first begin to articulate their appointments and policy agendas, and coverage was considered "hypercritical." A study by the Center for Media and Public Affairs found that nearly two-thirds of the coverage on Clinton during the first 18 months of his administration was negative, compared to only 50 percent negative coverage for Bush during the same time frame. Even as time passed for the new administration, stories became less focused on policy and more focused on the alleged scandal of the Whitewater affair.[12] Especially by 1995, as the Republican takeover of Congress and the O.J. Simpson trial were dominating the news media, stories generated by the White House press corps on substantive policy proposals were scarce. Many argued that reporters in Washington had become lazy, relying on practiced rituals to get news from key sources without leaving the White House press area. What reporters seemed to lack, as evidenced by coverage of the Clinton administration, was "a sense that their responsibility involved something more than their standing up to rehash the day's announcements when there was room for them again on the news."[13]

Even well-known political journalists tried to understand the nature of Clinton's critical coverage, which at times seemed to be worse than any previous president had received. Eleanor Clift of *Newsweek* admitted that the White House press corps might have gone too far in their criticisms:

> [T]he White House press room has never been as relentlessly petty and mean as it is today. It's hard to know who deserves the blame— the reporters or their handlers—but the impact on Clinton is clear: he gets even worse press coverage than he deserves.[14]

She concluded that both the press and the President were to blame for the negative coverage; Clinton's attempts to bypass the Washington media hurt him since the administration had not done enough "schmoozing" with reporters. The press, as a result, was all too happy to focus on the failures, however small, of the White House, especially during the early months of the administration.[15] A column appearing in the June 1993 issue of *The New Republic* also provided a theory about the negative coverage—that most reporters just did not like Clinton, likening the relationship to "tribal hatred." The gripes from the press corps, whether legitimate or not, included Clinton's lack of availability, at least compared to during the 1992 campaign; Clinton's lack of consideration, since he was routinely late and appeared oblivious to any inconveniences he caused as a result; and that Clinton aides were constantly in a state of overspin, thinking that they could talk their way out of any mess.[16]

Clinton, it seemed, was a victim of bad timing, entering the White House at a point in history when the press had become even more contentious for a president to deal with than ever before. A large factor contributing to the assault on the Clinton presidency was the prevailing attitude of members of the press. The news media was not immune to the recession of the early 1990s; budget cuts and smaller audiences made reporters more competitive, which led to less-responsible journalism and more tabloid-style stories. Being first was often more important than being right, which lent itself to pack journalism. Also, the focus on presidential coverage was personality, not only the president's, but the reporters' as well. Reporters wanted to make a name for themselves, and that meant asking "tough" questions and reporting on what the president did wrong rather than right. Also, resentment existed among many Washington reporters over the manipulation and management of news by the Reagan, and in part the Bush, administrations.[17]

While Clinton's overall press strategy may not have been well orchestrated or organized from the start, many scholars blame the national news media for being overly critical, hostile, and personalized in their coverage of the White House. And while presidents seem to have begun closely following public opinion polls to guide their policy decisions, journalists have developed their own agenda, independent of poll results, which drives press coverage. While American citizens seem to be most concerned about federal policies that will directly affect them, all Washington journalists wish to talk about is the political game inside the Beltway, which perhaps best described Clinton's fate with the news media during his first term:

> When ordinary citizens have a chance to pose questions on political leaders, they rarely ask about the game of politics. They mainly want

to know how the reality of politics will affect them—through taxes, programs, scholarship funds, wars. Journalists justify their intrusiveness and excesses by claiming that they are the public's representatives, asking the questions their fellow citizens would ask if they had the privilege of meeting with presidents and senators. In fact, they ask questions no one but their fellow political professionals care about.[18]

No other administration better defined the term "the public presidency" than the Clinton White House, which was "based on a perpetual campaign to obtain the support of the American people and fed by public opinion polls, focus groups, and public relations memos." Following the Republican victory in the 1994 midterm congressional elections, the Clinton administration was forced to shift its communication strategy from offense to defense. Following that, Clinton defended his moderate positions against many of the views of the Republican Party, and was forced to adopt many Republican initiatives, including smaller government, welfare reform, and balancing the federal budget: "The President benefited from standing in counterpoint to the Republicans."[19] This shift in strategy helped Clinton to rebound in public opinion polls and remind Americans that as President, he was still relevant, in spite of Newt Gingrich and the Republican-controlled Congress. This aided his reelection bid greatly, in spite of the sexual harassment lawsuit filed against him by Paula Jones.

However, Clinton's biggest public relations challenge would come after his reelection in 1996. The entire year of 1998, dubbed by some "the year of Monica," placed the Clinton presidency in a state of crisis (at least according to the labels used for the story by most media outlets). But even with Independent Counsel Kenneth Starr's attempts to bring down the Clinton administration, all the public revelations about Clinton's relationship with Lewinsky, and an impeachment trial in the Senate, Clinton's approval ratings remained in the 60 percent range throughout the scandal. Americans were able to compartmentalize their view of Clinton—most approved of his job performance, in part because of the strong economy, but most had little respect left for Clinton as a person.[20] Most of Clinton's public wounds were self-inflicted, and the seemingly never-ending scandal atmosphere of his administration crippled his ability to govern: "Campaigning, posturing, and pronouncing, although it may have been Clinton's strength, is not governance—certainly not in the usual sense of precipitating great national debates on important questions of public policy or of driving legislation through Congress."[21] Clearly, if the name of the game in Washington was survival, then Clinton won hands down. But the effect of his communication strategy, along with the perpetual White House spin in an attempt to control the message and survive scandal, may have left a bitter legacy for future presidents in what is now one of the most important jobs of the office—communicating with the press and the American public.

CLINTON'S PUBLIC ACTIVITIES

The rhetorical aspect of the presidency was a key component of Clinton's leadership strategy. Not only did he enjoy a high frequency of public speeches, they were usually long (often an hour or more), and packed with detailed discussions of policy initiatives. During his acceptance speech at the 1992 Democratic Convention, Clinton jokingly referred to his excruciatingly long nomination speech for Michael Dukakis in 1988, for which he received bad reviews in the press. Throughout both the 1992 and 1996 presidential campaigns, Clinton would often talk himself hoarse. In terms of delivery of speeches, Clinton's style was dynamic, and he relied on different types of deliveries for different audiences. For example, he appeared formal and somber during national addresses, while informal and at ease during townhall meetings. Clinton's speeches were greatly influenced by the words of John F. Kennedy, Robert Kennedy, and Martin Luther King, Jr., all known for their oratory skills. The strengths of Clinton's speeches relied on his ability to weave the significance of distinct policies together, especially between domestic and foreign issues. Clinton also possessed a vast memory for facts and figures, a skill that helped him during his national address on health care in August 1993. The teleprompter in the House chamber contained an earlier address on the economy, and Clinton was seven minutes into his health care address before aides corrected the problem. While the content of his speeches may not be as memorable as that of Kennedy's, Clinton was nonetheless considered, especially during his first term, a "dynamic communicator struggling to mobilize a lethargic Congress and a skeptical public to a new season of American renewal."[22]

As for the speechwriting process in the Clinton White House, as with the making of other decisions, a large number of advisors and staff usually became involved. For several major speeches during the first term, a "war room" similar to the one used as the headquarters for the 1992 presidential campaign would be set up within the White House for the group effort to prepare the speech. Often, more than a dozen people would be used to write a speech, with many aides working through the night, a trend that was considered "a badge of honor" in the early days of the Clinton White House. First Lady Hillary Rodham Clinton would also often take part in the speech writing process, reading aloud drafts to aides in an attempt to have the speech sound more like the President's style. Clinton was also extensively involved in writing his speeches, providing suggestions along the way and often making his own revisions right up to the scheduled delivery of the speech.[23]

When assessing Clinton's public activities during the first term (see Table 6.1), especially when compared with the other presidents during the television age, the numbers are both impressive and overwhelming. Clearly, Clinton preferred both a leadership style and a communication strategy that relied heavily on public appearances. The formats for those appearances were also diverse, ranging from traditional presidential activities, such as White House press conferences and addresses to the nation, to newer formats, such as teleconference remarks to various groups and townhall meetings with citizens. Clinton also continued Reagan's trend of weekly radio addresses from the time he first took office, gave several policy addresses each year, and participated in frequent exchanges with the White House press corps. He also held several press conferences with foreign dignitaries each year, as well as the traditional presidential press conferences. And while his yearly average for press conferences was somewhat low (excluding those with foreign dignitaries), his access to the press seemed to make up for a lack of more formal questioning. The yearly totals for public activities also remained quite consistent throughout the first term; the drop in 1995 could reflect the Republican congressional victory and the ensuing struggle over the national agenda with Speaker Gingrich and the Republican Contract With America. In total, Clinton participated in 2,450 public events between his inauguration on January 20, 1993 and December 31, 1996.

Table 6.1. Clinton—Public Activities.[24]

	1993	1994	1995	1996
National Addresses	7	5	3	1
Policy Addresses	42	27	48	58
Press Conferences	13	18	9	5
Radio Addresses	48	53	53	52
Brief Statements/Nonpolicy Remarks	256	320	287	229
Partisan Remarks/Campaign Speeches	19	51	20	144
Press Conferences with Foreign Dignitaries	25	27	19	16
Signing Ceremonies	27	17	11	23
Teleconference Remarks	11	20-	12	8
Roundtable Discussions	2	6	5	17
Town Meetings/Q&A Sessions	28	15	11	1
Remarks to/Exchanges with Reporters	165	79	63	74
Total	643	638	541	628
Daily Average	1.86	1.75	1.48	1.72

THE CLINTON POLICY AGENDA

From the time he took office in January 1993, Clinton showed great passion, interest, and energy in his domestic policy agenda. He extensively discussed domestic issues during the 1992 presidential campaign, and unlike Bush, whose White House years seemed mostly focused on foreign affairs, Clinton was eager to prove to the American public that they now had a president who would focus on issues at home. And that list of issues was quite extensive, including economic stimulus, health care reform, welfare reform, campaign finance and lobbying reform, a national service plan, a middle-class tax cut, and passage of the Brady bill, the Motor Voter bill, and the Family and Medical Leave Act (all previously vetoed by Bush), among others. However, the Clinton transition team was slow and ineffective at organizing its game plan, and as a result, the policy message was unfocused during Clinton's first weeks in office, a critical time for a new president to move on his policy agenda. Newspaper headlines and top stories on the nightly news focused on a new administration that seemed unorganized and inexperienced, and especially inept at handling the issue of gays in the military and the selection of an attorney general. The lack of a focused agenda also hurt Clinton's relationship with Congress, making coalition building difficult, especially for expansive programs like health care reform. However, Clinton did prove to be effective at lobbying and, despite his defeat on the 1993 budget stimulus package and health care reform in 1994 and the loss of control of Congress to the Republicans in the 1994 midterm elections, he did manage to pass many items on his agenda during his first term.[25]

From the start of the 1992 presidential election, Clinton campaigned as a "New Democrat" who would move beyond the traditional tax-and-spend liberal policies of past Democrats. His policy agenda was also shaped by the national political environment—the expanding influence of interest groups in Washington, the stagnation of middle-class incomes, and a national debt and entitlement spending that appeared to voters as out of control.[26] When assessing the Clinton agenda during the first term as related to major public addresses, it becomes clear that the President's priority list was both expansive and diverse (see Table 6.2). Domestic fiscal and monetary policies ranked first in priority during 1993 and 1995, with health care first in 1994, and unemployment and job creation ranking first in 1996; unlike many of his predecessors, diplomatic/military issues never ranked highest during the first term. Also important to note is how closely grouped many of the categories are—even those policy categories ranked first only held the top spot by a slim margin, followed closely by several other categories. For example, edu-

Table 6.2. Clinton's Public Agenda (Major Public Addresses).[27]

	1993	1994	1995	1996
Domestic				
Education	519 - 9%	445 - 9%	709 - 11%	999 - 14%
Health Care	1037 - 18%	1276 - 26%	246 - 4%	392 - 5%
Welfare/Entitlements	305 - 5%	175 - 4%	941 - 15%	926 - 13%
Anticrime	243 - 4%	675 - 14%	559 - 9%	986 - 14%
Political Reform	98 - 2%	51 - 1%	256 - 4%	72 - 1%
Science/Technology/ Transportation	78 - 1%	12 - <1%	53 - 1%	235 - 3%
Environment/Energy/ Land Management	42 - 1%	31 - 1%	146 - 2%	180 - 3%
Defense	138 - 2%	63 - 1%	115 - 2%	104 - 1%
International				
Diplomatic/Military	569 - 10%	1006 - 21%	1065 - 16%	864 - 12%
Trade/Economic	652 - 11%	403 - 8%	478 - 7%	334 - 5%
Economic				
Domestic Fiscal/Monetary	1244 - 21%	346 - 7%	1148 - 18%	860 - 12%
Unemployment/Jobs	973 - 16%	346 - 7%	736 - 11%	1236 - 17%
Total	N - 5898	N = 4829	N = 6452	N = 7185

cation, welfare/entitlements, and anticrime issues were discussed quite regularly during each year. And, as compared with his television age predecessors, not only did Clinton outperform them in the number of public activities, but his major public addresses were much more issue intensive, as witnessed by the total number of policy references for each year studied.

THE FIRST TIER: THE ANTI-CRIME BILL OF 1994

The Issue and White House Strategy

The issue of how the federal government could aid the nation's fight against crime was not new with the Clinton administration. As early as 1989, during the Bush administration, Congress had begun consideration on various types of anticrime legislation, but due to partisan differences, most legislative attempts failed. By the 1992 presidential campaign, public opinion polls showed crime as a top concern among voters; a political urgency existed as well, as even lawmakers who were "skeptical of federal involvement in what was basically a state and local issue began to insist that Congress act."[28] Clinton himself had long been a supporter of tough anticrime initiatives, which helped to identify him as a self-proclaimed "New Democrat." By 1993, efforts to fight crime still ranked as an urgent issue among voters, as reflected by continuing polls by both the news media and the White House. As a result, Clinton moved his anticrime proposal towards the top of his agenda in 1993 in response to the "sense of national crisis" among the public.[29]

Clinton introduced his anticrime proposal during an August 1993 speech in which he detailed the main aspects of the plan: federal funding to hire 100,000 new police officers; new federal death penalties and changes in the appeals process for death row inmates; a ban on assault weapons; and support for the Brady bill, which required a waiting period and background check before purchase of a handgun. But from the start, the bill represented a tough partisan fight in Congress between conservatives, who wanted tougher penalties imposed on criminals without preventative programs, and liberals, who wanted more prevention without "overzealous incarceration."[30] By the end of 1993, Clinton's public addresses began to focus more heavily on the fight against crime and winning passage of the Democratic anticrime package. By 1994, the issue had moved to the top of the Clinton policy agenda, and in policy prioritization in major addresses, the issue ranked third behind health care reform and diplomatic and military concerns (see Table 6.2). Clinton spoke to diverse audiences on the issue, including law enforcement, religious, and minority groups, among others, and he often would effectively tie the issue of violent crime into the urgent need for health care reform, citing statistics on shootings and other violence that drove up medical expenses for hospital emergency rooms.

By the summer of 1994, the anticrime bill represented an opportunity for crucial political momentum for Clinton. White House aides believed that a legislative victory on the bill would provide a much-needed public boost to Clinton's health care reform package, which like the Clinton presidency, had been taking a beating in public. Clinton and his staff waged a full offensive over the summer months in an attempt to not only win supporters among moderate Republicans, but also among Democrats who had abandoned the party line as well. Clinton ultimately won passage of the bill, watered down from its initial version, due in part to the upcoming midterm elections as members of Congress on both sides of the aisle did not want to appear to voters as having entirely blocked a measure to fight crime.[31] Clinton signed the $30.2 billion anticrime bill into law on September 13, 1994. In the end, the Clinton anticrime bill "narrowly avoided Congressional sabotage," but the victory was perceived as tenuous at best following the 1994 Republican victory in Congress, after which the new majority party announced that it would begin revision on various parts of the bill.[32]

Press Coverage

The *New York Times* provided fairly extensive coverage of Clinton's anti-crime package between August 1993 and September 1994, with a news item appearing, on average, once every three days. However, more than half of all the stories on the issue were generated by congressional activity; the White House generated only slightly more stories than did interest groups (see Table 6.3). Of the stories on Clinton's activities, the tone seemed evenly distributed between support and opposition to the bill (see Table 6.4). Clinton received good coverage in most news stories, mostly accounts of his public addresses on the issue of crime. One story, appearing on November 14, 1993, praised Clinton's speech to a Southern church about the ill effects of crime on society as a "moving" and "emotional and intense" address. Most editorials, however, were not as supportive of the President's policy, often supporting the idea of taking a tougher stance on crime, but critical of various aspects of the bill, including tougher death penalty requirements. And, as the political wrangling in Congress intensified before passage of the bill, the *Times* also criticized Clinton for ineffective leadership on the issue.

THE SECOND TIER: THE NATIONAL SERVICE PLAN OF 1993

The Issue and White House Strategy

During the 1992 presidential campaign, Clinton had outlined a plan to reform the existing federal student loan program by creating a national service trust fund. The goal was to reward those willing to work in community service jobs with money to fund a college education prior to attending, or by wiping out portions of loans after college by taking community service jobs. Clinton wanted to model the program after the Peace Corps, created by the Kennedy administration, which encouraged young Americans to do their part by performing community service work in Third World countries. In his inaugural address in January 1993, reminiscent of Kennedy, Clinton urged young Americans to pledge themselves to "a season of service."[33]

Table 6.3. Amount and Type of *New York Times* Coverage of the Anti-Crime Bill (August 1993-September 1994).

	White House	Congress	Interest Group/Other
News Story	21	46	10
News Analysis	5	13	11
Column	4	4	5
Editorial	9	10	6
Total	39 - (27%)	73 - (51%)	32 - (22%)

Table 6.4. Tone of *New York Times* Coverage of Presidential Activities on the Anti-Crime Bill (August 1993-September 1994).

	Positive	Negative	Balanced/Mixed	Neutral
News Story	7	1	11	2
News Analysis	0	2	3	0
Column	0	3	1	0
Editorial	1	4	4	0
Total	8	10	19	2

The national service plan, later dubbed Americorps, may have been a favorite policy of Clinton's, but it did not merit extensive attention in Clinton's public addresses as a top policy priority. Clinton would introduce the plan in a speech at Rutgers University on March 1, 1993, using a "vocabulary of military combat to talk about service, again attempting to place civilian service closer to a par with military." But following the announcement speech, Clinton would then discuss national service only in a handful of major address, or briefly in other addresses throughout the rest of the year, mostly referring to the plan as one of many items on his list of proposed policy initiatives. Clinton advisors also did not consider the proposal to be a top priority, and they did not provide the press with many off-the-record comments or leaks about the plan, which can often help to generate stories. The national media seemed uninterested, for the most part, in the story; Clinton received no questions during press conferences on his national service plan, and administration officials were not appearing on weekend news shows to promote its passage in Congress.[34]

Despite Republican concerns over creating a new entitlement program and spending too much money, Clinton won congressional passage of his proposal, and he signed the national service bill into law on September 21, 1993. A program designed to "send young people from across the country into communities to serve others," the final plan offered up to $4,725 a year for no more than two years to anyone age 17 or older who performed community service before, during or after college. The amount of the award, due to a political compromise in Congress, had been trimmed dramatically from the $10,000 amount that Clinton had initially proposed.[35] The national service plan ranked among other new initiatives promoted by Clinton in the early months of his administration that helped define his "New Democrat" policy agenda, and it gave the President "his most clear-cut win among new initiatives in the first [congressional] session."[36]

Press Coverage

Like other members of the national press, the *Times* did not give much coverage to Clinton's national service plan. Only a total of 35 news items appeared in the *Times* between February and September 1993, with an average of just over one news item every ten days. Both the White House and Congress generated equal amounts of coverage, with 40 percent each (with two front page stories for White House activities); while interest group activity generated the remaining 20 percent of coverage (see Table 6.5). However, the *Times* seemed to approve of the plan, as Clinton received no negative coverage on this issue; most coverage was either positive or balanced in tone (see Table 6.6). The low overall numbers for amount of news coverage in the *Times* are not surprising, considering that Clinton did not aggressively pursue the issue publicly, and that the plan was not a hotly contested political issue for Congress.

CONCLUSION

As this chapter shows, Clinton may have been able to blame the press for some of his troubles, but his leadership style also contributed to a mixed record on the public perception of his administration. He seemed to ignore the emerging catch phrase of the 1990s that "more is not necessarily better." His first term in office supported both the notion of a pres-

Table 6.5. Amount and Type of New York Times Coverage of the National Service Plan (February 1993-September 1993).

	White House	Congress	Interest Group/Other
News Story	6	12	6
News Analysis	2	0	0
Column	4	0	0
Editorial	2	2	1
Total	14 - (40%)	14 - (40%)	7 - (20%)

Table 6.6. Tone of New York Times Coverage of Presidential Activities on the National Service Plan (February 1993-September 1993).

	Positive	Negative	Balanced/Mixed	Neutral
News Story	1	0	3	2
News Analysis	0	0	2	0
Column	1	0	3	0
Editorial	1	0	1	0
Total	3	0	9	2

ident's willingness to now go public quite often to promote his agenda, as well as that of the perpetual campaign presidency. Clinton's willingness to discuss policy issues with both the press and the public was evident in the sheer volume of his public activities. Clearly, Clinton was never at a loss for not only a public response to a policy issue, but also a venue in which to provide it. Also, in his major public addresses, Clinton discussed an extensive list of issues, often in great detail. However, a general observation can be made about the pattern of Clinton's major public addresses; that is, many of his addresses in 1993 showed inconsistencies in their policy focus, with a willingness on his part to discuss a lot of issues in great detail in many speeches. But by 1994, a clearer, more methodical pattern emerged in terms of continuing to mention several policies in each speech, but more briefly, allowing more of a focus to emerge on one or two key policy proposals.

While the final assessments on the Clinton administration have yet to be made, he provides a challenge to any student of the American presidency. The goals and strategies of the Clinton White House were certainly complex. Not to discount the depth of previous administrations in their policy orientations or legislative goals, the Clinton team outpaced most predecessors in both the amount of public activities by the President, and the amount of issues on the policy agenda. Like most presidents, Clinton had his successes, and he seemed to learn from early miscues, at least in terms of his communication strategy. But if the ultimate goal of any administration is to win reelection, then despite Clinton's troubles with an ever-increasingly critical news media, like Nixon and Reagan, he must have done something right, at least in the eyes of the electorate of 1996.

In retrospect, news media coverage of scandals during the 1992 campaign seems to pale in comparison to the top story, and at times the only story, of 1998. Scholars and political pundits alike will continue to assess the impact of the Lewinsky scandal on the Clinton presidency for many years to come. For the purposes of this discussion, it is important to point out that, while the press has been increasingly cynical and critical of presidents since Watergate, the Clinton years have set new precedents for a tabloid style of journalism among the national political press. Particularly evident in 1998, competition among news outlets to break the latest detail of presidential scandal has not only damaged the image of the presidency, but created a backlash from the public against the press as well. The 24-hour television news cycle also allows stories to break before all details have emerged or facts can be accurately checked and verified. Clinton's high public approval ratings throughout Starr's investigation, the House deliberations on impeachment, and the Senate trial seem to suggest that, not only did the public separate their personal and political views of Clinton, but that they ignored much of the news media's characterization of the story as a "crisis" of tremendous proportion at the highest levels of government. Perhaps most evident in this later chapter of the Clinton saga was the disconnect between the national news media and the public at large. This trend has been building for many years, as more Americans feel alienated from Washington politics, and as reporters continue a discussion among themselves and other political elites about inside-the-Beltway issues. This represents a challenge for the next occupant of the Oval Office, especially in developing a communication strategy. Clinton's advisors recognized the need to create the means to circumvent the White House press corps as they looked for more positive coverage of the President. But thanks to Clinton, the "personal" is now the "political" more than ever, which may represent his greatest legacy, albeit a negative one, for the development of future White House communication strategies.

ENDNOTES

1. William Clinton, *Public Papers of the Presidents, 1993*, Vol. I (Washington, DC: Government Printing Office, 1994).
2. David Shaw, "Not Even Getting a First Chance," *Los Angeles Times*, 15 September 1993, A10-11.
3. David Lauter, "Year After Election, Clinton Alters His View of Change," *Los Angeles Times*, 7 November 1993, A1, 28-9.
4. Tom Rosenstiel, *The Beat Goes On: President Clinton's First Year With the Media* (New York: Twentieth Century Fund Press, 1994), 18-22.
5. Martha Joynt Kumar, "President Clinton Meets the Media: Communications Shaped by Predictable Patterns," in *The Clinton Presidency: Campaigning, Governing, and the Psychology of Leadership*, Ed. Stanley A. Renshon (Boulder, CO: Westview Press, 1995), 167-93.
6. Bob Woodward, *The Agenda: Inside the Clinton White House* (New York: Simon & Schuster, 1994), 111-3.
7. Fred I. Greenstein, "The Two Leadership Styles of William Jefferson Clinton," *Political Psychology* 15 (1994): 351-61.
8. George C. Edwards, III, "Campaigning is Not Governing: Bill Clinton's Rhetorical Presidency," in *The Clinton Legacy*, Eds. Colin Campbell and Bert A. Rockman (New York: Chatham House Publishers, 2000), 37.
9. Robert E. Denton, Jr. and Rachel L. Holloway, "Clinton and the Town Hall Meetings: Mediated Conversation and the Risk of Being 'In Touch,'" in *The Clinton Presidency: Images, Issues, and Communication Strategies*, Eds. Robert E. Denton, Jr. and Rachel L. Holloway (Westport, CT: Praeger Publishers, 1996), 30.
10. John Anthony Maltese, *Spin Control: The White House Office of Communications and the Management of Presidential News*, 2nd rev. ed. (Chapel Hill, NC: The University of North Carolina Press, 1994), 234.
11. Elizabeth Drew, *On the Edge: The Clinton Presidency* (New York: Simon & Schuster, 1994), 54.
12. Dean E. Alger, *The Media and Politics*, 2nd ed. (Belmont, CA: Wadsworth Publishing, 1996), 202-3.
13. James Fallows, *Breaking the News: How the Media Undermine American Democracy* (New York: Vintage Books, 1997), 34-5.
14. Eleanor Clift, "Don't Mess With the Media," *Newsweek*, 7 June 1993, 23.
15. Ibid.
16. Mickey Kaus, "Tribal Hatred," *The New Republic*, 21 June 1993, 4.
17. David Shaw, "Not Even Getting a First Chance," *Los Angeles Times*, 15 September 1993, A-10-1.
18. Fallows, 24.

19. George C. Edwards, III and Stephen J. Wayne, *Presidential Leadership: Politics and Policy Making*, 5th ed. (New York: St. Martin's Press, 1999), 124-5.
20. Edwards, "Campaigning is Not Governing," 43.
21. Ibid., 44.
22. Stephen C. Wood and Jean M. DeWitt, "Bill Clinton," in *U.S. Presidents as Orators: A Bio-Critical Sourcebook*, Ed. Halford Ryan (Westport, CT: Greenwood Press, 1995), 361-74.
23. Drew, 77-8.
24. Compiled from the *Public Papers of the Presidents: William Clinton, 1993-1996* (Washington, DC: Government Printing Office, 1994-1998).
25. See William W. Lammers, "Domestic Policy Leadership in the First Year" in *Understanding the Presidency*, Eds. James P. Pfiffner and Roger H. Davidson (New York: Longman, 1997), 224-9; and James P. Pfiffner, *The Strategic Presidency: Hitting the Ground Running*, 2nd rev. ed. (Lawrence, KS: University Press of Kansas, 1996), 173-82.
26. David Stoesz, *Small Change: Domestic Policy Under the Clinton Presidency* (New York: Longman, 1996), 195-7.
27. Compiled from the *Public Papers of the Presidents: William Clinton, 1993-1996* (Washington, DC: Government Printing Office, 1994-1998).
28. *Congressional Quarterly Almanac, 1994*, Vol. L (Washington, DC: Congressional Quarterly Service, 1995), 274.
29. Drew, 416.
30. *Congressional Quarterly Almanac, 1994*, 273.
31. Drew, 432-3.
32. Stoesz, 109.
33. *Congressional Quarterly Almanac, 1993*, Vol. XLIX (Washington, DC: Congressional Quarterly Service, 1994), 400.
34. Steven Waldman, "The Cynical White House Media," in *Understanding the Presidency*, Eds. James P. Pfiffner and Roger H. Davidson (New York: Longman, 1997), 99-103.
35. *Congressional Quarterly Almanac, 1993*, 400.
36. Charles O. Jones, "Campaigning to Govern: The Clinton Style," in *The Clinton Presidency: First Appraisals*, Eds. Colin Campbell and Bert A. Rockman (Chatham, NJ: Chatham House Publishers, 1996), 38.

7

Is Governing from Center
Stage Possible?

A comparison of White House communication strategies during the last
four decades—an era of politics that has been greatly defined by the
mass media's participation—shows not only how communicating to various groups and in various venues has become an integral part of a president's daily routine, but also shows that most presidents are limited in
their capacity to control both the image and message of their administrations. The president has emerged, especially during the television age, as
a dominant rhetorical figure in American politics, representing a national constituency, and having many opportunities to influence the national
agenda. This analysis of eight administrations suggests that presidents
are capable of developing successful communication strategies to get
their message out to the public although some presidents have been
more successful than others. The institutional nature of the presidency,
and the role that the press plays within it, can limit a president's options
in the development and implementation of strategies, but attempts to
influence the public's perception of the president are not always futile.
Most presidents in recent years have attempted to improve upon their
early mistakes while in office, especially when dealing with the press
and in other public activities, and most experience something of a learning curve as they become accustomed to the responsibilities of the office.
But the uniqueness of each president's leadership style cannot be com-

pletely ignored since every president leaves his mark, in one way or another, on the Oval Office, especially where communication strategies are concerned. As a result, each administration, at least in recent years, has served in the development of an institutional learning curve on press and public relations for future presidents to follow. Each has also affected the political environment, in part through their communication strategies, that future presidents must contend with in order to govern. But an important question remains—is a president who is successful at communicating his message to the public truly fulfilling the requirements for governing the nation?

A COMPARISON OF PRESIDENTS

A comparative analysis between the eight presidents considered here can be made to assess the effectiveness of the use of a communication strategy in two respects: first, how do presidents attempt to use public activities to communicate and set their agendas; and second, what type of press coverage results from such public activities? More broadly considered, why does this matter? The news media plays a crucial role in helping a president communicate, and communication is an integral part of presidential leadership. Understanding the relationship between the institutions of the presidency and the news media is important in understanding the presidential role within the constitutional framework. By constitutional design, presidents are limited in their capacity for leadership, and developing an effective communication strategy is now an additional burden that presidents must face. Also, both the public and the press have high expectations of presidents in the area of communication, therefore, much of what presidents and their advisors now do, whether it has an impact on policymaking or not, centers on delivering a message. Understanding the impact that individual presidents have had on the evolution of communication strategies helps to explain the institutionalized nature of communicating that now exists in the White House, which in turn limits the potential for national leadership. Effective communication may not be effective governance, yet presidents still devote a great deal of attention to the activities discussed below.

The Presidential-Press Relationship

All presidents are concerned with the flow of news from the executive branch, and all strive to achieve positive, or at the very least, fair, coverage. Each administration since the Kennedy years has struggled in its attempt to speak in one voice when representing the president's agenda to the press. This is a tremendous challenge, especially due to the growth of both the executive branch and the news media. Not only are there more people to give comments to the press on the president's policies, but more people within the news media now listen, record, and interpret the responses. Reporters are also quick to jump on dissension within an administration, which occurs if executive branch officials make conflicting responses. The Reagan administration was perhaps the most successful at managing their "line of the day" message to the press, but complete control in this area is virtually impossible with so many conflicting political agendas within one administration.

By most accounts, Kennedy and Reagan had effective communication strategies and both had a good relationship with the press. Johnson, Nixon, Ford, Carter, and Bush are viewed as poor communicators for various reasons, and they did not enjoy a good relationship with the press. The verdict on the Clinton years has yet to be fully determined; Clinton survived various onslaughts of negative coverage, but he certainly did not master the press. The impact of Kennedy's relationship with the press is still being felt today. No subsequent president has been able to live up to the image portrayed on television by Kennedy. Also, the medium of television is no longer novel or new, yet many presidents have longed for that golden, innocent era during the early 1960s when personal and political scandal did not dominate political reporting from Washington. The current political environment with the news media that presidents must face—which has steadily evolved since Vietnam and Watergate—is one that breeds mistrust, cynicism, and fierce competition among members of the White House press corps and their respective publications and news shows. The Reagan administration was especially skilled at controlling the message that came out of the White House, and this may have spoiled the press for anything less than the complete media package that sold both the president's image and his agenda. Presidents may now be doomed from the start, unable to establish what they consider to be a good relationship with the press; the Reagan years may have been a temporary respite that allowed skillful media advisors to partially control the content of the message. But while presidents work hard to achieve "good" press coverage, determining what is good for the president in terms of control over the message may not be the same as presenting substantive information about the political process to the American electorate.

For nearly 40 years, presidents have been developing specific strategies in their attempts to effectively manage the White House press corps. Other strategies have been developed to circumvent these same reporters. No one can dispute the fact that each side needs the other to do its job; the White House certainly aids the news media in providing a tremendous amount of information on the president and his policies. The Office of Communications has evolved into an effective public relations arm of the White House since its inception during the Nixon years. And since the Kennedy years, all presidents have recognized the value of promoting their agendas through non-Washington media, whether it is through regional press briefings and interviews, extensive press advance efforts, or invitations for regional and local news executives to Washington for White House events. The daily news summary has also grown into an important informational tool for presidents in the development of their daily communications. But despite these many efforts, presidents must always deal with the White House press corps and other representatives from the national news media. Striking the balance as to how much exposure and the type of relationship that the president will have with these individuals is perhaps the most important strategy.

Promising an "open" presidency, or a president promising to be honest with the press, does not guarantee a beneficial relationship for the president and his agenda with the press. Johnson lied to the press, Nixon both lied to and hid from the press, and Ford, Carter, and Bush were all the victims of bad timing with the press. (Any president to hold office in the first years after Watergate would have experienced an uphill battle with the press, as would any president following the successful news management during the Reagan years.) Not only do Americans expect too much from their presidents, but both the public and presidents may also expect too much from the press. If Kennedy and Reagan truly did have a good relationship with the press, it may not be a situation that is easily duplicated by other presidents. Kennedy had success due to his image, personality, friends among the White House press corps, and timing in office, entering when the medium of television was still so new. Reagan had skilled advisors who knew how to use his best leadership attributes, mostly his communication skills in front of a camera, to his best advantage. He also benefited from timing, as his advisors filled the informational needs of an expanding medium with well-packaged stories and ample photo opportunities. But even Reagan was not always able to completely control his image or his message in the press. Understanding the institutionalized "how" and "why" of White House news coverage should suggest to presidents that much of what the press does is beyond their control. Perhaps the best that any president can hope for is fair and accurate information (although the question of accuracy was certainly raised during coverage of the Monica Lewinsky scandal in 1998).

Public Activities

Not surprisingly, presidents now "go public" more often than ever before, in part because there are more outlets for presidential communications than ever before (see Table 7.1). The increase in presidential activities over the years can be attributed to not only the historical context of the role and capability of the news media during each administration, but to the president's public style as well. Since many presidential activities are now planned for optimum coverage on television, the White House relies more heavily, as especially witnessed during the Reagan administration, on using photo opportunities to achieve their few seconds of airtime on network newscasts. Also not surprising is an increase in the number of public activities during an election year, whether the event is in support of the president's own reelection efforts or in support of other members of his party.

The Clinton yearly totals for his first term in office certainly show a marked increase from the Kennedy years, which are more than double in the number of public activities. Like Clinton, other totals reflect the public leadership style of the particular president; for example, Nixon's totals decrease with each passing year in office. This reflects his unwillingness for extensive access to the press, and his administration's belief that less was better so as to protect the "myth" of the presidency. However, it is important to remember that presidential public events during the 1960s and early 1970s were not tailored to television coverage, but mostly to the audience in attendance, as well as the traditional Washington press corps, which at the time was still dominated by print journalists. Ford and Carter both attempted to return the presidency to the people, and many of their public appearances were geared at interacting with not only the press, but citizens as well. And of these eight presidents, Ford holds the record for most public activities during a particular year—681 in 1976, which includes the first weeks of January 1977—a presidential campaign year. The trend for increased public appearances continues with Reagan, whose advisors learned early on that he "packaged" well for television photo opportunities; the amount of Reagan's yearly public activities remains fairly consistent throughout his eight years in office. The 1980s, and even more so for Bush and Clinton in the 1990s, was also a time of increasing technological capabilities for the broadcast press, with instant "you are there" coverage available through satellite transmissions. Unlike earlier eras, the years from Reagan to Clinton required a press strategy that prepared for the ongoing political coverage found on CNN, in addition to the traditional network news. The Clinton numbers peak in 1994, but even as they decline slightly during 1995 and rebound again in 1996, Clinton's activities still greatly outpace most of his predecessors, reflecting the Clinton campaign style of aggressively promoting many items on his policy agenda.

Table 7.1. Comparison of Total Presidential Public Activities (By Years During Each Term).

	1st Year	2nd Year	3rd Year	4th Year	5th Year	6th Year	7th Year	8th Year
Kennedy (1961-1963)	198	291	284*	—	—	—	—	—
Johnson (1963-1969)	507**	256	318	267	332	—	—	—
Nixon (1969-1974)	266	230	170	156	138	103*	—	—
Ford (1974-1977)	157*	403	681	—	—	—	—	—
Carter (1977-1981)	326	362	285	458	—	—	—	—
Reagan (1981-1989)	252	378	405	441	317	317	366	394
Bush (1989-1993)	427	481	501	583	—	—	—	—
Clinton (1993-1996)	643	638	541	628	—	—	—	—

*Represents less than a full year in office
**Includes the last 40 days of 1963

What has changed since the Kennedy years is the number of public venues available to presidents. Again, expanding technology has aided this trend. An appearance via satellite is now commonplace for a president that cannot attend a convention in person. Roundtable discussions, townhall meetings, and question and answer sessions with either reporters or citizens are now also popular venues for presidents. This trend began with Ford and has continued with every administration since, functioning as a means to answer questions directly from citizens, members of particular interest groups involved in the policymaking process, or members of the local and regional press. The appeal is that, while the national news media may choose whether they cover the event, they are usually not in charge of the questions asked or the topics that the president must discuss. During the 1992 presidential campaign and early in his administration, Clinton made headlines as the first presidential candidate, and then president, to appear on a forum for MTV (where he received the now infamous question regarding "boxers or briefs"). Television events such as this, other townhall meetings), or appearances on *Larry King Live* may give presidents more options in delivering their message unfiltered to the audience, but television has also adversely affected the president's leadership potential:

> The television presidency operates on television's terms. As the medium personalizes government, so does it accelerate it and politicize it. Skillful presidents have learned how to use the medium to communicate their version of events to the nation, but this advantage is balanced by the rapidity with which presidents in the television age are expected to accomplish objectives and by the self-serving political manner in which their actions are cast.[1]

The up-close-and-personal look at our presidents that television now provides through the plethora of public venues has also altered the political environment in which the president must lead. The high public approval ratings maintained by Clinton throughout 1998 seem to suggest that, not only do Americans now expect the personal lives of our presidents to make headlines, but we are also desensitized to tabloid-style reporting about personal indiscretions.

The definition of what constitutes a major presidential public address has also changed since the Kennedy era. All presidents continue to address a joint session of Congress for annual State of the Union messages or when other events necessitate such an address, such as Bush's address following the Gulf War. Presidents also continue to address the nation from the Oval Office or perhaps from a more relaxed setting within the White House, such as the library, for issues of national importance (for example, Kennedy on the Cuban missile crisis and civil rights,

Johnson and Nixon on Vietnam, Carter on energy). But other public venues, such as national conventions for interest groups or other organizations, have become increasingly popular venues for presidents to deliver major policy addresses. Kennedy, Johnson, and Nixon all relied on traditional speaking engagements—such as meetings for labor, business, or law enforcement groups, commencement addresses at major universities, or annual addresses to the United Nations General Assembly each September—to deliver remarks outside of the White House about policy initiatives. But over the years, presidents attend even more national conventions, both in and out of Washington, and participate in more speaking engagements for the purpose of delivering a major policy address, especially evident with Clinton. While every other president studied here averaged between 10 and 20 major policy addresses each year, Clinton averaged more than 40 major policy addresses each year during his first term.

Presidential press conferences with the White House press corps, with some televised coverage, still remains a mainstay in presidential public venues. However, with the exception of Bush's ill-fated attempt to hold more press conferences, the frequency of these events has been on a steady decline with recent presidents. The reason is that presidents now prefer to focus on providing a targeted message to the American public, which is compatible with the news routines on television. But this decreases the desire for a president to hold regular press conferences, where he will be asked a wide variety of questions, many of which he may wish to avoid. It is not surprising that Clinton held so few press conferences. First, he used a wide variety of other venues, and second, the press conference lacks control:

> His venue of choice is most often limited to events emphasizing the routine rather than the extraordinary about the presidency. The controlled White House event is his venue. Such events are focused around a specific policy, make full use of the ornaments of the presidency, involve a brief appearance by the President, a few supporting administration and outside figures related to the substance of the event, and are events that can be scripted beforehand. They are short, targeted, and fairly risk free.[2]

Perhaps the lesson to be learned from Clinton is that a press conference is good for discussing broader policy objectives, but not a good thing if the president is facing critical questions about personal behavior.[3]

While no president during the twentieth century made better use of radio addresses than did Franklin Roosevelt with his "fireside chats," both Reagan (starting in 1982) and Clinton relied on weekly radio addresses to supplement their public activity agenda. Nixon, with the urging of several advisors, used a limited number of radio addresses while in office, most notably in 1973, with six policy addresses that substituted for a State of the Union address. Both Ford and Carter gave a handful of radio addresses during their presidential campaigns in 1976 and 1980, respectively, and Bush gave 5 in 1991 and 13 in 1992. Both Reagan and Clinton have relied on radio addresses to target specific policies, most often domestic or economic, as an additional means to reach citizens who may not watch television, and on the news media for additional coverage of a controlled event. (The president's weekly radio address, in addition to the opposing party's response, routinely makes the weekend news on CNN and a variety of other news sources.)

Given the number of public activities in which presidents now participate, speechwriting plays an increasingly important role in preparing the president for his public addresses. The irony, however, is that while speechwriting serves an important function in the White House, especially in an attempt to mold the president's image and overall policy message, most presidential speeches get little or no media coverage. Traditional speeches, such as the State of the Union or important foreign policy announcements, especially those involving U.S. military action, will always make headlines. However, as many studies on the content of political news have demonstrated in recent years, or as any regular viewer of network news can attest, coverage of substantive policy issues is not action oriented, and as such, is not usually newsworthy on television. Many of Clinton's speeches during the late summer and fall of 1998 received live coverage on CNN and MSNBC, but not because of their policy statements. Instead, the news media wanted to be front and center just in case the President decided to publicly apologize yet again for his affair with Lewinsky, or make other comments related to the scandal and his subsequent impeachment hearings.

Policy Prioritization and the Public Agenda

Also not surprising, presidents use major public addresses to talk about foreign policy matters more often than any other topic (see Table 7.2). As the public agendas of all eight presidents show, international diplomatic and military concerns are a frequent topic of major public addresses (national addresses, policy addresses, radio addresses, and opening statements at press conferences). Also of considerable importance are domestic fiscal and monetary matters; rarely do other domestic issues merit frequent discussions in major addresses. However, these results can also be explained, at least in part, by historical context as well as by presidential leadership style. The Kennedy era represented both a time period and a president focused on the Cold War and anticommunist

Table 7.2. Comparison of Policy Prioritization of the Public Agenda (Top Issue by Years in Office).

	1st Year	2nd Year	3rd Year	4th Year	5th Year	6th Year	7th Year	8th Year
Kennedy (1961-1963)	Diplomatic/ Military	Diplomatic/ Military	Diplomatic/ Military	—	—	—	—	—
Johnson (1963-1969)	Diplomatic/ Military	Diplomatic/ Military	Diplomatic/ Military	Diplomatic/ Military	Diplomatic/ Military	—	—	—
Nixon (1969-1974)	Diplomatic/ Military	Diplomatic/ Military	Diplomatic/ Military	Diplomatic/ Military	Domestic Fiscal/ Monetary	Domestic Fiscal/ Monetary	—	—
Ford (1974-1977)	Trade/ Economic	Domestic Fiscal/ Monetary	Domestic Fiscal/ Monetary	—	—	—	—	—
Carter (1977-1981)	Diplomatic/ Military	Diplomatic/ Military	Diplomatic/ Military	Diplomatic/ Military	—	—	—	—
Reagan (1981-1989)	Domestic Fiscal/ Monetary	Domestic Fiscal/ Monetary	Diplomatic/ Military	Diplomatic/ Military	Diplomatic/ Military	Diplomatic/ Military	Diplomatic/ Military	Diplomatic/ Military
Bush (1989-1993)	Diplomatic/ Military	Diplomatic/ Military	Diplomatic/ Military	Diplomatic/ Military	—	—	—	—
Clinton (1993-1996)	Domestic Fiscal/l Monetary	Health Care	Domestic Fiscal/ Monetary	Unemploy ment/ Jobs	—⋅	—	—	—

policies. Both Johnson and Nixon were consumed with the American involvement in the Vietnam War, and while Nixon's public activities were limited, he used national televised addresses quite frequently in order to update the public on the ongoing situation in Southeast Asia. Nixon also had a much higher interest in foreign affairs, and his policies of détente with the Soviet Union and his historic trip to China during his first term took top priority over domestic issues. Carter worked extensively to bring peace to the Middle East, attempted to negotiate new arms treaties with the Soviets, brokered the Panama Canal treaty, and had to face the Iranian hostage crisis beginning in November 1979. Reagan was elected, in part, on his promise to reverse the sagging American economic trends of the late 1970s; once he achieved passage of his extensive economic package in 1981, his priorities shifted to foreign affairs, including U.S.-Soviet relations and American military involvement in the Middle East and Grenada. Bush also focused more often on foreign affairs than domestic issues, and he held office at a time when major international events, such as the fall of the Soviet block, were occurring, and the U.S. military was involved in military actions in Panama and the Persian Gulf.

Ford and Clinton are the only two presidents of these eight to break the trend of focusing more on international issues than domestic ones. As those of an unelected president, the Ford years are unique in many ways. His two and a half years in the White House were more like a long presidential campaign instead of presidential leadership, with Ford first trying to introduce himself to the American public and then running for election to the office in his own right. But his time in the Oval Office was also plagued by a sharp economic downturn and the energy crisis, which is where most of his attention was focused. Like both Ford and Reagan, Clinton also faced a downturn in economic conditions upon taking office, and true to his campaign pledges, he aggressively pursued changes in domestic fiscal and monetary policies in 1993. By 1994, attempts to win passage of his sweeping health care reform proposal took top priority, but that was followed closely by international diplomatic and military issues, such as the ongoing civil war in Bosnia and American military involvement in Haiti. The Clinton totals were closely grouped in 1995 and 1996, with domestic economic concerns only slightly edging out the Diplomatic/Military and Welfare/Entitlement categories. Presidents, it seems, are expected to talk most often about foreign and economic matters in their public addresses. Whether or not Clinton has set a precedent for a new trend in this area has yet to be determined.

White House Strategies on Domestic Issues

Finally, the question remains: Did each president, through his public activities, influence news coverage of key domestic agenda issues? In other words, did White House communication strategies for the selected domestic policies succeed or fail? Again, the results are mixed, as this question raises several important considerations. And, since only one major news source was used for this analysis, the results are also limited in their breadth. However, specific trends did emerge across coverage for the eight presidencies, and therefore, the results are suggestive of other trends that may exist across various sources within the news industry. First, most news items in the *New York Times* were news stories and editorials for first-tier issues, with a few columns and/or news analyses, while second-tier issues mostly garnered news stories, with few editorials, columns, or news analyses. The formats of news items did not change much throughout the time period studied.

Nor did the content of news items change in terms of tone over time. At least in the *Times,* a leading source of news in the United States, news stories that were neutral or balanced/mixed in tone—and even a handful that portrayed the president and his policy in a positive light— still appeared as frequently for Clinton as they did for Kennedy nearly 40 years earlier. Editorials also remain consistent in content and tone; the *Times* can be supportive of a president's policy initiatives, but is not afraid to take the president to task for policy stances with which the editorial board does not agree, or for what it perceives as ineffective political leadership on the part of the president. This trend was consistent for each president and policy included in this study.

Overall, for all news items included, coverage seemed balanced for each policy studied. Expecting ongoing positive coverage for any president, even on an issue the *Times* may support, seems unrealistic. Editorials especially seem to reflect an impatience and dismay at political bickering on certain issues although it seems unrealistic to expect the policy making process to go smoothly in a government system destined for gridlock by its very design. So, does that mean that the editorial board at the *Times* is naive about the political process? More than likely, no; instead, perhaps the formats and content of covering political issues have become institutionalized within the organization of the news room, providing a predictable routine for the editorial staff to follow. Also, recent studies have discussed how news coverage of presidential campaigns, due in part to television's influence, has changed from a descriptive and more objective style during the 1950s and 1960s to a more interpretive and subjective style during the 1980s and 1990s.[4] While this sample of news coverage is limited, this trend did not appear in news coverage of presidential domestic policies. Most news items in the *Times* would provide a textbook example of how to write a news story for any introductory journalism course.

Finally, did a partisan difference or ideological bias exist in the news coverage in the *Times*? By historical circumstance, the eight presidents included in this study break down evenly with four from each major party, which provides a good sample to determine if the *Times*, always perceived as liberal in its political leanings, provided more favorable coverage of Democrats than of Republicans in the White House. Again, the limitations of this study do not allow for a conclusive assessment; however, in terms of partisan differences in coverage, any ideological bias that may appear results from the standpoint of specific policies, not of specific presidents. Many assumptions exist that, based on party identification and policy objectives, Republicans get worse coverage than do Democrats. Also, another safe assumption might be that Republican presidents like Nixon, whose administration waged open warfare against the press, would receive less than positive coverage from a charter member of the biased "Eastern establishment" press. However, at least on the domestic front, Nixon's policies were often well received by *Times* editorials. Again, negative coverage would show up later in the policy making process, especially as Congress began considering the policies. At least from this limited perspective, presidents seem to be interchangeable for the news media's purposes; the president has always been a key newsmaker in Washington, but they only seem to take priority in patterns of news coverage at the beginning and end of the policy making process. Perhaps when a president receives critical news coverage of his policies, his anger may be best directed at Congress, whose partisan activities on Capitol Hill can at times promote unfavorable and even cynical news coverage.

Press Coverage of Domestic Policies

When looking at the news coverage in the *Times* of selected domestic policies, a majority of the coverage was not generated by presidential activities. This is somewhat surprising given the president's status as the national leader, and as such, is most often in the best position to influence the national policy agenda. In most cases, the president receives more coverage than does any other political leader, but it is important to note that "although this imbalance in news coverage may reflect a bias toward the presidency and the office's occupant, it is not a bias toward a particular person, party, or ideology."[5] However, first-tier policy issues are higher priority agenda items, and they are also broad and/or sweeping policies. As a result, as Congress begins to consider legislation to create the laws of the land, the political give-and-take on and off Capitol Hill during the process provides a more action-packed news story than a presidential sound byte. For seven of the eight first-tier policies considered (with the exception of Bush and education), Congress by far generated the most news stories in the *Times;* the White House ranked a distant third in generating stories for Kennedy's tax cut proposal of 1963, Johnson's Medicare proposal in 1965, Nixon's welfare reform proposal in 1971-1972, Carter's national energy plan in 1977-1978, and Reagan's position on social security reform in 1982-1983. Both Ford's proposed tax cut in 1975 and Clinton's anticrime bill in 1994 barely beat out stories generated by interest group activity to rank second. Bush's education initiative in 1989-1990 received little coverage in general, due mostly to the lack of a substantive policy proposal submitted to Congress. Of interest here is the fact that the expansion of the rhetorical presidency presumes to exclude Congress from the public debate on policy issues:

> Today the pace of policy development follows less the rhythms of Congress and more the dynamics of public opinion. The consequence of this development is not only that Congress will often be left out of the deliberative stages of policy formation and that rhetorical imperatives will play a large role, but also that Congress will be forced to respond in kind.[6]

While this is certainly true, this data would suggest that Congress is considered a high priority in news media coverage of the policymaking process, which is an important source of information for other political actors and the public as well.

The results, however, were somewhat mixed for second-tier policy issues. Kennedy, who did not give domestic issues high priority on his public agenda, still ranked third in story generation behind Congress and interest group activity for his aid to education proposal in 1961, as did Johnson's Safe Streets Act in 1968, Carter's civil service reform in 1978, and Bush's proposed amendments to the Clean Air Act of 1990. Nixon, on the other hand, held the lead in generating stories on environmental protection in 1970, due in part to his use of executive powers in creating the EPA without extensive involvement from Congress. The Ford White House ranked second behind stories generated by interest group activity with the proposed Energy Corporation in 1975, but Congress took little action on the proposal, which left out an important source for most stories on the policymaking process. When Reagan proposed cuts to student loans and other federal education aid programs in 1982, interest groups and other political actors took center stage in news coverage in the *Times.* And finally, Clinton tied with Congress in generating the most stories on his pet project, the National Service Plan, in 1993. In general, the *Times* gave significantly less coverage to most second-tier issues when compared to first-tier issues.

WHITE HOUSE COMMUNICATION STRATEGIES: USEFUL OR FUTILE?

The larger question still remains as to the usefulness of White House communication strategies—can presidents make a difference in this area in determining the overall success of their administrations? Clearly, presidents and their administrations do develop communication strategies; so, on the surface that would suggest that those within the White House believe that a strategy can make a difference. Each president, and his administration, has distinct strengths and weaknesses. In the public realm, a charismatic speaking style, such as Kennedy's, or successful news management as seen during the Reagan years, can alter the public's perception of the president, which can, in turn, affect public approval. So, while a successful communication strategy does not make or break a presidency, it becomes a key component of the complex nature of the current state of presidential leadership. Dealing with the press has always been a part of being president, but in the twentieth century, the press has emerged as an even bigger political player. Therefore, as part of the job description, presidents and their advisors have devised strategies in an attempt to use the press to their advantage—some successfully, some not. As the mass media's role in politics continues to change and evolve, so too does the office of the presidency. And when considering communication strategies, the learning curve becomes apparent. Every administration has a different game plan, but most administrations during the last half of the twentieth century seem to have built on those of previous administrations, usually learning something from the mistakes of other presidents or continuing activities that were successful.

While presidents and their communication strategies have evolved with the news media, the Kennedy years still define the epitome of a successful president during the television age of politics. Since then, Reagan has been the only other president who came close, but even so with a much different style. In developing a communication strategy, style does matter since not every president will be comfortable in every format. Clinton, for example, was at his best during a townhall meeting or question and answer session with the public, while Reagan excelled at well-staged, scripted, and controlled media events. When portraying the president, the news media can accentuate the positive and hide the negative, as with Kennedy, whose youth and vigor seemed to always come through in his televised appearances, hiding his various health problems. The opposite can also be true, as with Johnson and Nixon, whose less appealing personality attributes seemed accentuated with news media exposure. Kennedy's use of television, thanks to timing, was also successful because his use of the medium was new and innovative; he developed the standard which his successors would try to emulate. The Reagan administration, on the other hand, took the use of television to a new level, thanks to technological advancements and the ability of his advisors to "package and sell" the President to the American public.

For American presidents, Kennedy seemed to open the Pandora's box using the news media, leaving in his wake many consequences for the state of presidential leadership. Presidents now find themselves facing several dilemmas: having the most influence to set the national agenda while at the same time providing unrealistic expectations to the public about policy capabilities; being aided by a large and resourceful staff of advisors, but risking abuses of power in the name of the presidency by a cumbersome staff whose actions are impossible to monitor at all times; and enjoying tremendous national visibility to reaffirm the leadership position of the president, but often becoming the public's scapegoat when things go awry. The presidency has often been characterized as a "no-win" office, where leadership strategies and often the president himself are considered insignificant.[7] Despite the fact that the Founders, in writing the Constitution, sought to limit the powers of the executive branch, presidents have found ways to become significant political players through both enumerated powers, such as the legislative veto, and prerogative powers, such as using the presidential bully pulpit to sway public opinion. But ultimately, whether or not a president accomplishes anything on his agenda depends on the entire political environment at any given time.

Past studies on the presidency have suggested many trends in leadership; among them, the limited window of opportunity soon after taking office, which means a president must "hit the ground running"[8] with his legislative agenda. Also, studies have pointed out that presidents can only successfully affect the legislative agenda "at the margins,"[9] and that in an attempt to control the political agenda, presidents now rely on a leadership strategy of "going public."[10] These studies have been quite instructive and insightful in developing a better understanding of the modern presidency. Yet, as presidency scholars grapple with the methodological question of studying the institution versus the president, no study can explain every president in every situation. Reagan was certainly successful in terms of winning passage of his broad economic plan during his first year in office, but his legislative success tailed off quite dramatically during his remaining years in office. Clinton, on the other hand, has had legislative success at various points during his time in office, even remaining productive with the Republican Congress elected in 1994, in part because he was willing to compromise, and he co-opted many of their legislative priorities. The point here is that presidents react differently given different circumstances; by 1983, Reagan's domestic agenda consisted of many conservative social issues, from which he was not interested in deviating and which Congress was not overly interested in pursuing. So, a lack of legislative success later during Reagan's first term was not solely dictated by the fact that the honeymoon with Congress was over. Timing during an administration does matter, but other circumstances in the political environment cannot be ignored, and all must be considered collectively in order to assess a president's success.

Therefore, communication strategies have become an important and permanent part of the everyday operation of the White House. And while presidents have incorporated a leadership strategy of "going public" more often in recent years, the use of public activities goes beyond being a strategy, which implies a choice.[11] Public activities are now part of the overall package of the White House and the president's job description. Presidents do not necessarily choose to go public just to get their message out to other political participants, namely Congress, nor do they give national addresses hoping that citizens will call their congressional representatives in support of their policies. Do presidents attempt to influence public opinion through major addresses? Yes. And do presidents use public activities in an attempt to influence other political actors? Again, the answer is yes. But claiming that a president's strategy relies on reaching only one group or the other misses the bigger picture. Concerns over press coverage, public opinion, Congressional support, interest group activity, and many other factors all work together in unison to create the current state of the presidency. Given the current political environment, it seems unlikely that any future president would regularly choose not to go public. Presidents must recognize what they can and cannot control; the public aspect of the presidency is now expected by both the press and the public, but presidents can still control the content of their message, just not how it is interpreted. However, presidential communications are "as much the product of situation and political climate as of individual choice."[12]

The presidency has become more institutionalized and politicized, and presidents and their staffs have learned over time how best to deal with the news media, which has become more institutionalized in its own right. Presidents must use the press to govern, but they do not have much control over the final message and are often at the mercy of the two-step flow of communication: "The news media now stand between politicians and their constituents. Politicians speak to the media; the media then speak to the voters. The media can filter, alter, distort or ignore altogether what politicians have to say."[13] Presidents have often tried to go over the heads of the traditional media, as witnessed by Clinton's efforts to find new public forums in which to discuss policy issues. But that type of effort by an administration is part of the continuing evolution of the president/press relationship and the overall communication strategy. And in the end, a successful White House communication strategy may be one that either circumvents the traditional news media, where innovation can provide at least some temporary control over the message, or a strategy that, based on the leadership strengths of the president, discovers how to use the news media to the president's best advantage.

The impact of the evolution of communication strategies on governing means that, while more messages may be coming out of the White House regarding the president's agenda, less substantive information seems to reach the public. While it is important to keep the news media part of the daily political give-and-take between the president and Congress, communication strategies that rely on substance over image seem to be ignored on a regular basis by the mainstream national press. In terms of strategy, Nixon may have been wrong to hide from the press since more exposure is not always better. But every president, on some level, has had difficulty in controlling the White House message to the public, which is the nature of the presidential/press relationship, regardless of strategy. While Clinton was considered the perpetually campaigning president, governing as campaigning actually started with Ford, and it has continued ever since through an increase in public activities. Clinton survived as president, in part, due to his communication skills. But political survival, like skillful communications that meet the needs and expectations of the news media, does not always equate with true leadership or effective governance. That may only come from a president whose leadership goes beyond just giving the public and press what they expect, but whether a future president can achieve that within the American system of government is a much larger question—one that remains open to debate.

ENDNOTES

1. Matthew Robert Kerbel, *Remote & Controlled: Media Politics in a Cynical Age*, 2nd ed. (Boulder, CO: Westview Press, 1999), 106.
2. Martha Joynt Kumar, "The Place of the Press Conference in a Constellation of Presidential Publicity Settings," paper prepared for delivery at the annual Midwest Political Science Association meeting in Chicago, April 1999.
3. Ibid.
4. For example, see Thomas E. Patterson, *Out of Order* (New York: Alfred A. Knopf, 1993).
5. George C. Edwards III, *The Public Presidency: The Pursuit of Popular Support* (New York: St. Martin's Press, 1983), 156.
6. Jeffrey Tulis, *The Rhetorical Presidency* (Princeton, NJ: Princeton University Press, 1987), 178.
7. Fred Greenstein, "Toward a Modern Presidency," in *Understanding the Presidency*, Eds. James P. Pfiffner and Roger H. Davidson (New York: Longman, 1997), 38-9. Greenstein, however, argues against this claim, supporting the notion that presidents can and do make a difference in defining leadership capabilities.
8. James P. Pfiffner, *The Strategic Presidency: Hitting the Ground Running*, 2nd rev. ed. (Lawrence, KS: University of Kansas Press, 1996).
9. George C. Edwards, III, *At The Margins: Presidential Leadership of Congress* (New Haven: Yale University Press, 1989).
10. Samuel Kernell, *Going Public: New Strategies of Presidential Leadership*, 3rd ed. (Washington, DC: CQ Press, 1997).
11. Kernell defines going public as a technique where "the ultimate object of the president's designs is not the American voter, but fellow politicians in Washington," ix.
12. Mary Stuckey, *Strategic Failures in the Modern Presidency* (Cresskill, NJ: Hampton Press, 1997), 175.
13. Stephen Ansolabehere, Roy Behr, and Shanto Iyengar, *The Media Game: American Politics in the Television Age* (New York: Macmillan Publishing, 1993), 1.

Bibliography

Alger, Dean E. *The Media and Politics.* 2nd ed. Belmont, CA: Wadsworth Publishing Company, 1996.

Allen, Craig. *Eisenhower and the Mass Media.* Chapel Hill: University of North Carolina Press, 1993.

Ambrose, Stephen E. *Nixon: The Triumph of a Politician 1962-1972.* New York: Simon & Schuster, 1989.

Ansolabehere, Stephen, Behr, Roy, and Iyengar, Shanto. *The Media Game: American Politics in the Television Age.* New York: Macmillan Publishing, 1993.

Barrow, John C. "An Age of Limits: Jimmy Carter and the Quest for a National Energy Policy." In *The Carter Presidency: Policy Choices in the Post-New Deal Era.* Eds. Gary M. Fink and Hugh Davis Graham. Lawrence, KS: University of Kansas Press, 1998.

Baumgartner, Frank R., and Jones, Bryan D. *Agendas and Instability in American Politics.* Chicago: University of Chicago Press, 1993.

Behr, Roy L., and Iyengar, Shanto. "Television News, Real-World Cues, and Changes in the Public Agenda." *Public Opinion Quarterly* 49 (1985): 38-57.

Bennett, W. Lance. *The Governing Crisis: Media, Money, and Marketing in American Elections.* 2nd ed. New York: St. Martin's Press, 1996.

Berman, Larry. *The New American Presidency.* Boston: Little, Brown and Company, 1987.

Bochin, Hal W. "Richard Milhous Nixon." In *U.S. Presidents as Orators: A Bio-Critical Sourcebook.* Ed. Halford Ryan. Westport, CT: Greenwood Press, 1995.

Brace, Paul, and Hinckley, Barbara. *Follow the Leader: Opinion Polls and the Modern Presidents.* New York: HarperCollins Publishers, 1992.

Bradlee, Benjamin C. *Conversations With Kennedy.* New York: W.W. Norton & Company, 1975.

Broder, David S. *Behind the Front Page: A Candid Look at How the News is Made.* New York: Simon & Schuster, 1987.

Brody, Richard A. *Assessing the President: The Media, Elite Opinion, and Public Support.* Stanford: Stanford University Press, 1991.

Browder, Joe. "Decision-Making in the White House." In *Nixon and the Environment: The Politics of Devastation.* Ed. James Rathlesberger. New York: Village Voice, 1972.

Burke, John. *The Institutional Presidency.* Baltimore: Johns Hopkins University Press, 1992.

Burke, Vincent J., and Burke, Vee. *Nixon's Good Deed: Welfare Reform.* New York: Columbia University Press, 1974.

Campbell, Karlyn Kohrs, and Jamieson, Kathleen Hall. *Deeds Done in Words: Presidential Rhetoric and the Genres of Governance.* Chicago: University of Chicago Press, 1990.

Cannon, Lou. *President Reagan: The Role of a Lifetime.* New York: Simon & Schuster, 1991.

_____. "The Press and the Nixon Presidency." In *The Nixon Presidency: Twenty-Two Intimate Perspectives of Richard M. Nixon.* Ed. Kenneth W. Thompson. Lanham, MD: University Press of America, 1987.

Carter, Jimmy. *Keeping Faith: Memoirs of a President.* New York: Bantam Books, 1982.

Christian, George. "Another Perspective." In *The Johnson Presidency: Twenty Intimate Perspectives of Lyndon B. Johnson.* Ed. Kenneth W. Thompson. Lanham, MD: University Press of America, 1986.

Clift, Eleanor. "Don't Mess With the Media." *Newsweek,* 7 June 1993, 23.

Cobb, Roger W., and Elder, Charles D. *Participation in American Politics: The Dynamics of Agenda-Building.* Boston: Allyn and Bacon, 1972.

Cohen, Jeffrey E. "Presidential Rhetoric and the Public Agenda." *American Journal of Political Science* 39 (February 1995): 87-107.

Cornwell, Elmer E., Jr. *Presidential Leadership of Public Opinion.* Westport, CT: Greenwood Press, 1965.

Cronin, Thomas E., and Genovese, Michael A. *The Paradoxes of the American Presidency.* New York: Oxford University Press, 1998.

Crothers, A.L. "Asserting Dominance: Presidential Transitions From Out-Party to In-Party." *Polity* (Summer 1994).

Dallek, Robert. *Flawed Giant: Lyndon Johnson and His Times 1961-1973.* New York: Oxford University Press, 1998.

_____. *Ronald Reagan: The Politics of Symbolism.* Cambridge: Harvard University Press, 1999.

Deaver, Michael K. *Behind the Scenes.* New York: William Morrow, 1987.

Denton, Robert E., Jr. *The Primetime Presidency of Ronald Reagan: The Era of the Television Presidency.* New York: Praeger Publishers, 1988.

Denton, Robert E., Jr., and Hahn, Dan F. "Reagan's Persuasiveness: An Exploratory Interpretation." In *Presidential Communication, Description and Analysis.* Eds. Robert E. Denton, Jr. and Dan F. Hahn. New York: Praeger Publishers, 1986.

Denton, Robert E., Jr., and Holloway, Rachel L. "Clinton and the Town Hall Meetings: Mediated Conversation and the Risk of Being 'In Touch.'" In *The Clinton Presidency: Images, Issues, and Communication Strategies.* Eds. Robert E. Denton, Jr. and Rachel L. Holloway. Westport, CT: Praeger Publishers, 1996.

Donovan, Hedley. *Roosevelt to Reagan: A Reporter's Encounters with Nine Presidents.* New York: Harper & Row, 1985.

Drew, Elizabeth. *On the Edge: The Clinton Presidency.* New York: Simon & Schuster, 1994.

Edwards, George C., III. *At The Margins: Presidential Leadership of Congress.* New Haven: Yale University Press, 1989.

_____. "Campaigning is Not Governing: Bill Clinton's Rhetorical Presidency." In *The Clinton Legacy.* Eds. Colin Campbell and Bert A. Rockman. New York: Chatham House Publishers, 2000.

_____. "George Bush and the Public Presidency: The Politics of Inclusion." In *The Bush Presidency: First Appraisals.* Eds. Colin Campbell and Bert A. Rockman. Chatham, NJ: Chatham House Publishers, 1991.

_____. *The Public Presidency: The Pursuit of Popular Support.* New York: St. Martin's Press, 1983.

Edwards, George C., III, and Wayne, Stephen J. *Presidential Leadership: Politics and Policy Making.* 5th ed. New York: St. Martin's Press, 1999.

Ehrlichman, John. "The White House and Policy-Making." In *The Nixon Presidency: Twenty-Two Intimate Perspectives of Richard M. Nixon.* Ed. Kenneth W. Thompson. Lanham, MD: University Press of America, 1987.

Emery, Michael, and Emery, Edwin. *The Press and America: An Interpretive History of the Mass Media.* 8th ed. Needham Heights, MA: Simon & Schuster, 1996.

Erickson, Paul D. *Reagan Speaks: The Making of an American Myth.* New York: New York University Press, 1985.

Fallows, James. *Breaking the News: How the Media Undermine American Democracy.* New York: Vintage Books, 1997.

_____. "The Presidency and the Press." In *The Presidency and the Political System.* Ed. Michael Nelson. Washington, DC: CQ Press, 1990.

Fishel, Jeff. *Presidents and Promises: From Campaign Pledge to Presidential Performance.* Washington, DC: CQ Press, 1985.

Fitzwater, Marlin. *Call the Briefing! Bush and Reagan, Sam and Helen: A Decade with Presidents and the Press.* New York: Random House, 1995.

Ford, Gerald R. *A Time to Heal: The Autobiography of Gerald R. Ford.* New York: Harper & Row, 1979.

_____. "The President and Political Leadership." In *Twenty Years of Papers on the Presidency.* Ed. Kenneth W. Thompson. Lanham, MD: University Press of America, 1995.

Genovese, Michael A. *The Nixon Presidency: Power and Politics in Turbulent Times.* New York: Greenwood Press, 1990.

Giglio, James N. *The Presidency of John F. Kennedy.* Lawrence, KS: University Press of Kansas, 1991.

Gold, Victor. "George Bush Speaks Out." *Washingtonian,* February 1994.

Goldzwig, Steven R., and Dionisopoulos, George N. *"In A Perilous Hour": The Public Addresses of John F. Kennedy.* Westport, CT: Greenwood Press, 1995.

Graber, Doris. *Mass Media and American Politics.* 5th ed. Washington, DC: CQ Press, 1997.

Gray, C. Boyden. "The President as Leader." Presented in a Forum at the Miller Center of Public Affairs on 2/17/94. In *The Bush Presidency: Ten Intimate Perspectives of George Bush.* Ed. Kenneth W. Thompson. Lanham, MD: University Press of America, 1997.

Greene, John Robert. "'A Nice Person Who Worked at the Job': The Dilemma of the Ford Image." In *Gerald R. Ford and the Politics of Post-Watergate America,* Vol. 2. Eds. Bernard J. Firestone and Alexej Ugrinsky. Westport, CT: Greenwood Press, 1993.

_____. *The Presidency of Gerald R. Ford.* Lawrence, KS: University Press of Kansas, 1995.

Greenstein, Fred I. "Toward a Modern Presidency." In *Understanding the Presidency.* Ed. James P. Pfiffner and Roger H. Davidson. New York: Longman, 1997.

_____. "The Two Leadership Styles of William Jefferson Clinton." *Political Psychology* 15 (1994).

Grossman, Michael Baruch, and Kumar, Martha Joynt. *Portraying the President: The White House and the News Media.* Baltimore: Johns Hopkins University Press, 1981.

Haas, Garland A. *Jimmy Carter and the Politics of Frustration.* Jefferson, NC: McFarland and Company, 1992.

Hahn, Dan F., and Ryan, Halford. "Jimmy Carter." In *U.S. Presidents as Orators: A Bio-Critical Sourcebook*. Ed. Halford Ryan. Westport, CT: Greenwood Press, 1995.

Hargrove, Erwin C. *Jimmy Carter as President: Leadership and the Politics of the Public Good*. Baton Rouge, LA: Louisiana State University Press, 1988.

_____. *The President as Leader: Appealing to the Better Angels of Our Nature*. Lawrence, KS: University Press of Kansas, 1998.

_____. "Presidential Personality and Leadership Style." In *Researching the Presidency: Vital Questions, New Approaches*. Ed. George C. Edwards, III, John H. Kessel, and Bert A. Rockman. Pittsburgh: University of Pittsburgh Press, 1993.

Hart, Roderick P. *The Sound of Leadership: Presidential Communication in the Modern Age*. Chicago: University of Chicago Press, 1987.

Heith, Diane J. "Presidential Polling and the Leadership of Public Thought." Paper prepared for delivery at the "Presidential Power: Forging the Presidency for the 21st Century" conference, Columbia University, New York, November, 1996.

Heller, Walter W. "Why We Must Cut Taxes." *Nation's Business*, November 1962, 281-84.

Hertsgaard, Mark. *On Bended Knee: The Press and the Reagan Presidency*. New York: Farrar Straus Giroux, 1988.

Hess, Stephen. *Presidents and the Presidency*. Washington, DC: Brookings Institution, 1996.

Hoff, Joan. *Nixon Reconsidered*. New York: HarperCollins Publishers, 1994.

Ingraham, Patricia W. and Perry, James L. "The Three Faces of Civil Service Reform." In *The Presidency and Domestic Policies of Jimmy Carter*. Eds. Herbert D. Rosenbaum and Alexej Ugrinsky. Westport, CT: Greenwood Press, 1994.

Johnson, Lyndon Baines. *The Vantage Point: Perspectives of the Presidency 1963-1969*. New York: Holt, Rinehart and Winston, 1971.

Jones, Charles O. "Campaigning to Govern: The Clinton Style," in *The Clinton Presidency: First Appraisals*, Eds. Colin Campbell and Bert A. Rockman. Chatham, NJ: Chatham House Publishers, 1996.

_____. *The Trusteeship Presidency: Jimmy Carter and the United States Congress*. Baton Rouge, LA: Louisiana State University Press, 1988.

Kahn, Kim Fridkin. *The Political Consequences of Being a Woman: How Stereotypes Influence the Conduct and Consequence of Political Campaigns*. New York: Columbia University Press, 1996.

Kaus, Mickey. "Tribal Hatred." *The New Republic*, 21 June 1993, 4.

Kearns, Doris. *Lyndon Johnson and the American Dream*. New York: Harper & Row, 1976.

Kellerman, Barbara. *The Political Presidency: Practice of Leadership*. New York: Oxford University Press, 1984.

Keogh, James. "Nixon, The Press and the White House." In *The Nixon Presidency: Twenty-Two Intimate Perspectives of Richard M. Nixon*. Ed. Kenneth W. Thompson. Lanham, MD: University Press of America, 1987.

Kerbel, Matthew Robert. *Remote and Controlled: Media Politics in a Cynical Age*. 2nd ed. Boulder, CO: Westview Press, 1999.

Kernell, Samuel. *Going Public: New Strategies of Presidential Leadership*. 3rd ed. Washington, DC: CQ Press, 1993.

Kingdon, John W. *Agendas, Alternatives, and Public Policies*. New York: HarperCollins Publishers, 1995.

Kumar, Martha Joynt. "The Place of the Press Conference in a Constellation of Presidential Publicity Settings." Paper prepared for delivery at the annual Midwest Political Science Association meeting in Chicago, April 1999.

_____. "President Clinton Meets the Media: Communications Shaped by Predictable Patterns." In *The Clinton Presidency: Campaigning, Governing, and the Psychology of Leadership*. Ed. Stanley A. Renshon. Boulder, CO: Westview Press, 1995.

_____. "The Relationship Between the White House and the Press: One Hundred Years in the Making." Paper prepared for delivery at the 1997 Annual Meeting of the Midwest Political Science Association, Chicago, Illinois.

Kutler, Stanley I. *The Wars of Watergate: The Last Crisis of Richard Nixon*. New York: Alfred A. Knopf, 1990.

Lammers, William W. "Domestic Policy Leadership in the First Year." In *Understanding the Presidency*. Eds. James P. Pfiffner and Roger H. Davidson. New York: Longman, 1997.

_____. "Presidential Attention-Focusing Activities." In *The President and the Public*. Ed. Doris Graber. Philadelphia: Institute for the Study of Human Issues, 1982.

_____. "Presidential Press-Conference Schedules: Who Hides, and When?" *Political Science Quarterly* 96 (Summer 1981): 261-78.

Lauter, David. "Year After Election, Clinton Alters His View of Change." *Los Angeles Times*, 7 November 1993, A1, 28-9.

Leuchtenburg, William E. "Jimmy Carter and the Post-New Deal Presidency." In *The Carter Presidency: Policy Choices in the Post-New Deal Era*. Eds. Gary M. Fink and Hugh Davis Graham. Lawrence, KS: University of Kansas Press, 1998.

Light, Paul C. *Artful Work: The Politics of Social Security Reform*. New York: Random House, 1985.

_____. "Presidential Policy Making." In *Researching the Presidency: Vital Questions, New Approaches*. Eds. George C. Edwards, III, John H. Kessel, and Bert A. Rockman. Pittsburgh: University of Pittsburgh Press, 1993.

_____. *The President's Agenda: Domestic Policy Choice from Kennedy to Reagan*. Rev. ed. Baltimore: Johns Hopkins University Press, 1991.

Littlefield, Robert S. "Carter and the Media: An Analysis of Selected Strategies Used to Manage the Public Communication of the Administration." In *The Presidency and Domestic Policies of Jimmy Carter*. Eds. Herbert D. Rosenbaum and Alexej Ugrinsky. Westport, CT: Greenwood Press, 1994.

Lowi, Theodore J. *The Personal President: Power Invested, Promise Unfulfilled*. Ithaca, NY: Cornell University Press, 1985.

Maltese, John Anthony. *Spin Control: The White House Office of Communications and the Management of Presidential News*. 2nd rev. ed. Chapel Hill: University of North Carolina Press, 1994.

_____. "Spin Control in the White House." In *Understanding the Presidency*. Eds. James P. Pfiffner and Roger H. Davidson. New York: Longman, 1977.

Medhurst, Martin J. "A Tale of Two Constructs: The Rhetorical Presidency Versus Presidential Rhetoric." In *Beyond the Rhetorical Presidency*. Ed. Martin J. Medhurst. College Station, TX: Texas A&M University Press, 1996.

Mervin, David. *George Bush and the Guardianship Presidency*. New York: St. Martin's Press, 1996.

Moe, Terry M. "The Politicized Presidency." In *The New Direction in American Politics*. Ed. John E. Chubb and Paul E. Peterson. Washington, DC: Brookings Institution, 1985.

_____. "Presidents, Institutions, and Theory." In *Researching the Presidency: Vital Questions, New Approaches*. Eds. George C. Edwards, III, John H. Kessel, and Bert A. Rockman. Pittsburgh: University of Pittsburgh Press, 1993.

Muir, William Ker, Jr. *The Bully Pulpit: The Presidential Leadership of Ronald Reagan*. San Francisco: ICS Press, 1992.

Nathan, Richard P. "The Reagan Presidency in Domestic Affairs." In *The Reagan Presidency: An Early Assessment*. Ed. Fred I. Greenstein. Baltimore: Johns Hopkins University Press, 1983.

Nessen, Ron. *It Sure Looks Different from the Inside*. Chicago: Playboy Press, 1978.

Neustadt, Richard. *Presidential Power and the Modern Presidents: The Politics of Leadership From Roosevelt to Reagan*. New York: The Free Press, 1990.

Nixon, Richard M. *In the Arena: A Memoir of Victory, Defeat and Renewal*. New York: Pocket Books, 1990.

_____. "A Statement from President Nixon." In *The Environment: A National Mission for the Seventies*. Ed. Fortune Magazine. New York: Harper & Row Publishers, 1970.

Noonan, Peggy. *What I Saw at the Revolution: A Political Life in the Reagan Era.* New York: Random House, 1990.

O'Hara, William T. *John F. Kennedy on Education.* New York: Teachers College Press, 1966.

Page, Benjamin I., and Shapiro, Robert Y. *The Rational Public: Fifty Years of Trends in Americans' Policy Preferences.* Chicago: University of Chicago Press, 1992.

Paletz, David L., and Entman, Robert M. *Media Power Politics.* New York: The Free Press, 1981.

Patterson, Thomas E. *Out of Order.* New York: Alfred A. Knopf, 1993.

Peterson, Paul E., and Rom, Mark. "Lower Taxes, More Spending, and Budget Deficits." In *The Reagan Legacy: Promise and Performance.* Ed. Charles O. Jones. Chatham, NJ: Chatham House Publishers, 1988.

Pfiffner, James P. *The Strategic Presidency: Hitting the Ground Running.* 2nd rev. ed. Lawrence, KS: University Press of Kansas, 1996.

Quirk, Paul J. "Domestic Policy: Divided Government and Cooperative Presidential Leadership." In *The Bush Presidency: First Appraisals.* Eds. Colin Campbell and Bert A. Rockman. Chatham, NJ: Chatham House Publishers, 1991.

Ragsdale, Lyn. "The Politics of Presidential Speechmaking, 1949-1980." *American Political Science Review* 78 (December 1984): 971-84.

_____. *Vital Statistics on the Presidency: Washington to Clinton.* Washington, DC: CQ Press, 1996.

Reeves, Richard. *A Ford, not a Lincoln.* New York: Harcourt Brace Jovanovich, 1975.

_____. *President Kennedy: Profile of Power.* New York: Simon & Schuster, 1993.

Regan, Donald T. *For the Record: From Wall Street to Washington.* New York: Harcourt Brace, 1988.

Reston, James. *Deadline: A Memoir.* New York: Random House, 1991.

Ritter, Kurt. "Ronald Reagan." In *U.S. Presidents as Orators: A Bio-Critical Sourcebook.* Ed. Halford Ryan. Westport, CT: Greenwood Press, 1995.

Roberts, Charles. "JFK and the Press." In *Ten Presidents and the Press.* Ed. Kenneth W. Thompson. Washington, DC: University Press of America, 1983.

_____. "Kennedy and the Press: Image and Reality." In *The Kennedy Presidency: Seventeen Intimate Perspectives of John F. Kennedy.* Ed. Kenneth W. Thompson. Lanham, MD: University Press of America, 1985.

Rose, Richard. *The Postmodern President.* Chatham, NJ: Chatham House Publishers, 1991.

Rosenstiel, Tom. *The Beat Goes On: President Clinton's First Year With the Media.* New York: Twentieth Century Fund Press, 1994.

Rozell, Mark J. *The Press and the Carter Presidency.* Boulder, CO: Westview Press, 1989.

_____. *The Press and the Ford Presidency.* Ann Arbor: University of Michigan Press, 1992.

Sabato, Larry. *Feeding Frenzy: How Attack Journalism Has Transformed American Politics.* New York: Free Press, 1991.

Safire, William. *Before the Fall: An Inside View of the Pre-Watergate White House.* New York: Da Capo Press, 1975.

Salinger, Pierre. *With Kennedy.* New York: Doubleday, 1966.

Schattschneider, E.E. *The Semisovereign People: A Realist's View of Democracy in America.* New York: Harcourt Brace, 1975.

Schlesinger, Arthur M., Jr. *A Thousand Days: John F. Kennedy in the White House.* New York: Fawcett Premier, 1965.

Schram, Martin. *The Great American Video Game: Presidential Politics in the Television Age.* New York: William Morrow, 1987.

Shaw, David. "Did the Press Apply the Teflon to Reagan's Presidency?" *Los Angeles Times,* 27 October 1992, A20.

_____. "Not Even Getting a First Chance." *Los Angeles Times,* 15 September 1993, A 10-1.

Shesol, Jeff. *Mutual Contempt: Lyndon Johnson, Robert Kennedy, and the Feud That Defined a Decade.* New York: W.W. Norton & Company, 1997.

Sigelman, Lee. "Presidential Inaugurals: The Modernization of a Genre." *Political Communication* 13 (January-March 1996): 81-92.

Silvestri, Vito N. "John Fitzgerald Kennedy." In *U.S. Presidents as Orators: A Bio-Critical Sourcebook.* Ed. Halford Ryan. Westport, CT: Greenwood Press, 1995.

Sloan, John W. "Groping Toward a Macrotheme: Economic Policymaking in the Ford Presidency." In *Gerald R. Ford and the Politics of Post-Watergate America,* Vol. I. Eds. Bernard J. Firestone and Alexej Ugrinsky. Westport, CT: Greenwood Press, 1993.

Smith, Carolyn. *Presidential Press Conferences: A Critical Approach.* New York: Praeger Publishers, 1990.

Smith, Craig Allen. "Gerald R. Ford." In *U.S. Presidents as Orators: A Bio-Critical Sourcebook.* Ed. Halford Ryan. Westport, CT: Greenwood Press, 1995.

Smith, Craig Allen, and Smith, Kathy B. *The White House Speaks: Presidential Leadership as Persuasion.* Westport, CT: Praeger Publishers, 1994.

Smith, Craig R. "George Herbert Walker Bush." In *U.S. Presidents as Orators: A Bio-Critical Sourcebook.* Ed. Halford Ryan. Westport, CT: Greenwood Press, 1995.

Sorensen, Theodore C. *Kennedy.* New York: Harper And Row, 1965.

_____, Ed. "Let the Word Go Forth:" The Speeches, Statements, and Writings of John F. Kennedy. New York: Delacorte Press, 1988.

Speakes, Larry. *Speaking Out: The Reagan Presidency from Inside the White House*. New York: Charles Scribner's Sons, 1988.

Spear, Joseph C. *Presidents and the Press: The Nixon Legacy*. Cambridge: MIT Press, 1984.

Stoesz, David. *Small Change: Domestic Policy Under the Clinton Presidency*. New York: Longman, 1996.

Stuckey, Mary E. *Playing the Game: The Presidential Rhetoric of Ronald Reagan*. New York: Praeger Publishers, 1990.

_____. *The President as Interpreter-in-Chief*. Chatham, NJ: Chatham House Publishers, 1991.

_____. *Strategic Failures in the Modern Presidency*. Cresskill, NJ: Hampton Press, 1997.

Tebbel, John, and Watts, Sarah Miles. *The Press and the Presidency: From George Washington to Ronald Reagan*. New York: Oxford University Press, 1985.

Thomas, Norman C., Pika, Joseph A., and Watson, Richard A. *The Politics of the Presidency*. 3rd rev. ed. Washington, DC: CQ Press, 1994.

Thompson, Kenneth W., ed. *Ten Presidents and the Press*. Washington, DC: University Press of America, 1983.

Tulis, Jeffrey K. *The Rhetorical Presidency*. Princeton: Princeton University Press, 1987.

Waldman, Steven. "The Cynical White House Media," in *Understanding the Presidency*. Ed. James P. Pfiffner and Roger H. Davidson. New York: Longman, 1997.

Waterman, Richard W., Wright, Robert, and St. Clair, Gilbert. *The Image-Is-Everything Presidency: Dilemmas in American Leadership*. Boulder, CO: Westview Press, 1999.

Weber, Robert Philip. *Basic Content Analysis*. 2nd ed. Newbury Park, CA: Sage Publications, 1990.

Weko, Thomas J. *The Politicizing Presidency: The White House Personnel Office, 1948-1994*. Lawrence, KS: University of Kansas Press, 1995.

Whitaker, John C. *Striking A Balance: Environment and Natural Resources Policy in the Nixon-Ford Years*. Washington, DC: American Enterprise Institute for Public Policy Research, 1976.

Wood, Stephen C., and DeWitt, Jean M. "Bill Clinton." In *U.S. Presidents as Orators: A Bio-Critical Sourcebook*. Ed. Halford Ryan. Westport, CT: Greenwood Press, 1995.

Woodward, Bob. *The Agenda: Inside the Clinton White House*. New York: Simon & Schuster, 1994.

Yeutter, Clayton. "Accomplishments and Setbacks." Presented in a Forum at the Miller Center of Public Affairs on 4/30/93. In *The Bush Presidency: Ten Intimate Perspectives of George Bush*. Ed.

Kenneth W. Thompson. Lanham, MD: University Press of America, 1997.

Zagacki, Kenneth S. "Lyndon Baines Johnson." In *U.S. Presidents as Orators: A Bio-Critical Sourcebook.* Ed. Halford Ryan. Westport, CT: Greenwood Press, 1995.

Zernicke, Paul Haskell. *Pitching the Presidency: How Presidents Depict the Office.* Westport, CT: Praeger Publishers, 1994.

Author Index

A

Alger, D.E., 18(*n*59), 25, 232(*n*12), 245, 267
Allen, C., 28(*n*1), 43, 267
Allin, M., 81(*n*92, *n*93), 82(*n*98, *n*99), 106, 107
Ambrose, S.E., 86(*n*116, *n*117), 108, 267
Ansolabehere, S., 264(*n*13), 265, 267

B

Baker, J., 186(*n*19, *n*20), 222
Bario, P., 142(*n*75), 145(*n*80), 148(*n*89, *n*91), 154(*n*107), 174, 175, 176
Baroody, M., 200(*n*64), 224
Barrow, J.C., 158(*n*119), 160(*n*123), 163(*n*134), 176, 177, 267
Bauer, P., 148(*n*90), 175
Baumgartner, F.R., 11(*n*38), 24, 267

Behr, R.L., 12(*n*42), 24, 264(*n*13), 265, 267
Bennett, W.L., 199(*n*61), 224, 267
Berman, L., 36(*n*36), 45, 66(*n*59), 90(*n*128), 104, 109, 130(*n*51), 141(*n*72), 170(*n*144), 173, 174, 178, 196, 223, 267
Bochin, H.W., 87(*n*121), 108, 268
Brace, P., 8(*n*21), 9(*n*27), 23, 33(*n*25, *n*26), 45, 268
Bradlee, B.C., 32(*n*21), 45, 268
Broder, D.S., 181(*n*5), 221, 268
Brody, R.A., 8(*n*22), 23, 268
Browder, J., 97(*n*144), 109, 268
Buchanan, P., 83(*n*104), 85(*n*113), 86(*n*115), 87(*n*119), 94(*n*136), 107, 108, 109, 113(*n*8), 114(*n*9), 171
Burke, J., 2(*n*1), 21, 268
Burke, V., 93(*n*133), 109, 268
Burke, V.J., 93(*n*133), 109, 268
Busby, H., 59(*n*40), 72(*n*73), 104

279

Bush, G., 213(*n*98-100), 214(*n*104), 217(*n*107, *n*108, *n*110), 226

C

Campbell, K.K., 6(*n*15), 10(*n*30), 22, 23, 268

Cannon, L., 79(*n*85), 106, 193(*n*44), 194(*n*48), 199(*n*58), 223, 224, 268

Carter, J., 147(*n*87), 151(*n*97), 153(*n*104), 160(*n*122, *n*125) 161(*n*126, *n*129), 162(*n*131), 166(*n*137, *n*139, *n*140),168(*n*141), 175, 176, 177, 178, 268

Cater, D., 55(*n*22), 103

Cavanaugh, J., 120(*n*37), 172

Chancellor, J., 113(*n*7), 171

Cheney, D., 138(*n*64), 173

Christian, G., 49(*n*3), 52(*n*14), 55(*n*27), 58(*n*38), 102, 103, 104, 268

Clift, E., 232(*n*14), 233(*n*15), 245, 268

Clinton, W., 229(*n*1), 245

Cobb, R.W., 11(*n*36), 23, 268

Cohen, J.E., 12(*n*43), 24, 268

Colson, C., 84(*n*109), 107

Cornwell, E.E., 4(*n*5), 22, 268

Cronin, T.E., 4(*n*7), 22, 268

Crothers, A.L., 9(*n*29), 23, 268

Cuval, M., 126(*n*37), 172

D

Dallek, R., 49(*n*4), 69(*n*64), 71(*n*72), 75(*n*77), 76(*n*81), 102, 105, 106, 193(*n*43, *n*44), 223, 269

Darman, R., 185(*n*18), 222

Deaver, M.K., 187(*n*25), 222, 269

DeCair, T., 124(*n*71), 172

Denton, R.E., 182(*n*8), 183(*n*9), 193(*n*45), 221, 223, 231(*n*9), 245, 269

DeWitt, J.M., 235(*n*22), 246, 276

Dionisopoulos, G.N., 33(*n*28, *n*29, *n*30), 35(*n*33), 45, 270

Donovan, H., 144(*n*79), 174, 269

Drew, E., 232(*n*11), 236(*n*23), 239(*n*29, *n*32), 245, 246, 269

E

Edwards, G.C., 14(*n*50), 24, 80(*n*88), 106, 205(*n*74, *n*75), 206(*n*81), 207(*n*84), 210(*n*94), 224, 225, 231(*n*8), 234(*n*19-21), 245, 246, 259(*n*5), 262(*n*9), 265, 269

Ehrlichman, J., 90(*n*129), 109, 269

Eizenstat, 162(*n*130), 167(*n*138), 177

Elder, C.D., 11(*n*36), 23

Emery, E., 12(*n*44), 18(*n*59), 24, 25, 30(*n*9), 32(*n*22), 44, 45, 48(*n*2), 61(*n*47), 81(*n*92), 83(*n*103), 102, 104, 106, 107, 112(*n*2, *n*3), 171, 170(*n*145), 178, 206(*n*83), 225, 269

Emery, M., 12(*n*44), 18(*n*59), 24, 25, 30(*n*9), 32(*n*22), 44, 45, 48(*n*2), 61(*n*47), 81(*n*92), 83(*n*103), 102, 104, 106, 107, 112(*n*2, *n*3), 171, 170(*n*145), 178, 206(*n*83), 225, 269

Entman, R.M., 14(*n*49), 24, 274

Erickson, P.D., 193(*n*44), 223, 194(*n*47), 269

F

Fallows, J., 13(*n*48), 24, 143(*n*76), 143, 156(*n*113, *n*115), 176, 232(*n*13), 234(*n*18), 245, 269-270

Fishel, J., 12(*n*41), 17(*n*57), 24, 25, 36(*n*36), 45, 196(*n*55), 223, 270

Fitzwater, M., 196(*n*52), 223, 207(*n*87), 225, 209(*n*90), 270

Ford, G.R., 112(*n*6), 123(*n*30), 127(*n*41), 133(*n*54, *n*56), 137(*n*63), 138(*n*65), 139(*n*66, *n*67), 171, 172, 173, 270

Frantz, J., 49(*n*5), 50(*n*7), 51(*n*12), 52(*n*15), 53(*n*16), 54(*n* 19, *n*20),

55(*n*24), 57(*n*31, *n*34), 59(*n*39),
64(*n*53), 65(*n*54), *102, 103, 104*
Friendly, A., 142(*n*75), 145(*n*80),
148(*n*89, *n*91), 154(*n*107), *174,
175, 176*
Fuller, C., 185(*n*18), *222*

G

Genovese, M.A., 4(*n*7), *22*, 79(*n*83),
89(*n*125), 90(*n*126), 93(*n*132),
96(*n*141), 97(*n*143), *106, 108, 109,
268, 270*
Gaither, J., 74(*n*76), *105*
Gergen, D., 126(*n*37), *172*, 129(*n*47),
190(*n*33), 196(*n*53), *222, 223*
Gerig, L., 184(*n*12), *221*
Giglio, J.N., 31(*n*15), 32(*n*22),
33(*n*24), *44, 45, 270*
Gold, V., 208(*n*89), *225, 270*
Goldzwig, S.R., 33(*n*28-30),
35(*n*33), *45, 270*
Goode, M., 84(*n*107, *n*108), *107*
Graber, D., 13(*n*45), 18(*n*59), *24, 25,
270*
Granum, R., 142(*n*75), 145(*n*80),
148(*n*89, *n*91), 154(*n*107), *174,
175, 176*
Gray, C.B., 206(*n*82), 209(*n*92),
214(*n*105), *225, 226, 270*
Greene, J.R., 112(*n*1, *n*4), 115(*n*12),
118(*n*20), 128(*n*44, *n*45),
130(*n*50), *171, 172, 173, 270*
Greenstein, F.I., 231(*n*7), *245,
262(*n*7), 265, 270*
Grossman, M.B., 13(*n*46), *24,
18(*n*58), 25*, 31(*n*18), *44, 270*

H

Haas, G.A., 145(*n*81), 147(*n*86),
161(*n*127), *175, 177, 270*
Hahn, D.F., 155(*n*111), *176,
193(*n*45), 223, 269, 271*
Haldeman, H.R., 81(*n*94), *106*

Hargrove, E.C., 5(*n*9), *22*, 70(*n*66),
71(*n*71), *105*, 156(*n*112), *176, 271,*
Hart, B., 184(*n*14), *221*
Hart, R.P., 6(*n*12), *22, 271*
Heith, D.J., 9(*n*26), *23, 271*
Heller, W.W., 37(*n*41, *n*43),
38(*n*44), *46, 271*
Hertsgaard, M., 181(*n*3, *n*4),
186(*n*21), 202(*n*67), *221, 222, 224,
271*
Hess, S., 13(*n*47), *24, 271*
Hinckley, B., 8(*n*21), 9(*n*27), *23,*
33(*n*25, *n*26), *45, 268*
Hoff, J., 94(*n*138), 96(*n*139),
97(*n*145), *109, 271,*
Holloway, R.L., 231(*n*9), *245, 269*
Hunter, R.E., 65(*n*55, *n*57), *104*
Hushen, J., 117(*n*17, *n*18), *171*

I

Ingraham, P.W., 166(*n*135),
168(*n*143), *177, 178, 271*
Iyengar, S., 12(*n*42), *24*, 264(*n*13),
265, 267

J

Jamieson, K.H., 6(*n*15), 10(*n*30), *22,
23, 268*
Jenkins, R., 142(*n*75), 145(*n*80),
148(*n*89, *n*91), 154(*n*107), *174,
175, 176*
Johnson, L.B., 70(*n*67, *n*68), 71(*n*69,
*n*72), 72(*n*74), 74(*n*75),
100(*n*149), *105, 110, 271,*
Johnson, T., 59(*n*41), 75(*n*78),
76(*n*80-82), *104, 105, 106*
Jones, B.D., 11(*n*38), *24, 267*
Jones, C.O., 158(*n*118), *176,*
242(*n*36), *246, 271*

K

Kahn, K.F., 18(*n*58), *25, 271*
Kaus, M., 233(*n*16), *245, 271*
Kaysen, C., 37(*n*39, *n*42), 38(*n*45,
*n*48), *46*

Kearns, D., 50(n8), 56(n28, n29), 65(n56), 66(n58), 102, 103, 104, 271,

Kellerman, B., 40(n54), 41(n55), 46, 93(n135), 109, 138(n55, n57), 160(n124), 163(n133), 173, 177, 271

Keogh, J., 85(n111), 88(n122), 107, 272, 108

Kerbel, M., 3(n3), 15(n52), 22, 24, 253(n1), 265, 272

Kernell, S., 8(n19, n20), 23, 203(n71), 205(n77), 224, 225, 262(n10), 263(n11), 265, 272

Kingdon, J.W., 11(n37), 23, 272

Kumar, M.J., 12(n43), 13(n46), 18(n58), 24, 25, 31(n18), 44, 230(n5), 245, 254(n2, n3), 265, 270, 272

Kutler, S.I., 81(n95), 85(n112), 106, 108, 272

L

Lammers, W.W., 9(n28), 10(n33), 23, 237(n25), 246, 272

Lauter, D., 229(n3), 245, 272

Leibach, D., 142(n75), 145(n80), 148(n84, n91), 154(n107), 174, 175, 176

Leuchtenburg, W.E., 158(n120), 176-177, 272

Light, P.C., 5(n10), 12(n39), 22, 24, 36(n38), 40(n53), 46, 90(n127), 109, 139(n69), 174, 197(n56), 199(n59, n62), 223, 224, 272-273

Littlefield, R.S., 153(n103), 176, 273

Lowi, T.J., 4(n5), 22, 273

M

Maguire, C., 59(n42), 104

Maltese, J.A., 2(n2), 14(n51), 22, 24, 82, 107, 124(n32), 125(n34), 126(n38), 146(n84, n85), 172, 175, 184(n13, n16), 203(n70), 205(n76,

n78), 221, 224, 225, 232(n10), 245, 273(n101)

Martin, P., 31(n19), 44

McNulty, J., 56(n30), 103

McPherson, H., 54(n21), 64(n51), 103, 104

Mead, B., 125(n36), 172

Moore, R., 82(n96), 107

Medhurst, M.J., 7(n17), 22, 273

Mervin, D., 204(n72, n73), 224, 209(n91), 225, 273

Moe, T.M., 2(n1), 21, 273

Moyers, B., 103, 58(n35-37), 104, 62(n50), 71(n70), 105

Muir, W.K., 194(n49), 223, 273

N

Nathan, R.P., 199(n60), 224, 273

Nessen, R., 115(n11), 116(n15), 125(n35), 133(n58), 135(n61), 171, 172, 173, 273

Neustadt, R., 4(n4), 22 273

Nixon, R.M., 79(n84), 84(n106), 85(n114), 87(n120), 96(n140), 106, 107, 108, 109, 273

Noonan, P., 194(n49), 223, 274

O

O'Hara, W.T., 40(n50), 46, 274

Osborne, S., 117(n16), 171

P

Page, B.I., 8(n23), 23, 274

Paletz, D.L., 14(n49), 24, 274

Patterson, T.E., 258(n4), 265, 274

Pearson, D., 52(n13), 102

Perry, J.L., 166(n135), 168(n143), 177, 178, 271

Peterson, P.E., 200(n65), 224, 274

Pfiffner, J.P., 12(n40), 24, 211(n96), 225, 237(n25), 246, 262(n8), 265, 274

Pika, J.A., 202(n66), 224

Potter, P., 50(n10), 51(n11), 53(n17), 61(n46), 102, 104

Powell, J., 142(*n*74), 142(*n*75), 144(*n*77), 145(*n*80), 146(*n*82) 148(*n*89, *n*91), 149(*n*92), 151(*n*99), 152(*n*100), 153(*n*102), 154(*n*107), *174, 175, 176,*

Q

Quirk, P.J., 214(*n*103), 216(*n*106), *226, 274*

R

Reagan, R., 202(*n*69), *224*
Rafshoon, G., 144(*n*78), 146(*n*83), 149(*n*93), 150(*n*94-96), 152(*n*101), 154(*n*108), 156(*n*114), 157(*n*116), 163(*n*132), 168(*n*142), *174, 175, 176, 176, 177, 178*
Ragsdale, L., 5(*n*8), 9(*n*24, *n*25, *n*27), 16(*n*53, *n*54), 17(*n*57), *22, 23, 24, 25,* 205(*n*79), *225, 274*
Reedy, G., 60(*n*45), 62(*n*49), *104*
Reeves, R., 30(*n*12), *44,* 112(*n*5), 123(*n*29), *171, 172, 274*
Regan, D.T., 187(*n*24), *222, 274*
Reston, J., 141(*n*71), 154(*n*106), *174, 176,* 207(*n*86), *225, 274*
Ritter, K., 192(*n*40, *n*41), 194(*n*46), *223, 223, 274*
Roberts, C., 28(*n*4), 30(*n*14), *44, 274*
Rom, M., 200(*n*65), *224, 274*
Rose, R., 8(*n*20), *23, 274*
Rosenstiel, T., 230(*n*4), *245, 274*
Rowe, J.H., Jr., 48(*n*1), *102*
Rozell, M.J., 114(*n*10), 118(*n*19, *n*21), 126(*n*39, *n*40), 155(*n*109), *171, 172, 176, 275*
Rumsfeld, D., 124(*n*33), *172*
Ryan, H., 155(*n*111), *176, 271*

S

Sabato, L., 15(*n*52), *24, 275*
Safire, W., 79(*n*87), 82(*n*100), 88(*n*123), *106, 107, 108, 275*

Salinger, P., 28(*n*2), 29(*n*5-8), 30(*n*11, *n*13), 31(*n*16, *n*17), 32(*n*20, *n*23), *44, 45, 275*
Schattschneider, E.E., 11(*n*35), *23, 275*
Schlesinger, A.M., 28(*n*3), 40(*n*53), *44, 46, 275*
Schram, M., 186(*n*23), 191(*n*36), *222, 275*
Shapiro, R.Y., 8(*n*23), *23, 274*
Shaw, D., 180(*n*1), 186(*n*22), 206(*n*80), *221, 222, 225,* 229(*n*2), 233(*n*17), *245, 275*
Shesol, J., 53(*n*18), 70(*n*65), *102, 105, 275*
Shuman, J., 119(*n*22), 122(*n*27, *n*28), *171, 172*
Sidey, H., 142(*n*74), *174*
Sigelman, L., 10(*n*31), *23, 275*
Silvestri, W.N., 33(*n*27), 34(*n*32), *45, 275*
Sloan, J.W., 132(*n*53), *173, 275*
Smathers, G., 61(*n*48), *104*
Smith, C., 10(*n*32), *23, 275*
Smith, C.A., 6(*n*14), *22,* 128(*n*43), *172, 275*
Smith, C.R., 209(*n*93), *225, 275*
Smith, D., 20(*n*24), 119(*n*23), 121(*n*25), *171*
Smith, K.B., 6(*n*14), *22, 275*
Sorensen, T.C., 20(*n*12), 31(*n*16), 33(*n*29, *n*30), 34(*n*32), 37(*n*40), *44, 45, 46, 275*
Speakes, L., 184(*n*10, *n*11, *n*15), 185(*n*17), 188(*n*26-28), 189(*n*29-31), 190(*n*32, *n*34, *n*35), 220(*n*111), *221, 222, 276*
Spear, J.C., 86(*n*118), *108, 276*
St. Clair, G., 207(*n*85), *225, 276*
Stoesz, D., 237(*n*26), 240(*n*32), *246, 276*
Stuckey, M., 4(*n*6), 6(*n*13), 10(*n*34), *22, 23,* 155(*n*110), *176,* 182(*n*7), *221,* 263(*n*12), *265, 276*

T

Tebbel, J., 30(*n*10), 44, 51(*n*11),
  59(*n*43, *n*44), 60(*n*43), 79(*n*83),
  82(*n*97), 83(*n*102), 83(*n*105),
  85(*n*110), *102, 104, 106, 107*,
  115(*n*13, *n*14), 127(*n*42), *171, 172*,
  181(*n*2), 182(*n*6), 192(*n*38, *n*39),
  222, 221, 276
Theis, P., 129(*n*48), *172*
Thomas, N.C., 202(*n*66), *224, 276*
Thompson, K.W., 79(*n*86), *106*,
  191(*n*37), *222, 276*,
Townsend, C., 142(*n*75), 145(*n*80),
  148(*n*89, *n*91), 154(*n*107), *174*,
  175, 176
Tulis, J.K., 6(*n*11), 7(*n*18), 22,
  260(*n*6), *265, 276*

W

Waldman, S., 242(*n*34), *246, 276*
Waterman, R.W., 207(*n*85), *225*,
  276
Watson, R.A., 202(*n*66), *224*
Watts, S.M., 30(*n*10), 44, 50(*n*43*,
  *n*44), 51(*n*11), 60(*n*43), 79(*n*83),
  82(*n*97), 83(*n*102), 84(*n*105),
  85(*n*110), *102, 104, 106, 107*,
  115(*n*13, *n*14), 127(*n*42), *171, 172*,
  181(*n*2), 182(*n*6), 192(*n*38, *n*39),
  221, 222
Wayne, S.J., 205(*n*74), *224*,
  234(*n*19), *246, 269*
Weber, R.P., 16(*n*56), *25, 276*
Weinberg, M., 193(*n*42), *223*
Weko, T.J., 2(*n*1), *21-22, 276*
Whitaker, J.C., 96(*n*142), 98(*n*147),
  109, 276
White, M.E., 134(*n*59), *173*
White, T., 29(*n*5-7), 30(*n*13), 44,
  49(*n*6), *102*
Wood, S.C., 235(*n*22), *245, 276*
Woodward, B., 231(*n*6), *245, 276*
Wright, R., 207(*n*85), *225, 276*

Y

Yeutter, C., 208(*n*88), *225, 276-277*

Z

Zagacki, K.S., 64(*n*52), *276, 104*
Zernicke, P.H., 7(*n*16), 22,
  142(*n*73), *174, 276*
Ziegler, R., 80(*n*89, *n*90), *106*

Subject Index

A

Agnew, Spiro, 79, 111
Allin, Mort, 82
Alsop, Joe, 81
Anderson, Jack, 81
Associated Press, 31

B

Baird, Zoe, 229
Baker, James, 183, 185, 186, 188, 190, 196
Bario, Patricia, 154
Begala, Paul, 231
Bradlee, Benjamin, 32, 183
Brinkley, David, 80-81
Broder, David, 81, 143, 181, 183
Buchanan, Patrick, 83, 85-87, 113
Buckley, William F., 81
Bundy, McGeorge, 29
Busby, Horace, 59
Bush, George, 6, 20, 182, 228
  Clean Air Act, 216-219
  and press coverage, 217-219
  Education Excellence Act, 212-216
  and press coverage, 215-216
  and Office of Communications, 205
  policy agenda, 210-212
  and Presidential Campaign of 1988, 206
  and Presidential Campaign of 1992, 208
  and the press, 203-209
  press conferences, 203, 205
  and press coverage of the Gulf War, 205
  and press coverage of the recession, 205-206
  public activities, 209-210, 251
  public agenda/major public addresses, 211-212
  radio addresses, 255
  speech writing, 209
Byrd, Harry, 71

C

Caddell, Pat, 148
Califano, Joseph, 58
Cannon, Lou, 79
Carlson, John, 118
Carter, Jimmy, 7, 19-20, 128, 180, 249
  Civil Service reform, 165-169
  and press coverage, 168-169
  and daily news summary, 147-148
  Energy policy, 159-165
  and press coverage, 163-165
  and local media outlets, 146
  and "malaise" speech, 154
  policy agenda, 158-159
  and polling, 148-149
  and the press, 141-155
  and press conferences, 146-147
  public activities, 155-157, 251
  public agenda/major public addresses, 158-9
  radio addresses, 255
  speech writing, 156-157
Carter, Rosalynn, 147
Carville, James, 231
Cater, Douglas, 64
Chancellor, John, 80
Chapin, Dwight, 108n
Chase, Chevy, 128
Cheney, Richard, 123, 128, 137
Christian, George, 48-49, 51-52, 55, 58, 63-64, 103n
Clift, Eleanor, 232-233
Clinton, Bill, 1, 7, 15, 20-21, 129, 142, 249, 261-264
  Anti-Crime Bill, 238-240
  and press coverage, 240-241
  and approval ratings, 234
  and impeachment, 234
  and leadership style, 231
  National Service Plan, 240-242
  and press coverage, 242-243
  and Office of Communications, 231-232
  policy agenda, 237-238
  and Presidential Campaign of 1992, 227-228
  and the press, 228-235
  and press conferences, 254
  public activities, 235-236, 251
  public agenda/major public addresses, 237-238
  radio addresses, 254-255
  and scandal, 244
  speech writing, 235-236
Clinton, Hillary Rodham, 235
CNN, 15
Colson, Charles, 84
Credibility Gap, 12, 32, 48
  see also Lyndon Johnson, John F. Kennedy, and Richard Nixon
Cronkite, Walter, 81, 142

D

Deaver, Michael, 185-187, 189, 196, 202, 220
DeCair, Tom, 123
Donaldson, Sam, 80
Donovan, Hedley, 144
Dukakis, Michael, 206, 235
Dwyer, Daniel, 58

E

Eisenhower, Dwight, 15, 30, 32, 35, 40, 43n, 56, 69
Eizenstat, Stuart, 162, 166-167
Erlichman, John, 90
Evans, Rowland, 81

F

Fallows, James, 142-143, 156
Fitzwater, Marlin, 207, 208
Flowers, Gennifer, 227
Ford, Gerald, 19, 199, 249, 264
  Energy Corporation, 137-141
  and press coverage, 140-141
  and image as president, 118-121

and local media outlets, 125
and Office of Communications,
    124-126
and pardon of Richard Nixon,
    112
policy agenda, 130
and the press, 112-127
and press conferences, 122-124
public activities, 128-130, 251
public agenda/major public
    addresses, 130-131
radio addresses, 255
and SALT II talks, 115
speech writing, 128-129
Tax Cut proposal, 132-137
and press coverage, 135-137
and Watergate, 114
and Whip Inflation Now cam-
    paign, 131-132

G

Gergen, David, 87, 126, 128, 186,
    190, 196, 220, 230
Gingrich, Newt, 234, 236
Goodwin, Richard, 33, 64
Gray, C. Boyden, 206, 209, 214
Grunwald, Mandy, 231

H

Haldeman, H.R., 80, 85
Hartmann, Robert, 126, 128
Heller, Walter, 37
Hunter, Robert, 65
Huntley, Chet, 81

I

Inaugural Addresses, 9-10
Internet, 15

J

Johnson, Lyndon, 6, 18-19, 38, 111,
    130, 141, 249, 262
and civil rights, 66-67
and credibility gap, 59-63
daily news summary, 58

Great Society, 47, 61, 67, 74
Medicare, 69-73, 100
and press coverage, 72-73
policy agenda, 66
and the press, 48-63
press conferences, 48, 54-55
public activities, 63-66
public agenda/major public
    addresses, 67
Safe Streets and Crime Control
    Act, 74-78, 100
and press coverage, 76-78
as Senate Majority Leader, 50-51
speech writing, 63-65
and Vietnam, 47, 59-60, 61-63,
    67, 257
Jones, Paula, 230, 234

K

Kalb, Marvin, 81
Kennedy, John F., 18, 63, 69, 228,
    230, 235, 240, 249, 261-262
Aid to Education proposal, 39-
    42, 43
and press coverage, 41-42
and Alliance for Progress, 35
and civil rights, 36
communication strategy, 27
and credibility gap, 32
editor and publisher luncheons,
    31
and foreign press, 31-32
New Frontier, 40
policy agenda, 34-36
and Presidential Campaign of
    1960, 27-28, 29, 36
and the press, 28-32
press conferences, 28-30
public activities, 33-34
public agenda/major public
    addresses, 35-36
and public opinion, 33
speech writing, 33
Tax Cut proposal, 35, 36-39, 43

and press coverage, 38-39
Kennedy, Robert, 53, 69, 76, 89, 235
Keogh, Jim, 85, 87-88
King, Martin Luther Jr., 69, 76, 89, 235
Kintner, Robert, 49-50, 52, 54, 57, 64, 103*n*
Klein, Herb, 114
Kondracke, Morton, 81
Kruschev, Nikita, 32

L

Lance, Bert, 161
Lewinsky, Monica, 1, 228, 234, 244, 250, 255

M

Martin, Paul, 31
McNulty, Jack, 103*n*
McPherson, Harry, 54, 58, 63-64
Meese, Ed, 185, 188
Middleton, Harry, 64
Mills, Wilbur, 69
Moore, Frank, 149
Moore, Richard, 81
Moyers, Bill, 51, 54, 58, 62, 64, 71
MSNBC, 15
Mudd, Roger, 80
Muskie, Edmund, 97

N

Nessen, Ron, 114-117, 125, 133, 134
New York Times, 17-19, 31, 48, 81
see also press coverage of policy issues for individual presidents
Nixon, Richard, 6, 18-19, 111, 141, 249, 259, 262, 264
and Alger Hiss, 78
and California Gubernatorial Campaign of 1962, 79, 83
Checkers Speech, 79
and credibility gap, 101
daily news summary, 82
enemies list/monitoring project, 79-82

Environmental Protection proposal, 96-99
and press coverage, 98-99
and Office of Communications, 82-83
and Pentagon Papers case, 79
policy agenda, 89-90
"PR Campaign," 85-86
and Presidential Campaign of 1960, 79, 83
and Presidential Campaign of 1968, 79, 83
and Presidential Campaign of 1972, 86
and the press, 78-87
press conferences, 83-84
public activities, 87-89, 251
public agenda/major public addresses, 90-92
radio addresses, 88, 254-255
speech writing, 87-88
and use of television, 83-84
and Vietnam, 89-90, 257
and Watergate, 79, 101
Welfare Reform proposal, 92-95
and press coverage, 94-95
Novak, Robert, 81

O

O'Donnell, Kenneth, 28-29
O'Mara, Walter, 57
Orben, Robert, 128
Osborne, John, 116

P

Pearson, Drew, 51
Potter, Philip, 50, 53, 61
Powell, Jody, 142, 144, 145, 148, 152, 153, 174*n*
Presidents
and communication strategy, 1-3, 15-18, 248, 250, 261-264
and Congress, 11-12

and domestic policy, 17, 258-259
and press coverage, 259-261
and leadership, 3-5
and major public addresses, 16, 253-254
and policy making, 4-5, 11
and press conferences, 10, 254
and press coverage, 8, 12-15, 248-250
and public activities, 7-9, 12, 16, 251-255
and public agenda, 11-12, 16, 255-257
and rhetoric, 3, 5-7, 8-9
and speechwriting, 255
and State of the Union Address, 12, 253
and transitions, 9
Press bias, 14
Price, Raymond K., 87
Public opinion, 8-9, 12

R

Rafshoon, Gerald, 144, 146, 149-50, 154, 156, 162, 168
Rather, Dan, 80
Reagan, Ronald, 6, 20, 128, 170, 228, 249, 261-3
and daily news summary, 185
and local media outlets, 184
and misstatements, 189-190
and news management, 181-182, 185-187, 220
policy agenda, 196-198
and the press, 180-192
press conferences, 10, 191
public activities, 192-196, 251
public agenda/major public addresses, 197-198
radio addresses, 183, 254-255
"Reaganisms," 194
Social Security reform, 199-201
and press coverage, 200-201
speech writing, 193-194

Student Aid cuts, 201-203
and press coverage, 203-204
and use of television, 182, 188
Reedy, George, 60, 62
Regan, Donald, 183, 186, 188
Reston, James, 81, 141, 154, 207
Reynolds, Frank, 80
Rockefeller, Nelson, 137, 139
Roosevelt, Franklin D., 10, 35, 55, 69, 158, 183, 254
Roosevelt, Theodore, 82
Rumsfeld, Donald, 124, 133
Rusk, Dean, 29

S

Safire, William, 79, 82, 87, 108n
Salinger, Pierre, 28-29, 31, 49
Schattschneider, E.E., 11
Schlesinger, Arthur Jr., 28, 32-33
Schlesinger, James R., 160
Schneiders, Greg, 147, 151, 162
Sevareid, Eric, 80
Shaw, David, 229
Shultz, George, 188
Shuman, Jim, 119, 121-122
Sidey, Hugh, 81
Smith, Howard K., 80, 84
Snow, Tony, 209
Sorenson, Theodore, 28-29, 33, 37-38, 41, 45n, 64
Speakes, Larry, 182, 186, 187, 188, 189, 190, 196, 220
Stahl, Leslie, 190-191
Starr, Kenneth, 234, 244
Stephanopoulos, George, 229-230
Stockman, David, 182, 183

T

terHorst, Jerald, 112-113, 115
Theis, Paul, 128
Townsend, Claudia, 148
Truman, Harry, 10, 35, 69, 71-72

U

United Press International, 31

V

Valenti, Jack, 55, 64
Vanocur, Sander, 80

W

Walters, Barbara, 84
Weinberger, Casper, 188
Wicker, Tom, 81
Whitaker, John, 97-98
White House Office of
    Communications, 2, 14

see also Richard Nixon, Gerald
    Ford, George Bush, and Bill
    Clinton
White, Margita, 125

Y

Yeutter, Clayton, 207

Z

Ziegler, Ronald, 80, 84